China's Energy Security and Relations with Petrostates

AF763213

This book examines the development of bilateral energy relations between China and the two oil-rich countries, Kazakhstan and Russia.

Challenging conventional assumptions about energy politics and China's global quest for oil, this book examines the interplay of politics and sociocultural contexts. It shows how energy resources become ideas and how these ideas are mobilized in the realm of international relations. China's relations with Kazakhstan and Russia are simultaneously enabled and constrained by the discursive politics of oil. It is argued that to build collaborative and constructive energy relations with China, its partners in Kazakhstan, Russia, and elsewhere must consider not only the material realities of China's energy industry and the institutional settings of China's energy policy but also the multiple symbolic meanings that energy resources and, particularly, oil acquire in China.

China's Energy Security and Relations with Petrostates offers a nuanced understanding of China's bilateral energy relations with Kazakhstan and Russia, raising essential questions about the social logic of international energy politics. It will appeal to students and scholars of international relations, energy security, Chinese and post-Soviet studies, along with researchers working in the fields of energy policy and environmental sustainability.

Dr. Anna Kuteleva is a postdoctoral research fellow at the School of International Regional Studies at the National Research University Higher School of Economics, Russia. Anna holds a PhD in Political Science from the University of Alberta, Canada, and an MA in World Politics from Shandong University, China. Over the past ten years, she has worked extensively in the realm of political science and Chinese studies. Her research is located in a broad constructivist tradition of IR and focuses on the nexus between politics and sociocultural contexts in international relations, with particular interests in energy politics, Russia, and China.

Routledge Contemporary China Series

Modern Art for a Modern China
Yiyan Wang

Ethnic Minorities, Media and Participation in Hong Kong
Creative and Tactical Belonging
Lisa Y.M. Leung

The Politics of Waste Management in Greater China
Environmental Governance and Public Participation in Transition
Natalie Wai Man Wong

Hegemony with Chinese Characteristics
From the Tributary System to the Belt and Road Initiative
Asim Dogan

Homeownership in Hong Kong
House Buying as Hope Mechanism
Chung-kin Tsang

Local Clan Communities in Rural China
Revolution and Urbanisation since the Late Qing Dynasty
Zongli Tang

China's Energy Security and Relations With Petrostates
Oil as an Idea
Anna Kuteleva

Ethnic Identity of the Kam People in Contemporary China
Government versus Local Perspectives
Wei Wang and Lisong Jiang

For more information about this series, please visit: https://www.routledge.com/Routledge-Contemporary-China-Series/book-series/SE0768

China's Energy Security and Relations with Petrostates

Oil as an Idea

Anna Kuteleva

Routledge
Taylor & Francis Group
LONDON AND NEW YORK

First published 2022
by Routledge
2 Park Square, Milton Park, Abingdon, Oxon OX14 4RN

and by Routledge
605 Third Avenue, New York, NY 10158

Routledge is an imprint of the Taylor & Francis Group, an informa business

© 2022 Anna Kuteleva

The right of Anna Kuteleva to be identified as author of this work has been asserted by her in accordance with sections 77 and 78 of the Copyright, Designs and Patents Act 1988.

All rights reserved. No part of this book may be reprinted or reproduced or utilised in any form or by any electronic, mechanical, or other means, now known or hereafter invented, including photocopying and recording, or in any information storage or retrieval system, without permission in writing from the publishers.

Trademark notice: Product or corporate names may be trademarks or registered trademarks, and are used only for identification and explanation without intent to infringe.

British Library Cataloguing-in-Publication Data
A catalogue record for this book is available from the British Library

Library of Congress Cataloging-in-Publication Data
Names: Kuteleva, Anna, author.
Title: China's energy security and relations with petrostates : oil as an idea / Anna Kuteleva.
Description: New York : Routledge, 2021. | Includes bibliographical references and index. |
Identifiers: LCCN 2021001426 | ISBN 9780367651329 (hardback) | ISBN 9780367651466 (paperback) | ISBN 9781000406313 (adobe pdf) | ISBN 9781000406320 (epub)
Subjects: LCSH: Energy policy--China. | Energy industries--China--International cooperation. | China--Commerce--Russia (Federation) | Russia (Federation)--Commerce--China. | China--Commerce--Kazakhstan. | Kazakhstan--Commerce--China. | Environmental policy--International cooperation.
Classification: LCC HD9502.C62 K88 2021 | DDC 333.8/2320951--dc23
LC record available at https://lccn.loc.gov/2021001426

ISBN: 978-0-367-65132-9 (hbk)
ISBN: 978-0-367-65146-6 (pbk)
ISBN: 978-1-003-12804-5 (ebk)

Typeset in Times New Roman
by Deanta Global Publishing Services, Chennai, India

I dedicate my work to my grandfather, Vadim Filippov, and the memory of my grandmother, Antonina Filippova. Ultimately nothing could have been possible without the unwavering support of my mother, Olga Kuteleva.

Contents

Illustrations

Tables

Preface

At the heart of this book is the interplay between politics and sociocultural contexts in international energy politics. I explore this interplay by examining the development of bilateral energy relations between China and two oil-rich countries, Kazakhstan and Russia, from 2005 to 2017. The goal is to challenge conventional assumptions about energy politics and, particularly, about China's global quest for oil by showing how energy resources become ideas and how these ideas are mobilized in the realm of international relations.

Building my analysis on constructivist and poststructuralist insights, I demonstrate that China's energy relations with Kazakhstan and Russia are simultaneously enabled and constrained by the discursive politics of energy. I also reveal that China's external energy strategy is crucially dependent on its domestic discursive politics of energy. Hence, to build collaborative and constructive energy relations with China, its partners in Kazakhstan, Russia, and elsewhere must consider not only the material realities of China's energy industry (e.g., energy resources available in China, its mining, refining, and storage capacity, and the existing and planned transportation routes) and the institutional settings of China's energy policy (e.g., China's legal frameworks and the structure of China's energy government) but also the multiple symbolic meanings that energy resources acquire in China.

Overall, this book not only provides a nuanced understanding of China's bilateral energy relations with Kazakhstan and Russia but also raises and brings to the fore questions about the social logic of international energy politics in general. Thus, it offers an important addition to the literature critical of mainstream approaches to international relations and helping to promote discourse analysis within the discipline further.

Acknowledgments

This book is the result of a six-year-long research adventure. It is based on the PhD thesis which I prepared and defended at the University of Alberta in Canada. In the course of this research project, I have been fortunate enough to receive support and advice from many people.

First of all, I owe infinite thanks to my supervisor Ian Urquhart. This research project would not be the same without your constructive feedback, gentle guidance, and encouragement. From our first meeting, you took me, my writing, and my ideas seriously. I never felt lonely but always felt supported and valued. You are the best mentor I could ask for. Thank you for your insightful discussions and for always being there for me. Thank you for your humor, kindness, and patience.

Thank you very much to my supervisory committee members, Roger Epp and Gordon Houlden, for the enthusiastic guidance of my research. Roger, thank you for assisting me in each step to complete my PhD program. Your thought-stimulating questions not only encouraged me to critically evaluate my research practices and scholarly analysis but also instilled confidence in me and empowered me as an independent thinker. Gordon, thank you for being generous with your time and advice. Thank you for welcoming me into the China Institute and for giving me the opportunity to be a part of a top-notch research team.

I would like to thank Rob Aitken and Jeremy Paltiel for reading my work so thoughtfully and offering insightful comments. Thank you to Malinda Smith, Siobhan Byrne, Greg Anderson, Patrick von Maravic, Yasmeen Abu-Laban, Judy Garber, and Mojtaba Mahdavi for advice, feedback, challenging questions, guidance, and encouragement at various stages of my work at the University of Alberta. Thank you to Stephen Kuntz, associate director of the Academic Success Centre at the University of Alberta, for helping me to build my confidence in writing.

I also would like to thank my friends and colleagues, Theodor Tudoroiu, Valeriy Semikashev, Justin Leifso, Chad Cowie, Renée Beausoleil, and Jennifer Boivin, who read my early drafts, took the time to discuss my work and gave many helpful suggestions for its improvements. And thank you to all my interviewees in China, Kazakhstan, and Russia for taking the time to share their knowledge with me.

My PhD "gang," Justin Leifso, Chad Cowie, Michael Burton, and Emrah Keskin, I am incredibly lucky to share this journey with you. Thank you for sharing ideas, experiences, books, contacts, as well as hopes, victories, fears, tears, and laughs. Justin, Chad, and Mike thank you for being excellent ambassadors for Canada and welcoming me to your country with open arms. I am grateful for everything I learned from you (except for the nonsense about those 1972 hockey games).

Thank you to my friends and peers, Danyel Evseev, Alexander Bajev, Samreen Ahmed, Prachi Mishra, Owuraku Kusi-Ampofo, Sevan Beukian, Nicole Lugosi, Hajar Amidian, Mia Tulli, Dax D'Orazio, Megan Aiken, Isaac Odoom, Geoff Salomons, and Alexandra Savchenko. I am deeply grateful for your support, inspiration, friendship, and shoulder to lean on.

Finally, thank you to Mariam Georgis and Nisha Nath for becoming inspirational academic role models for me. Mariam and Nisha, please know that I cannot imagine having done this without you. You have had a profound influence on my attitudes toward my research and scholarly focus. I am a better scholar having worked alongside you.

Abbreviations

BP	British Petroleum
BRI	Belt and Road Initiative
CEO	Chief Executive Officer
CNOOC	China National Offshore Oil Corporation
CNPC	China National Petroleum Corporation
CPC	Communist Party of China
EIA	Energy Information Administration
ESPO	Eastern Siberia–Pacific Ocean
EU	European Union
GDP	Gross Domestic Product
IWEP ACSS	Institute World Economics and Politics Chinese Academy of Social Sciences
KMG	KazMunayGas
KCP LLP	Kazakhstan-China Pipeline Limited liability partnerships
NBSC	National Bureau of Statistics of China
NFRK	National Fund of the Republic of Kazakhstan
NOC	National oil company
MFA of the PRC	Ministry of Foreign Affairs of the Peoples' Republic of China
Mtoe	Million Tons of Oil Equivalent
PLA	People's Liberation Army of China
PRC	People's Republic of China
SCO	Shanghai Cooperation Organization
UN	United Nations
US	United States
USSR	Union of Soviet Socialist Republics

1 What do you imagine when you think about oil?

Oil.
What do you imagine when you think about oil?
What is the first thing that comes to your mind?

Do you imagine highways full of fast cars? Do you think about climate change and imagine pipeline protests in North Dakota? Do you think about a small toy factory in China's Guangdong? Maybe, you think about the 2003 invasion of Iraq? I was born and raised in post-Soviet Russia, and when I think about oil, the first thing that comes to my mind is corruption. When I think about oil, I imagine Vladimir Putin being the president of my country for yet another decade.

Since the early 20th century, we have lived in "the world of oil" (e.g., Yeomans 2004; Heinberg 2003; Shiva 2008; Yergin 2011a; Bridge and Le Billon 2012). With the rapid development of the natural gas industry, electricity, biofuels, and non-traditional energy sources over the past decades, oil has been losing ground. In the past decades, oil also has been pushed politically to defensive positions in many parts of the world by environmental activists and the international politics of climate change mitigation. However, we still largely depend on oil, and in the near future it will stay entrenched in literally all systems of our societies. Oil is *the* energy of our civilization.

Crude oil is a form of bitumen composed principally of hydrocarbons. It is extracted from natural reservoirs and transported through pipelines to a refinery or to a port, where it is loaded into a tanker and continues its journey to a refinery by water. More than half of all the crude oil used in the world crosses an international border, which makes oil one of the most internationally traded commodities in the world (Yergin 2011a).

Oil powers over 90 percent of the world's transportation that underpins modern economies and lifestyles. Our industrial food supply systems also consume a lot of oil. Petrochemicals from oil are used to make everything from clothes to mobile phones to perfumes to vitamins. Nothing moves without oil in the modern world. This makes oil a globally sought-after commodity (Wenar 2016; Yergin 2011b). Nonetheless, oil is concentrated only in a few geographic areas, and concerns about its scarcity are widespread and strong. The temporal aspect and declining availability of oil that reflect technological and geological constraints of oil extraction add another dimension to its scarcity.

From economic, geological, and technological perspectives, oil is a concrete and real thing, yet it animates such abstract ideas as freedom, mobility, and independence. When we think about oil, we think not only about pumpjacks, pipelines, tankers, price charts, and long supply chains but also about capitalism, security, development, environment, democracy, and modernity. Importantly, both material and imagined constructions of oil are socially and culturally specific. In other words, while we all live in the world of oil, we all think about oil and imagine it differently.

These ideas have inspired the central question of this book: *How do different states understand oil, and how do these understandings influence relations between them?* At its heart is a general interest in the nexus between politics and sociocultural contexts in international energy politics, and the book explores this nexus by drawing on the analysis of the development of bilateral energy relations between China and two oil-rich countries – Kazakhstan and Russia.

The book centers on China because its case is unique. In the late 19th and the early 20th centuries, economically dilapidated and politically unstable, China posed a potential threat to some states and served as a space for geopolitical invasion for others. Despite that, by the beginning of the 21st century, China has successfully lifted a record number of people out of poverty and achieved a rapid increase in living standards, and reached a sustained level of economic growth, gaining stature and influence in world affairs. To quote Giovanni Arrighi (2007, 95), at the end of the 20th century China pioneered "the social and economic empowerment of the peoples of the global South." Given China's size and scale, it is evident that its rapid and powerful rise is bringing about a new age in economic and political history (e.g., Arrighi 2007; Jacques 2009; Harvey 2005). China's extreme transformation from energy self-sufficient to energy-dependent development over the past three decades is one of the driving factors of these changes.

Since the early 1990s, China has emerged as "the world's factory floor." Around half of all energy consumed in China is absorbed by the industrial sector and can be attributed to international trade (Du and Lin 2015). The increased output of China's industrial sector drives the high demand for electricity, refined petroleum products, and materials that are energy-intensive to produce, such as chemicals, steel, and aluminum (Ma et al. 2009; Fu et al. 2014; Du and Lin 2015). The industry has also contributed to the total energy demand by boosting energy consumption in the transport sector (Leung 2010; Meidan et al. 2015). Socioeconomic changes, such as the marketization of the economy, rapid urbanization, and rising incomes, have added additional pressure to China's demand for energy. The dynamic consumer culture emerging in China promotes lifestyles that are fundamentally dependent on ecologically destructive and non-renewable sources of energy. High fossil-fuel use and carbon-intensive behavior are now the major consumer patterns of China's households (Liu et al. 2009; Feng et al. 2011; Dai et al. 2012).

As a result of these deep and rapid changes, in the first decade of the 21st century, the fluctuations in Chinese energy consumption deviated considerably from global trends. While primary energy consumption has only risen by 13 percent in OECD countries and by 30 percent for the whole world, China increased its primary energy consumption by 70 percent. Rising demand for energy has turned China from a net energy exporter to a net energy importer. China's energy production was 11.6 percent more than consumption in the mid-1980s; since 2005 its consumption has surpassed output by approximately 10 percent. China became a coal importer in 2002 and a natural gas importer in 2007. However, the switch is particularly marked for petroleum products: in the 1980s China's oil production was 35 percent more than its consumption, but since 2003 over one-half of the total oil consumption has been imported. Importantly, there is strong evidence to suggest that the expansion in demand for energy will continue for about another two decades, inasmuch as China's economy is still in the process of "take-off" in industrialization and socioeconomic transformation (EIA 2015).

Over the past decade, the productivity of China's oilfields has worsened, and the quality of domestic production has declined steadily because of resource depletion. While in the 1960s the development of internal energy capacity was the principal solution to China's energy security challenges, in the future substantial new fossil-fuel reserves will not likely be discovered. In other words, almost all radical options for the development of domestic energy capacity have already been exhausted; in the near to medium term, China will be unable to overcome its foreign energy dependence on fossil fuels. Currently, Chinese state-owned enterprises are prospecting for and extracting crude oil in 42 states (EIA 2015, 9). Three-fourths of China's crude oil imports come from the Middle East (52 percent) and Africa (23 percent)[1] (EIA 2015, 10). Even so, there is ample evidence to suggest that China aims to broaden the geographical scope of its foreign energy quest.

It is important to recognize and analyze China's emergence as a new influential actor in international energy politics. From the standpoint of enlightened self-interest, mutual vulnerabilities within the global energy system should be a sufficient pragmatic reason for studying the way China understands energy and constructs its relations with energy exporters in different parts of the world. It is also important to inquire what, on a relative basis, makes China an attractive partner for various energy exporters and how their interactions with China transform the way they view their own energy wealth.

To explain how China's quest for energy security transforms the global attitudes toward oil, this book examines China's relations with Russia and Kazakhstan. The China–Russia case is significant because both states play major roles in shaping global trends in energy politics. In contrast, news from Kazakhstan rarely hit international headlines, yet Kazakhstan is a significant oil producer and has become an increasingly important supplier to China over the past 20 years. Importantly, the China–Kazakhstan case provides novel insights into China's approach to South–South cooperation and its strategy in Central Asia.

By examining China's relations with Kazakhstan and Russia, this book not only provides a nuanced understanding of energy relations between these individual states but also raises and brings to the fore questions about the social logic of international energy politics in general. Specifically, it demonstrates that the material and discursive structures of energy politics are complexly interwoven and interdependent through diverse social, cultural, economic, and political encounters with energy, and thus, energy relations are determined not only by material realities but also by discursive politics of energy. In this sense, the analytical focus of this book is not on why a particular outcome was obtained in China–Kazakhstan and China–Russia energy relations but rather on how and with what effect diverse discursive structures of energy politics are socially constructed in the course of these relations.

Two key theoretical propositions anchor my analysis. First, the realities of energy production and consumption (e.g., volume and destinations of oil exports, domestic oil demand) are treated as material referents of identities that are constructed by states in international energy politics. Second, the material realities of energy acquire their meanings and significance only in the process of narrative-making and discursive symbolization. Hence, if we want to understand how an agent constructs its identity and the identities of its counterparts in international energy politics, we need to know what meanings this agent attributes to energy resources. A structured and systematic intertextual discourse analysis based on Lene Hansen's methodology (2006) of a heterogeneous collection of texts allows me to achieve two primary analytical goals:

- to reveal the discourses that dominate China's energy relations with Kazakhstan and Russia; and
- to examine how these dominant discourses support and sustain specific interpretations of China's energy relations with Kazakhstan and Russia while excluding or rendering marginal others.

To map and elucidate the development of discursive politics of energy in China, Kazakhstan, and Russia, I use textual documents and diverse cultural artifacts (e.g., works of fiction, popular song lyrics, paintings, photographs, films, museum exhibits, and architecture). My research is bilingual, with textual documents in Chinese and Russian being the major sources of data. I take language seriously and explore its power to construct social reality. Moreover, I show that diverse competing discourses about extraction, production, and consumption of energy and redistribution of energy revenues emerge and disseminate themselves through different forms of visual art, popular entertainment, architecture and city planning, museums, cultural spaces, and other sociocultural structures and practices. This allows me not only to advance the understanding of official energy discourses but also to unravel critical discourses about the economic, environmental, social, and political impacts associated with the expansion of the energy industry and the increase of energy exports.

The rest of the book proceeds in five chapters. In Chapter 2, I explain where the book is located within the major theoretical debates that provide the basis for the study of energy politics in the realm of International Relations. I start with a broad and diverse but not overly detailed review of the existing mainstream realist and liberal scholarship that is heavily preoccupied with the dichotomy of conflict and cooperation and explains international energy relations through the prism of energy security. Problematizing the concept of energy security, I present constructivism as an alternative that can lead to valuable insights. In the last part of this chapter, I define major concepts and develop a constructivist methodology for studying international energy relations as a product of complex, dynamic, and interdependent social processes.

Chapter 3 focuses on China. I start with China's quest for "self-reliance" in the 1950s and the story of the Daqing oilfield. Further, I discuss the legacy of "self-reliance" and transition to the "going global" energy strategy in the era of "reform and opening-up" in the 1990s and the early 2000s. In the second part of this chapter, I examine the evolution of China's discursive politics of energy in the mid-2000s and the early 2010s. I identify the dominant discursive constructions in China's energy politics and trace how they shifted and changed over the past ten years. Finally, I determine how these discursive constructions support and sustain specific interpretations of China's energy strategy while excluding others or rendering them marginal. This allows me to define norms, meanings, and ideas that constitute China's energy paradigm.

Chapters 4 and 5 focus on China's relations with Russian and Kazakhstan, respectively. I start each case study with an analysis of national energy paradigms of China's counterparts and then examine what impact China's emergence as a key energy consumer has on them. These chapters show that while China is redefining global energy politics and conventional approaches to energy security, its understanding of oil has not changed much since the mid-1950s. Hence, China's quest for energy security strengthens the affirmation that there is no alternative for oil. At the same time, the two petrostates see China as striving to control their energy sector and, subsequently, as a threat to their sovereignty in the realm of international energy politics, which is key to their sense of identity. Overall, Russia's and Kazakhstan's energy cooperation with China simultaneously exposes contradictions within their energy paradigms and acts as a conduit through which perceptions of China as a threat find a stronger voice.

Finally, Chapter 6 emphasizes the need to take the constitutive power of language seriously and reflect on how the language we use influences the way we study and practice energy politics. It stresses that the external energy strategies of China and its energy-rich counterparts are crucially dependent on their discursive politics of energy. Hence, the work of building collaborative and constructive energy relations with China, its partners in Kazakhstan, Russia, and elsewhere must consider not only material realities of China's energy industry (e.g., energy resources available in China, its mining, refining, and storage capacity, and the existing and planned transportation routes) and institutional settings of China's energy policy (e.g., China's legal frameworks and the structure of China's energy government), but also multiple symbolic meanings that energy resources acquire in China.

Moving beyond China's relations with petrostates, the chapter returns to the concept of energy security. At the heart of China's energy paradigm is an unhealthy obsession with energy self-sufficiency, and its notion of security centers on avoiding sudden changes in the availability of energy relative to demand in the name of national security and ongoing economic growth. China's quest for oil empowers petrostates, like Russia and Kazakhstan, and reinforces the understanding of oil as a critical sought-after energy source.

We indeed live in the "world of our making," and this world, to a large extent, is talked into being. Hence, to redefine our understandings of energy security, we need to start taking the world of words and ideas as seriously as the world of pumpjacks, pipelines, tankers, price charts, and extended supply chains. The book ends by emphasizing that if we are to imagine the world without oil, we need to rethink our relations with it. Once we start viewing oil as a threat rather than an opportunity for our development and progress, we will be able to develop a new language that denaturalizes the dominant notions of energy (in)security and cooperate to produce sustainable international energy solutions.

Note

1 China's oil imports come from Saudi Arabia, Iraq, Iran, Oman, Angola, and Russia. In 2015, Russia temporarily overtook Saudi Arabia as the biggest crude exporter to China four times. While fluctuations in import numbers over 2015 indicate that Russia is gaining momentum in China's market, it is too early to draw conclusions. As for 2018, Saudi Arabia is still China's major supplier.

Bibliography

Arrighi, G. (2007). *Adam Smith in Beijing: lineages of the twenty-first century*. London; New York: Verso.

Bridge, G., and Le Billon, P. (2012). *Oil*. Cambridge: Polity Press.

Dai, H., Masuib, T., Matsuokac, Y., and Fujimor, S. (2012). The impacts of China's household consumption expenditure patterns on energy demand and carbon emissions towards 2050. *Energy Policy*, *50*(1), 336–350.

Du, K., and Lin, B. (2015). Understanding the rapid growth of China's energy consumption: a comprehensive decomposition framework. *Energy*, *90*(1), 570–577.

Energy Information Administration [EIA] (2015). China. International energy data and analysis [PDF file] Retrieved 27 June 2016 from https://www.eia.gov/beta/international/analysis_includes/countries_long/China/china.pdf.

Feng, Z., Zou, L., and Wei, M. (2011). The impact of household consumption on energy use and CO2 emissions in China. *Energy*, *36*(1), 656–670.

Fu, F., Ma, L., Li, Z., and Polenske, K.R. (2014). The implications of China's investment-driven economy on its energy consumption and carbon emissions. *Energy Conversion Management*, *85*, 573–580.

Hansen, L. (2006). *Security as practice: discourse analysis and the Bosnian War*. London: Routledge.

Harvey, D. (2005). *A brief history of neoliberalism*. New York: Oxford University Press.

Heinberg, R. (2003). *The Party's over: oil, war and the fate of industrial*. Gabriola Island: New Society Publishers.

Jacques, M. (2009). *When China rules the world: the rise of the middle kingdom and the end of the western world*. New York: Allen Lane.

Leung, G. C. K. (2010). China's oil use, 1990–2008. *Energy Policy*, *38*(2), 932–944.

Liu, H., Guo, J., Dong, Q., and Xi, Y. (2009). Comprehensive evaluation of household indirect energy consumption and impacts of alternative energy policies in China by input-output analysis. *Energy Policy*, *37*(8), 3194–3204.

Ma, H., Oxley L., and Gibson J. (2009). Substitution possibilities and determinants of energy intensity for China. *Energy Policy*, *37*(5), 1793–1804.

Meidan, M., Sen, A., and Campbell, R. (2015). China: the "new normal." The Oxford Institute of Energy Studies. [PDF file] Retrieved 12 June 2016 from https://www.oxfordenergy.org/wpcms/wp-content/uploads/2015/02/China-the-new-normal.pdf.

Shiva, V. (2008). *Soil not oil: climate change, peak oil and food insecurity*. London: Zed Books.

Wenar, L. (2016). *Blood oil: tyranny, resources, and the rules that run the world*. New York: Oxford University Press.

Yeomans, M. (2004). *Oil: anatomy of an industry*. New York: New Press.

Yergin, D. (2011a). *The Prize: the epic quest for oil, money and power*. New York: Simon and Schuster.

Yergin, D. (2011b). *The Quest: energy, security, and the remaking of the modern world*. London: Penguin.

2 Discursive politics of energy and energy paradigms

Theoretical framework and methodology

Building my analysis on constructivist and poststructuralist insights, I seek to offer a nuanced perspective of energy politics that captures such variables as social context, intersubjective meanings, and identities. My research is divided into two parts. The first area that will be examined is the discursive politics of energy that includes identities and historical narratives about energy resources that are constructed by states to represent themselves and each other in energy relations. The second area of research involves developing a better understanding of how these identities and historical narratives about energy resources are reproduced in energy paradigms. This chapter introduces the theoretical framework that informs this analysis. It starts with a critique of the mainstream approaches to energy politics and then proceeds to develop a constructivist methodology for studying international energy relations as a product of social processes.

Realism vs. liberalism: The dichotomy of conflict and cooperation in the study of international energy politics

The major divisions within the scholarship on international energy relations are built on different approaches to international order and the nature of the state in providing and regulating this order. The literature on energy politics that seeks to incorporate International Relations (IR) theoretical perspectives most often refers to realist and liberal theories as "major," "dominant," or "traditional" schools of IR (the issue highlighted by Hancock and Vivoda 2014 and Stoddard 2013). Despite some notable exceptions (Bouzarovski and Bassin 2011; Mitchell 2011; DeBardeleben 2012; Casier 2011, 2013; Kratochvíl and Tichý, 2013; Campion 2016), the role of other IR traditions in the research on international energy relations is limited to the extent to which theorizing is reduced to a dialogue between realism and liberalism.

Realism assumes that the international system is characterized by anarchy, inasmuch as no authority is capable of regulating interactions of the "sovereign" states within it. This means that instead of following the prescriptions of a higher authority, states have to build relations with each other on their own. States are viewed as rational agents that always pursue their interests in the system of self-help, and thus the crucial goal of a state is to ensure its survival. In the quest for security, states try to accumulate resources, and the relative levels of military and economic power of states determine the relations between them. The majority of mainstream realists use the fixed and narrow concept of power offered by Kenneth Waltz (1979, 131), according to which the power of a state in international relations is measured in terms of the "size of population and territory, resource endowment, economic capability, military strength, political stability, and competence." This materialistic approach to power is one of the major appeals of mainstream realism because it allows its advocates to "justify both accommodation and the building up of armaments in the name of a balance of power" (Hollis and Smith 1990, 28). It also offers those advocates "the ingredients needed to explain the resilience of the modern international system of states" (Little 2007, 3).

When it comes to energy, proponents of the realist approach hold that energy relations, like any other field of international relations, are strictly determined by the national interests of states in which concerns of survival and power are highly prioritized. Following the realist tradition, scholars focus on categories such as resource competition (e.g., Klare 2008; Zweig and Bi 2005; Zweig and Hao 2015), energy dependence (e.g., Bilgin 2011; Bosse and Schmidt-Felzmann 2011; Orttung and Overland, 2011), and resource nationalism. From this perspective, China is a "hungry dragon" that needs to fight for energy resources – and particularly fossil fuels – to power its rapidly developing economy (e.g., Klare 2008; Zweig and Bi 2005; Zweig and Hao 2015); Russia has an "energy weapon" and is trying to use it to build a new "energy imperialism" (e.g., Baev 2008; Goldman 2008; Kropatcheva 2014; Mankoff 2009; Orban 2008); and Kazakhstan matters only as a space of geopolitical expansion for various great powers (e.g., Ahmad and Rubab 2015; Weitz 2006).

In sum, proponents of the realist approach to international energy relations examine a world of states that faces an ongoing battle over resources. They emphasize geostrategic aspects of energy relations and most often rather narrowly focus on the balance of power between energy exporters and import-dependent states, portraying energy relations as a zero-sum game. This, as advocates of the liberal tradition point out, leads realist analysis to many shortcomings since it disregards important institutional determinants of energy relations.

In the popular imagination and wide foreign policy discourse, liberalism is portrayed as being peace-orientated and more ethical when compared to realism. Discussion of energy relations is not an exception (e.g., Currier and Dorraj 2011; Stokes and Raphael 2010). On the contrary, however, the principal concern of liberal scholarship is not the attainment of peace or peaceful relations among individuals and states. In fact, similar to realist scholars, the majority of contemporary proponents of liberalism in IR offer pronounced utilitarian and rationalistic theories. At the same time, they all are still based on the belief in "a slow but inexorable journey away from the anarchic world the realists envision, as trade and finance forge ties between nations, and democratic norms spread" (Snyder 2004, 56). Even when liberal theorizing is detached from its historical, ideological inclinations – such as the celebration of progress and modernity, the balance of plurality and unity, the equality of opportunities, and the promotion of well-being – it is still logically cognate with a teleological definition of international relations as unfolding in the pursuit of mutually advantageous cooperation (e.g., Moravcsik 1997).

Liberal theorizing claims that if it is possible to identify instigators of a conflict, then it should be possible to form a coalition of law-abiding states that will jointly stand against aggressors (e.g., Claude 1964; Kupchan and Kupchan 1995). A global system of international organizations ought to fulfill legislative, executive, and, importantly, judicial functions and responsibilities, ensuring at the same time that each state would be able to retain its sovereignty, freedom, and independence (e.g., Smith 1992; Kingsbury and Robert 1993). Importantly, liberalism presupposes that it is governments that make wars, not people. Hence, according to the logic of reason, the best hope for peace is a democracy because it represents the will of the people who reject conflict in favor of cooperation (e.g., Owen 1994; Doyle 1997; Oneal and Russett 1997). Consequently, various versions of liberalism, regardless of their theoretical orientations, manifest the intent and restraint that announces the possibility of peace among the states that are bound by rational liberal norms. Liberal scholarship on energy relations perfectly illustrates this point.

The underlying assumption that guides the liberal approach to international energy politics is that energy relations are governed by diverse institutions, organizations, and regimes and thus involve both state and non-state agents. Liberal scholarship on energy relations focuses mainly on complex institutional arrangements that provide frameworks for cooperation between energy exporters and energy importers (Goldthau and Witte 2010). While liberal scholarship on international energy politics is diverse, all liberal contributions to the study of international energy politics are united by the "faith in the functioning of markets and the potential for institutional international cooperation to achieve mutually beneficial solutions between both economic actors and states" (Stoddard 2013, 445).

Advocates of the liberal approach are interested in strategies that transform energy relations into a positive-sum game and ensure greater economic efficiency of cooperation between energy exporters and energy importers. Examining energy relations as a positive-sum game, scholars turn to environmental aspects of energy cooperation and emphasize issues of long-term depletion of fossil-fuel reserves, efficient energy use, environmental protection, as well as the development of renewable energy sources. These themes are articulated particularly clearly in the literature on global energy governance that asks the questions: Who should govern global energy relations, and how should those relations be governed? (Florini and Sovacool 2009; Victor and Yueh 2010; Ghosh 2011) And what should be governed in energy? (Cherp et al. 2011; Araújo 2014; Bazilian et al. 2014). Some scholars focus on the potential of existing organizations, such as the G8, G20, or the International Energy Agency (e.g., Kirton and Kokotsis 2015; Downie 2015; Keohane 1978; Van de Graaf 2012), to govern global energy relations, while others propose establishment of new organizations (Victor and Yueh 2010). As regards the areas of energy governance, the vast majority of liberal scholars agree that emphasis needs to be put on the security of energy supply, environmental sustainability, and energy poverty – in each case, to offset presumed causes of international conflict.

Whether energy relations are perceived as a zero-sum game (realism) or as a positive-sum game (liberalism), their logic is explained through incentives provided by energy security. As Lynne Chester (2010, 891) points out, the very term "energy security" evidently promises that there is "a concept (an abstract idea) with some form of strategic intent" behind it. At the same time, the concept of energy security is vague: it covers a range of threats that vary in nature, time, and magnitude, and includes "the multiplicity of meanings that can be attributed to it establishes that there can be no 'one-size-fits-all' solution" (893). The only idea that unites diverse interpretations of energy security is an emphasis on avoiding sudden changes in the availability of energy relative to demand. In other words, energy security is always about the deficit of energy and this deficit is to be addressed mainly by increasing supply.

Both realist and liberal analyses of energy relations disregard their social logic, which creates a few blind spots. As the case in point, issues related to the extraction, production, and consumption of energy and the redistribution of energy rents become matters of security only when a powerful agent frames and responds to them as such. Hence, the very notion of "security" in energy relations should be problematized and conceptualized in ways that allow for an understanding of how various energy issues become matters of security.

What are the different ideas that the notion of security embodies in energy politics? How do particular responses to the challenges of extraction, production, consumption, and distribution of energy emerge as appropriate and rational? How do multiple and diverse understandings of energy shape the identities of states in international relations? How are different national narratives about energy resources connected at the international level? Constructivism and poststructuralism offer clues to these questions.

An alternative: Critical constructivism

One of the core insights of constructivism was formulated by Nicholas Onuf (1989): the subject of IR theory is a "world of our making." Social realities are then, following Onuf's argument, as influential as material realities in determining states' actions in the international arena. For instance, in the words of Alexander Wendt (1995), "social structures include material resources like gold and tanks" because "material resources only acquire meaning for human action through the structure of shared knowledge in which they are embedded" (73). Accordingly, primary units of analysis are diverse social constructs that are "real and objective, not 'just talk' … [but] this objectivity depends on shared knowledge" (Wendt 1995, 74). Importantly, social constructs exist "not in actors' heads nor in material capabilities, but in practices" (Wendt 1995, 74). This means that social constructs emerge through the processes of complex social interactions between agents and the existence of these social constructs is reinforced by practice.

As Brigit Locher and Elizabeth Prügl (2001) argue, "diverse constructivisms" embrace the "ontology of becoming" inasmuch as all of them "are describing the world not as one that is, but as one that is in the process of becoming" (114). Particularly, the ontology of becoming allows constructivists to examine "the constitution of international agents" and reveal historically contingent sets of agreed knowledge to explain transformations of strategies and develop a comprehensive understanding of social change (Locher and Prügl 2001, 114–115). The two overarching constructivist approaches are labeled as "conventional" (or "thin") and "critical" (or "thick") (e.g., Adler 1997; Price and Reus-Smit 1998; Zehfuss 2001). Both approaches assume that the material and social realities of international relations are complexly interwoven and interdependent, yet conventional constructivism puts at the center of analysis material factors, whereas critical constructivism prioritizes discursive structures. Striving to bridge epistemological relativism and epistemological rationalism, conventional constructivists perceive the international system "as an objective social fact" (Wendt 1999, 75). In contrast, critical constructivists focus on "how the world is 'talked into existence'" (Adler 2013, 122). For them, social facts emerge through the structures of language, which presupposes that "consciousness can be studied only as mediated by language" (Adler 2013, 97). Consequently, critical constructivist scholars take relations between symbolization, language, and power more seriously than conventional constructivists, which brings them close to poststructuralism.

James Der Derian (2009) defines poststructuralism as "a semio-critical activity ever searching for and seeking to dismantle the empirico-rational positions where power fixes meaning" (296). He offers a four-dimensional research agenda of poststructuralist theorizing:

> to interrogate present knowledge of international relations through past practices, to search out the margins of political theory, to listen for the critical voices drowned out by official discourses, and to conduct an inquiry into the encounter of the given text with reacting text.
>
> (Der Derian and Shapiro 1989, 6)

Subsequently, as Onuf (1989) accurately points out, poststructuralism takes the major ontological and epistemological assumptions of constructivist theorizing "as a dialectical necessity" and extends them to "a radical degree" (45–46).

Poststructuralist theorizing explicitly questions the very existence of independent and objective knowledge and explores "how the discursive distribution of power normalizes particular subject positions, regulates space and time, and surveils to ensure conformity" (McKenna 2004, 22). Following this logic, poststructuralist scholars see causal epistemology as "a particular discourse of knowledge, which cannot sustain its privilege outside of its own historical and political location" (Hansen 2006, 9).

Critical constructivists borrow freely and apply conceptual apparatus and methodological tools developed by poststructuralist IR scholars. Nonetheless, even when critical constructivists pose constitutive questions – "how is it possible?" (see

Doty 1993) – they do not diverge from the position of mild positivism and are not willing to abandon completely causal epistemology (e.g., Price and Reus-Smit 1998, 282 and Jackson 2016, 105–108). Operating within constitutive and intersubjective frameworks of social facts, they deliberately use existing meta-structures of international relations (e.g., state, sovereignty) to define and limit their theorizing. Importantly, as Emanuel Adler (1997, 333–334) argues, critical constructivists are "interested neither in emancipation per se, nor exclusively in uncovering the power structures that affect the marginalized in history but in providing better explanations of social reality." In this regard, critical constructivism is still a "rebel son" of mainstream IR traditions, realism, and liberalism (Agathangelou and Ling 2004, 28–29).

In sum, constructivism remains a diverse scholarship that is best described as a "heterogamous" research program (Hopf 1998, 196) or a "meta-theory" (Wæver 1997, 25). Hence, its engagement with and learning from poststructuralism is natural and appropriate. Building my research on constructivist and poststructuralist insights, I seek to demonstrate that identities of agents matter in international energy politics and examine these identities systematically through the adoption of a discourse analysis approach. In doing so, I move beyond the concept of energy security and focus on a set of research questions that emphasize the constitutive significance of representations of identity in formulating and debating diverse strategies in the realm of international energy politics. While my study is inspired by both constructivist and poststructuralist scholarship, it still firmly fits into an overarching constructivist research agenda because it is focused on "what is" rather than "what ought to be" or "what could possibly be."

Beyond energy security

Although the theory of securitization integrates classical realist understandings of international relations, it is grounded in constructivist ontological and epistemological assumptions. In this case, as Stefano Guzzini (2011, 331) puts it, "the constructivist horse has been put before the geopolitical cart." Securitization is "a set of interrelated practices, and the processes of their production, diffusion, and reception/translation that bring threats into being" (Balzacq 2010, xiii). The quintessence of the concept of securitization is that "it is by labeling something a security issue that it becomes one" (Wæver 2004, 13). This means that security is a social construct, and thus it does not have any pre-existent meaning but can be anything a securitizing agent claims it is. As Barry Buzan, Ole Wæver, and Jaap de Wilde (1998, 26) elaborate:

> [T]he task is not to assess some objective threats that "really" endanger some object to be defended or secured; rather, it is to understand the process of constructing a shared understanding of what is to be considered and collectively responded to as a threat.

Consequently, the concept of securitization represents the essence of what Buzan (2010) elsewhere refers to as the "social side" of security analysis and opens up a way to denaturalize the framing of certain events, issues, things, or people as posing existential threats to states and societies. The reverse process – politicization (desecuritization) – is understood as "the shifting of issues out of the emergency mode and into the normal bargaining process of the political sphere" (Buzan, Wæver, and de Wilde 1998, 4).

When applied to the study of energy relations, the theory of securitization offers insights into how an energy deficit becomes represented as either an existential threat to national sovereignty and international stability or a political matter. Importantly, by identifying energy issues as security or political matters, agents simultaneously determine the need for respective strategies. Consequently, the theory of securitization helps to explain the conceptual foundations of the dichotomy between conflict and cooperation that is at the center of the radical rift between realist and liberal views of energy relations. For example, Andrew Phillips (2013, 34) examines energy security as "the product of interlocking perceptions relating to questions of supply adequacy, the efficiency, flexibility, adaptability and resilience of allocative institutions, and the stability and benignity of the strategic order in which energy markets are anchored." According to him, securitization of energy is a result of China's and India's rise as "import-dependent energy superconsumers" (2013, 17). Along similar lines, re-examining Sino-Japanese energy and environmental relations, Elizabeth Wishnick (2009) concludes that diverse social and cultural factors prevent the two countries from forming a regional security community, even though they have shared risks. In sum, both Phillips' and Wishnick's analyses show that the failure of liberal theories does not mean the success of the realist approach to energy politics. Instead, they both demonstrate that the concept of energy security that lies at the center of both liberal and realist approaches to energy politics explains nothing and has to be explained itself.

Other scholars use the concept of securitization to call into question the givenness of the differential categories of security and insecurity in the realm of energy politics. As a case in point, Jonna Nyman (2018) argues that security is a practice, "something that people do" (24) and thus has neither an inherent meaning nor an intrinsic value but is never neutral. As a result, Nyman approaches security as "a powerful tool for change" (32) and distinguishes "negative" and "positive" energy security. Applying this theoretical framework to a detailed case study of China's energy security practices, Nyman (2018, 7) identifies a security paradox: "state energy security practices result in less security for states, human beings, and the environment" (see also Nyman and Zeng 2016).

To raise and bring to the fore questions about the social logic of energy relations, a constructivist analysis should move beyond the concept of energy security and focus on the role of identity in international energy politics. Hence, problematizing the idea of security in energy relations is not enough. The second step is to ask how particular responses to the challenges of extraction, production, consumption, and distribution of energy emerge as appropriate and rational. To do so, this book goes beyond the analysis of policy discourses and introduces a methodological framework that includes broader cultural artifacts and societal discourses.

Identity and the logic of appropriateness

Identity is a complicated concept: it "tends to mean too much (when understood in a strong sense), too little (when understood in a weak sense), or nothing at all (because of its sheer ambiguity)" (Brubaker and Cooper 2000, 1). In the theoretical framework offered by constructivist scholars, identity is perceived as a "relatively stable system of meanings with a well-consolidated context in which to act" (Tsygankov 2010, 16) and is located "at the core of national and transnational interests" (Adler 2013, 102). This does not imply, however, that each agent of international relations holds only one identity or that agents have a pre-social essence. On the contrary, identity is continually transforming in the process of social interaction. As Ted Hopf (1998, 175) points out, an agent "understands others according to the identity it attributes to them, while simultaneously reproducing its own identity through daily social practices." The central conceptual premise behind this assumption is threefold. First, agents' identities are shaped by the social structures of the environments in which they operate (Hansen 2006; Tannenwald 2007; Jackson 2016). Second, identities are constructed through the process of differentiation and linking (Wæver 2002; Hansen 2006). Third, identities are negotiated in a discursive competition between different social groups that represent agents (Tsygankov 2010). Consequently, here my version of constructivism deviates significantly from the conventional constructivist theorizing associated with the works of Wendt (1999).

In the constructivist conceptual framework that captures various identities constructed by agents to represent themselves and each other in international energy politics, energy relations appear as a product of complex, dynamic, and interdependent social processes. In this framework, identity has characteristics of a causal variable because it gives rise to and explains the logic of appropriateness in energy relations. The logic of appropriateness is a structure of meaning that justifies actions that are accepted by an agent (March and Olsen 1989, 2006, 2009). Agents evaluate courses of action according to the logic of appropriateness that corresponds best with their identities. This means that action always implies "evoking an identity or role and matching the obligations of that identity or role to a specific situation" (March and Olsen 1989, 951). In this light, the broad constructivist question about international energy politics can be put as follows: how does the way agents identify/label themselves and others shape the strategic choices they make?

Discursive politics of energy

As the preceding analysis shows, realist scholars securitize the deficits of energy resources and perceive them as a strategic commodity, control over which determines the power and influence of a state. Liberal scholars, on the other hand, politicize the deficits of energy resources, seeing them as a normal economic commodity that should be allocated by markets and regulated by international institutions. These two approaches present three idiosyncratic narratives about energy resources yet ignore the process through which these narratives are socially constructed. Energy, as E. F. Schumacher (1982, 1–2) highlights, "is not just another commodity, but the precondition of all commodities, a basic factor equal with air, water, and earth." Diverse social, cultural, economic, and political encounters with energy resources give them multiple symbolic meanings.

In the framework that I propose, the realities of energy production and consumption (e.g., volume and destinations of oil exports, domestic oil demand) are treated as material referents of identities that are constructed by states in international energy politics. However, narratives about energy resources define the meaning of these material referents. For example, when Russian political leaders identify Russia as an "energy superpower," they refer to oil, natural gas, coal, and other energy resources that are located within Russia's borders and often use the volume of Russia's energy imports as a material referent. In this case, the narrative about energy resources portrays them as a source of extraordinary national power. Nevertheless, the material realities of energy acquire their meanings and significance only in the process of narrative-making and discursive symbolization. The very same material realities of energy production and imports are successfully used as a referent by those who claim that Russia's energy wealth is the source of tremendous national vulnerability and identify Russia as an "energy appendage of the developed world."

Consequently, a material referent qualifies as a part of the "reality" of international energy politics not because it exists but because it is valued by agents. The reality, in general, is thought of as a quality that agents attribute to phenomena in the process of narrative-making by noticing them, talking about them with others, and acting as if these phenomena are important. Following this logic, if we want to understand how an agent constructs its identity and the identities of its counterparts in international energy politics, we need to know what meaning this agent attributes to energy resources.

The logic of appropriateness in energy relations: Energy paradigms

Diverse contestations of identity and narratives about energy resources are promoted by various actors in both public and private spaces. These contestations could be especially intense until one of the available visions of identity and a specific narrative about energy resources acquires a dominant status. More specifically, the persuasion part of the process is complete when the state appropriates an identity vision and a narrative about energy resources as a foundation of its energy paradigm.

I use the term "paradigm" in Thomas Kuhn's broad sense as standing for "the entire constellation of beliefs, values, techniques, and so on, shared by the members of a given community" (2012, 175). Energy paradigms are discursively constructed precisely in a way to appear to be objective representations of reality and provide a consolidated institutional context in which states operate in the realm of international energy politics. Energy paradigms represent the logic of appropriateness in international energy relations and, like any other expression of the logic of appropriateness, they are rooted in "structures of resources that make action possible" and "structures of meaning that explain and justify behavior" (March and Olsen 2006, 691). Energy paradigms are my constructivist roadmaps to energy relations: they represent relatively stable systems of norms, meanings, and ideas that shape the way states act in the field of energy relations.

Discourse analysis and texts: "From poststructuralist islands to the faraway shores of constructivism"

The chapter has thus far aimed to develop a critical constructivist research design for the study of international energy politics. In this section, I further elaborate on the methodology of this project by focusing on the methods of collecting, generating, and analyzing the data. I briefly outline the logic of discourse analysis in IR and then focus on the specific framework of discourse analysis that I utilize.[1] I also describe how the data was collected and generated and discuss some particular patterns in the data collection.

Discourse as a concept and discourse analysis as a methodology in the realm of IR had initially belonged to poststructuralist scholarship that entered the field in the late 1980s, and the early 1990s as a critical attitude and new approach to intellectual inquiry focused mainly on the ontological and epistemological shortcomings of conventional IR theorizing (e.g., Der Derian 2009; Walker 1993). However, as Anna Holzscheiter (2014, 43) points out, over the past two decades the study of discourse "has gradually traveled from poststructuralist islands to even the faraway shores of constructivism that works hard to reconcile constructivist ontology and positivist epistemology."

I borrow heavily from the poststructuralist discourse analysis methodology offered by Lene Hansen (2006), who in turn draws on Julia Kristeva's (1986, 37) theory of intertextual generation of meaning that implies that texts are "constructed as a mosaic of quotations; any text is the absorption and transformation of another." Hence, Hansen's intertextual discourse analysis examines texts as "simultaneously unique and united," meaning that each text "makes its own particular construction of identity, weaves a series of differentiations and juxtapositions, and couples them to a spatially, temporally, and ethically situated foreign policy" (Hansen 2006, 55). She develops a set of "intertextual research models," each of which has its own analytical focus, an object of analysis, and a goal of analysis (57). Using these intertextual research models, I organize all my texts into larger groups to structure and systematize my analysis (Table 2.1).

Mainly, I focus on Model 1 which captures discourses produced by "political leaders with official authority to sanction the foreign policies pursued as well as those with central roles in executing these policies" (Hansen 2006, 53). The analysis of cultural representation (Model 2A) and marginal discourses (Model 2B) helps to demonstrate how and with what effect official discourses emerge and disseminate themselves beyond the realm of foreign policy. These two models are specifically crucial in cases where official discourses achieve a hegemonic status (the discursive power of texts in Model 1 is extreme) and the space for a broader political discussion is limited.

Table 2.1 Intertextual Research Models

	Model 1	*Model 2A*	*Model 2B*
Sources of texts	National leaders, governments, senior civil servants, and diplomats	High and popular culture	NGOs, media, and academics
Object of analysis	Core official texts: official statements and speeches, reports of governmental institutions and policy-making agencies, and strategic policy documents	Films, fiction, photography, music, poetry, paintings, architecture, museum exhibits	Books, pamphlets, and reports produced by national and international NGOs Academic analysis Newspaper editorials
Goal of analysis	The stabilization of official discourses through intertextual links The response of official discourses to critical discourses	The support and critique of official discourses The broader historical, cultural, and social contexts of the study	The support and critique of official discourses
Number of texts			
China	234	24	212
Russia	165	47	121
Kazakhstan	77	21	68

Research question and analytical questions

Discursive politics of energy:

What identities and historical narratives about energy resources do China, Canada, Kazakhstan, and Russia construct to represent themselves and each other in energy relations?

- What is energy? What is oil?
- Who are "we" in relation to energy/oil?
- Who are "they" in relation to energy/oil?

Energy paradigms:

How are identities and historical narratives about energy resources constructed, manifested, and enacted in bilateral energy relations between China and Canada, Kazakhstan, and Russia?

- What are "we" going to do with energy?
- What are "they" going to do with energy?

In preparing my analysis, I formulated an overarching analytical question: What identities and historical narratives about energy resources do China, Russia, and Kazakhstan construct to represent themselves and others in energy relations? This question was further divided into three operational questions to "interrogate" all texts in the dataset when I read and coded each of them to identify recurring patterns, themes, concepts, and relations between them:

- Definition of the subject: What is energy? What is oil?
- Definition of actors (Self): Who are "we" in relation to energy/oil?
- Definition of actors (Other): Who are "they" in relation to energy/oil?
- Definition of action: What are "we" going to do with energy/oil?

I treat all texts included in Model 1 as primary sources, whereas Model 2B contains both primary and secondary sources. In the framework of intertextual discourse analysis, texts that are conventionally considered secondary sources (Halperin and Heath 2012, 180–181 and 255–256) might be treated as a primary source. For example, if a scholarly article from Model 2B is repeatedly quoted in official discourse or wider public debate, it could be treated as a primary source in some cases and as a secondary source in others. In this case, as Hansen (2006, 75) emphasizes, "the use of secondary sources does not prevent one from subjecting them to discourse analysis at a later stage of the research process."

I selected and examined 969 texts dating from 2005 to 2017. All textual sources were collected from official websites of individual institutions or through databases. Some of the texts were identified using "snowballing." For example, a significant photograph or a notable social media posting (Model 2A) surfaced in the analysis of newspaper editorials or expert reports (Model 2B). Finally, some of the sources were collected in the course of fieldwork. Model 2A includes interviews and observations made in China, Kazakhstan, and Russia between 2015 and 2018. Specifically, Model 2B includes 11 semi-structured interviews in China, Kazakhstan, and Russia with leading experts and academics conducted between May 2016 and May 2017. Respondents were chosen based on their practical or academic experience with international energy cooperation and foreign affairs. All the interviews were transcribed in the original language.

In sum, the analysis in this book is based on a comprehensive corpus of texts that are as representative as possible of various discursive layers in each state. Drawing on the notion of intertextuality, I can reveal how multiple and often contradictory discourses – circulating across different time-scales, levels, and layers – are linked to one another and how these discourses come together to constitute energy paradigms that shape the way China interacts with Russia and Kazakhstan in the field of energy politics and the way the three countries construct and reconstruct oil in this process.

Note

1 This methodological framework was also used to examine Canadian discursive politics of oil on provincial, federal, and international levels (Kuteleva and Leifso 2020) and Russia's energy relations with the European Union (Kuteleva 2020).

References

Adler, E. (1997). Seizing the middle ground: constructivism in world politics. *European Journal of International Relations*, *3*(3), 319–363.

Adler, E. (2013). Constructivism in international relations: sources, contributions, and debates. In W. Carlsnaes, T. Risse, and B. A. Simmons (Eds.) *Handbook of international relations* (pp. 112–144). London: SAGE Publications.

Agathangelou, A. M., and Ling, L. H. (2004). The house of IR: from family power politics to the poisies of worldism. *International Studies Review*, *6*(4), 21–49.

Ahmad, M., and Rubab, M. (2015). Great game of great powers in Central Asia: a comparative analysis. *Defence Journal*, *18*(11), 31.

Araújo, K. (2014). The emerging field of energy transitions: progress, challenges, and opportunities. *Energy Research and Social Science*, *1*, 112–121.

Baev, P. K. (2008). Russian super-giant in its liar: Gazprom's role in domestic affairs. In S. E. Cornell, and N. Nilsson (Eds.) *Europe's energy security: Gazprom's dominance and Caspian supply alternatives* (pp. 59–70). Washington, DC; Stockholm: Central Asia–Caucasus Institute, Silk Road Studies Programme.

Balzacq, T. (2010). *Understanding securitisation theory: how security problems emerge and dissolve*. London; New York: Routledge.

Bazilian, M., Nakhooda, S., and van de Graaf, T. (2014). Energy governance and poverty. *Energy Research and Social Science*, *1*, 217–225.

Bilgin, M. (2011). Energy security and Russia's gas strategy: the symbiotic relationship between the state and firms. *Communist and Post-Communist Studies*, *44*(2), 119–127.

Bosse, G., and Schmidt-Felzmann, A. (2011). The geopolitics of energy supply in the "Wider Europe." *Geopolitics*, *16*(3), 479–485.

Bouzarovski, S., and Bassin, M. (2011). Energy and identity: imagining Russia as a hydrocarbon superpower. *Annals of the Association of American Geographers*, *101*(4), 783–794.

Brubaker, R., and Cooper, F. (2000). Beyond "identity." *Theory and Society*, *29*(1), 1–47.

Buzan, B., Wæver , O., and de Wilde, J. (1998). *Security: a new framework for analysis*. London; Boulder: Lynne Rienner.

Campion, A. S. (2016). *The geopolitics of red oil: constructing the China threat through energy security*. London: Routledge.

Casier, T. (2011). Russia's energy leverage over the EU: myth or reality? *Perspectives on European Politics and Society*, *12*(4), 493–508.

Casier, T. (2013). The EU–Russia strategic partnership: challenging the normative argument. *Europe-Asia Studies*, *65*(7), 1377–1395.

Cherp, A., Jewell, J., and Goldthau, A. (2011). Governing global energy: systems, transitions, complexity. *Global Policy*, *2*(1), 75–88.

Chester, L. (2010). Conceptualising energy security and making explicit its polysemic nature. *Energy Policy*, *38*(2), 887–895.

Claude, I. (1964). *Swords into plowshares: the problems and progress of international organization* (3rd ed). New York: Random House.

Currier, C. L., and Dorraj M. (2011). *China's energy relations with the developing world*. London: The Continuum International Publishing Group.

DeBardeleben, J. (2012). Applying constructivism to understanding EU–Russian relations. *International Politics*, *49*(4), 418–433.

Der Derian, J. (2009). *Critical practices in international theory: selected essays*. London; New York: Routledge.
Der Derian, J., and Shapiro, M. (1989). *International/intertextual relations: postmodern readings of world politics*. Lexington: Lexington Books.
Doty, R. L. (1993). Foreign policy as social construction: a post-positivist analysis of US counterinsurgency policy in the Philippines. *International Studies Quarterly*, *37*(3), 297–320.
Doyle, M. (1997). *Ways of war and peace*. New York: W. W. Norton.
Downie, C. (2015). Global energy governance in the G-20: states, coalitions, and crises. *Global Governance: A Review of Multilateralism and International Organizations*, *21*(3), 475–492.
Florini, A., and Sovacool, B. K. (2009). Who governs energy? The challenges facing global energy governance. *Energy Policy*, *37*(12), 5239–5248.
Ghosh, A. (2011). Seeking coherence in complexity? the governance of energy by trade and investment institutions. *Global Policy*, *2*(1), 106–119.
Goldman, M. (2008). *Petrostate*. Oxford: Oxford University Press.
Goldthau, A., and Witte, J. M. (2010). *The role of rules and institutions in global energy: an introduction*. Berlin: Global Public Policy Institute.
Guzzini, S. (2011). Securitization as a causal mechanism. *Security Dialogue*, *42*(4), 329–341.
Halperin, S., and Heath, O. (2012). *Political research: methods and practical skills*. Oxford: Oxford University Press.
Hancock, K. J., and Vivoda, V. (2014). Energy research and social science. *Middle East*, *18*(92), 98.
Hansen, L. (2006). *Security as practice: discourse analysis and the Bosnian war*. London: Routledge.
Hollis, M., and Smith, S. (1990). *Explaining and understanding international relations*. Oxford: Clarendon Press.
Holzscheiter, A. (2014). Between communicative interaction and structures of signification: discourse theory and analysis in international relations. *International Studies Perspectives*, *15*(2), 142–162.
Hopf, T. (1998). The promise of constructivism in international relations theory. *International Security*, *23*(1), 171–200.
Jackson, P. T. (2016). *The conduct of inquiry in international relations: philosophy of science and its implications for the study of world politics*. London; New York: Routledge.
Keohane, R. (1978). The international energy agency: state influence and transgovernmental politics. *International Organization*, *32*(4), 929–951.
Kingsbury, B., and Robert, A. (1993). *United Nations, divided world: the UN's roles in international relations* (2nd ed.). Oxford: Clarendon Press; New York: Oxford University Press.
Kirton, J., and Kokotsis, E. (2015). *The global governance of climate change: G7, G20, and UN leadership*. London; New York: Routledge.
Klare, M. T. (2008). *Rising powers, shrinking planet: how scarce energy is creating a new world order*. New York: Metropolitan Books.
Kratochvíl, P., and Tichý, L. (2013). EU and Russian discourse on energy relations. *Energy Policy*, *56*, 391–406.
Kristeva, J. (1986). *The Kristeva reader*. New York: Columbia University Press.
Kropatcheva, E. (2014). He who has the pipeline calls the tune? Russia's energy power against the background of the shale "revolutions." *Energy Policy*, *66*, 1–10.

Kuhn, T. S. (2012). *The structure of scientific revolutions*. Chicago: University of Chicago Press.

Kuteleva, A. (2020). Discursive politics of energy in EU–Russia relations: Russia as an "energy superpower" and a "raw-material appendage." *Problems of Post-Communism*, *67*(1), 78–92.

Kuteleva, A., and Leifso, J. (2020). Contested crude: multiscalar identities, conflicting discourses, and narratives of oil production in Canada. *Energy Research & Social Science*, *70*, 101672.

Kupchan, Ch. A., and Kupchan, C. A. (1995). The promise of collective security. *International Security*, *20*(1), 52–61.

Little, R. (2007). *The balance of power in international relations: metaphors, myths and models*. Cambridge; New York: Cambridge University Press.

Locher, B., and Prügl, E. (2001). Feminism and constructivism: worlds apart or sharing the middle ground? *International Studies Quarterly*, *45*(1), 111–129.

Mankoff, J. (2009). *Russian foreign policy: the return of great power politics*. Lanham: Rowman and Littlefield Publishers.

March, J. G., and Olsen, J. P. (1989). *Rediscovering institutions: the organizational basis of politics*. New York: Free Press; London: Collier Macmillan.

March, J. G., and Olsen, J. P. (2006). The logic of appropriateness. In M. Moran, M. Rein, R. Goodin (Eds.) *The Oxford handbook of public policy* (pp. 689–708). Oxford: Oxford University Press.

March, J. G., and Olsen, J. P. (2009). The logic of appropriateness. ARENA Working Paper 04. Retrieved from https://www.sv.uio.no/arena/english/research/publications/arena-publications/workingpapers/working-papers2004/wp04_9.pdf/.

McKenna, B. (2004). Critical discourse studies: where to from here? *Critical Discourse Studies*, *1*(1), 9–39.

Mitchell, T. (2011). *Carbon democracy: political power in the age of oil*. London; New York: Verso Books.

Moravcsik, A. (1997). Taking preferences seriously: a liberal theory of international politics. *International Organization*, *51*(4), 513–553.

Nyman, J. (2018). *The energy security paradox: rethinking energy (in) security in the United States and China*. Oxford: Oxford University Press.

Nyman, J., and Zeng, J. (2016). Securitization in Chinese climate and energy politics. *Wiley Interdisciplinary Reviews: Climate Change*, *7*(2), 301–313.

Oneal, J. R., and Russett, B. (1997). The classical liberals were right: democracy, interdependence, and conflict, 1950–1985. *International Studies Quarterly*, *41*(2), 267–294.

Onuf, N. (1989). *World of our making: rules and rule in social theory and international relations*. Columbia, SC: University of South Carolina Press.

Orban, A. (2008). *Power, energy, and the new Russian imperialism*. Connecticut; London: Westport.

Orttung, R. W., and Overland, I. (2011). A limited toolbox: explaining the constraints on Russia's foreign energy policy. *Journal of Eurasian Studies*, *2*(1), 74–85.

Owen, J. (1994). How liberalism produces democratic peace. *International Security 19*(2), 87–125.

Phillips, A. (2013). A dangerous synergy: energy securitization, great power rivalry and strategic stability in the Asian century. *The Pacific Review*, *26*(1), 17–38.

Price, R., and Reus-Smit, C. (1998). Dangerous liaisons? Critical international theory and constructivism. *European Journal of International Relations*, *4*(3), 259–294.

Schumacher, E. F. (1982). *Schumacher on energy: speeches and writings of E. F. Schumacher*. London: Jonathan Cape.

Smith, M. J. (1992). Liberalism and international reform. In T. Nardin and D. Mapel (Eds.) *Traditions of international ethics* (pp. 201–224). Cambridge: Cambridge University Press.

Snyder, J. (2004). One world, rival theories. *Foreign Policy*, *145*, 52–62.

Stoddard, E. (2013). Reconsidering the ontological foundations of international energy affairs: realist geopolitics, market liberalism and a politico-economic alternative. *European Security*, *22*(4), 437–463.

Stokes, D., and Raphael, S. (2010). *Global energy security and American hegemony*. Baltimore, MD: JHU Press.

Tannenwald, N. (2007). *The nuclear taboo: The United States and the non-use of nuclear weapons since 1945*. Cambridge: Cambridge University Press.

Tsygankov, A. P. (2010). *Russia's foreign policy: change and continuity in national identity*. Lanham, MD: Rowman and Littlefield.

Van de Graaf, T. (2012). Obsolete or resurgent? The International Energy Agency in a changing global landscape. *Energy Policy*, *48*, 233–241.

Victor, D. G., and Yueh, L. (2010). The new energy order. *Foreign Affairs*, *89*(1), 61–73.

Walker, R. B. J. (1993). *Inside/outside: international relations as political theory*. Cambridge: Cambridge University Press.

Waltz, K. (1979). *Theory of international politics*. New York: McGraw-Hill.

Wæver, O. (1997). Alexander Wendt: a social scientist struggling with history. In I. B. Neumann and O. Wæver (Eds.) *The future of international relations: masters in the making?* (pp. 269–289). London; New York: Routledge.

Wæver, O. (2002). Identity, communities and foreign policy: discourse analysis as foreign policy theory. In L. Hansen and O. Wæver (Eds.) *European integration and national identity: the challenge of the Nordic states* (pp. 20–49). London: Routledge.

Wæver, O. (2004). *Aberystwyth, Paris, Copenhagen New Schools in Security Theory and the Origins between Core and Periphery*. Paper presented at the ISA Conference Montreal.

Weitz, R. (2006). Averting a new great game in central Asia. *Washington Quarterly*, *29*(3), 155–167.

Wendt, A. (1995). Constructing international politics. *International Security*, *20*(1), 71–85.

Wendt, A. (1999). *Social theory of international politics*. Cambridge: Cambridge University Press.

Wishnick, E. (2009). Competition and cooperative practices in Sino-Japanese energy and environmental relations: towards an energy security "risk community"?. *The Pacific Review*, *22*(4), 401–428.

Zehfuss, M. (2001). Constructivism and identity: a dangerous liaison. *European Journal of International Relations*, *7*(3), 315–348.

Zweig, D., and Bi, J. (2005). China's hunt for global energy. *Foreign Affairs*, *84*(5), 25–38.

Zweig, D., and Hao, Y. (2015). *Sino-US energy triangles: resource diplomacy under hegemony*. London; New York: Routledge.

3 China's energy security and discursive politics of energy

In the late 19th and the early 20th centuries, economically dilapidated, politically divided, and unstable, China served as a space for geopolitical invasion and imperial domination for Britain, Germany, Russia, France, Japan, and other nations. In October 1949, the People's Republic of China emerged from the crucible of the "century of humiliation" (百年国耻, *bainian guochi*). China's new leaders, led by Mao Zedong, introduced a centrally planned command economy patterned on that of the Soviet Union and set out an ambitious goal to develop a massive industrial complex by the end of the next decade. The period between 1953 and 1957, corresponding to the First Five-Year Plan, was largely successful. However, the Great Leap Forward campaign launched in 1958 resulted in an economic disaster that caused the most devastating famine in China's modern history (Zhou 2013; Dikötter 2011). The concurrent withdrawal of Soviet aid seriously affected the progress of the Third Five-Year Plan and further aggravated China's socioeconomic development (Adelman and Sunding 1987). Moreover, economic experiments of the Great Leap Forward were followed by social and political experiments of the Great Cultural Revolution (1966–1976) that led to a profound systemic crisis (MacFarquhar and Fairbank 1991).

The so-called "second generation of leaders," headed by Deng Xiaoping, came to power soon after Mao Zedong died in 1976 and made a sharp and decisive turn from "permanent revolution" (不断革命, *buduan geming*) to "socialism with Chinese characteristics" (中国特色社会主义, *zhongguo tese shehui zhuyi*). In the four decades after China's government officially initiated the "reform and opening up" policies in 1978, China has successfully lifted a record number of people out of poverty, achieved a rapid increase in living standards, reached a sustained level of economic growth, and emerged as an active participant in global trade, gaining stature and influence in world affairs and becoming a player of consequence on the international stage. Martin Jacques (2009, 185) enthusiastically summarizes China's developmental experience in the 21st century:

> The emergent Chinese model bears witness to a new kind of capitalism where the state is hyperactive and omnipresent in a range of different ways and forms: in providing assistance to private firms, in a galaxy of state-owned enterprises, in managing the process by which the renminbi slowly evolves

> towards fully convertible status and, above all, in being the architect of an economic strategy which has driven China's economic transformation. China's success suggests that the Chinese model of the state is destined to exercise a powerful global influence, especially in the developing world, and thereby transform the terms of future economic debate.

Despite such positive assessments, there are plenty of far less favorable aspects of China's extraordinary transformation. China's development so far has been extremely resource-intensive, and its current success cannot be divorced from the various domestic challenges related to the environmental and resource sustainability of its growth trajectory.

China's energy problems are vast, complex, and increase exponentially as China continues its development. Since the establishment of the People's Republic of China in 1949, energy resources have been perceived in China as a matter of national security and a source of chronic vulnerability. After struggling to achieve energy self-sufficiency throughout the 1950s, China enjoyed it for almost three decades. Energy exports were the major source of foreign exchange and played a vital role in China's modernization in the late 1970s and the mid-1980s. In the early 1990s, China began transitioning rapidly from self-sufficient to import-dependent development. China became a coal importer in 2002 and a natural gas importer in 2007. However, the shift is specifically noticeable for oil: in the 1980s China's oil production was 35 percent more than its consumption, but since 2003 over one-half of the oil consumed in China has been imported (BP 2017).

Between the 2000s and the 2010s, China's industrial sector accounted for 70 percent of final energy consumption. Contrary to popular assumptions, the rapid and extensive development of industry is not directly correlated to the accelerated growth of oil demand. Oil demand increased by 567 percent in industry, but in other sectors it has been growing faster (e.g., Leung 2010; Lin and Xie 2013; Pan et al. 2020). In fact, the industrial sector's share of total oil consumption even decreased from 59 percent in 1990 to 41 percent in 2014. Industry has been contributing to the total oil consumption by driving oil demand in the transport sector that went up by 2,097 percent between 1980 and 2012. While the share of oil in the total industrial energy fuel mix did not change since the early 1990s, fluctuating around 15–16 percent, the share of oil in the transportation sector fuel mix jumped to 90 percent in the mid-2000s (Leung 2010, 937). Specifically, the accelerated use of diesel for road transportation closely correlates to the development of heavy industries that boomed throughout the 1990s and 2000s, for example, construction, coal, shipbuilding, steel, and cement (Meidan et al. 2015, 4). For more than a decade after 2000, the demand for diesel grew with 8 percent annual average rates. Even though it started slowing down in 2011 and declined in 2013 for the first time in the past four decades, IWEP ACSS (2016, 132) predicts that domestic consumption and further development of the transport sector will likely continue to precipitate a modest growth of diesel consumption in the future.

Socioeconomic changes of the 2000s have also added additional pressure to oil consumption. China's urban population grew from 35.4 percent in 2000 to

57.35 percent in 2016 (NBSC 2017). At the same time, the disposable income per capita of urban residents skyrocketed, showing a 10 percent increase annually (NBSC 2017). China's new dynamic consumer culture promotes a lifestyle that is ecologically destructive and fundamentally dependent on non-renewable sources of energy. High fossil fuel use and carbon-intensive behavior are now the major consumer patterns of China's households (Dai et al. 2012; Feng et al. 2011; Liu et al. 2009). The spread of "car culture" that goes hand in hand with urbanization and the expansion of the urban middle class is one of the most vivid examples of the relationships between socioeconomic changes and oil consumption.

In the 2000s, Chinese cities became less pedestrian and cyclist-friendly, the daily travel distance of urban residents significantly increased, and the use of public transport escalated considerably at the expense of non-motorized transport modes (Pan et al. 2009; Wang et al. 2011). At the same time, owning a car became an essential badge of middle-class social status for the urban Chinese (Gerth 2010; Marks 2012). The overall number of civilian vehicles on the roads increased from 15.45 million in 2006 to 108.7 million in 2016, while the number of private passenger cars grew from 11.49 million to 101.5 million (NBSC 2017). Gasoline is the second-largest consumed oil product in China, with an estimated 23 percent share and, due to the growth in the number of vehicles, its consumption rose to 17,812 Mtoe in 2015 (IWEP ACSS 2016, 132). Besides, the massive boom in car ownership and rapid development of the transport sector, in general, spurred energy-hungry domestic auto production. China surpassed the US, Japan, Germany, and South Korea and became the largest auto manufacturer in 2012 (OICA 2017). In 2016, China's production of passenger cars reached 24.420 million units (OICA 2017) and continues to grow. To put China's car culture in the global perspective, the share of car owners in China is only 17 percent, whereas 88 percent of Americans have a car, Japan and South Korea trail closely behind the US with 81 percent and 83 percent of car owners respectively, and the median national share of car owners in the European Union is 79 percent (Pew Research Center 2015). China's share of car owners is significantly below the international average of 35 percent and is less than the share of car owners in countries such as El Salvador (19 percent), Nigeria (18 percent), and South Africa (31 percent) (Pew Research Center 2015). Given China's low numbers, it is reasonable to expect that the expansion of car culture in China will push the consumption of oil for quite some time.

Why does China's oil consumption matter? Many interdependences between China and the world are economic – most notable examples include trade relations and financial flows – while other, no less important, forms of mutual interdependencies concern global environmental degradation and natural resource shortage. Consequently, inasmuch as China now occupies a central place in an increasingly interdependent world, the sustainability of China's development is not "their" but "our" problem. Both inside and outside China, the consensus is that the country's resource-intensive model of development is unsustainable in the short and long terms. But how will China address the resource shortage? If

China's modern history is a guide, China will change swiftly and deliberately, solving the problems that it currently faces and moving on to the next set of problems that it will create in the interim. That is why it is particularly important to understand how China defines its development in the context of energy deficit, as well as how China imagines the future and prepares for it.

How does modern China define and communicate its identity in international energy relations and how does China make its energy choices? This is the central question that I address in this chapter. The first part of the chapter discusses the evolution of China's energy strategy from the mid-1950s to the early 2000s. It tells the story of China's oil that starts with the discovery of oil in Daqing in 1959 and goes all the way to China's commitment to "peaceful rise" and "world harmony" in the early 2000s. The second section focuses on China's discursive energy politics between 2005 and 2016. First, it examines the evolution and diversification of China's approach to energy security and explains the recent changes in China's framing of oil. Further, the chapter turns to contextualized actualizations of collective identities: Who are "we" and who are "they" in China's energy politics? It explains how and with what effect China defines itself as well as its allies and adversaries in international energy politics. The final section of the chapter maps China's energy paradigm by identifying discursive constructions that are institutionalized as China's energy strategy.

Evolution of China's energy strategy from the 1950s to the 2000s: "Self-reliance," "going out," and "scientific development"

Daqing: The "big celebration" in the history of China's oil

Right after the People's Republic of China was established, China joined the "battle for oil" (石油大会战, *Shiyou dahui zhan*). During the first decade of this battle, Soviet technical advisers and specialists controlled the development of China's petroleum industry. China also was dependent on the Soviet Union for approximately 80 percent of drilling equipment and machinery and imported Soviet crude oil and refined oil products (Cheng 1976, 128). As a result, the Sino-Soviet split of the mid-1950s created an acute shortage of oil that forced China's government to accelerate efforts to increase domestic extraction and production capacity. Soon Daqing, located in the northeastern part of the country in Heilongjiang Province, became the frontline of China's "battle for oil" and the axial symbol of China's economic and political independence.

Daqing is the largest oilfield in China. Official narratives link its discovery directly to the core of China's nation-building project by connecting it to the 10th anniversary of the foundation of the PRC. Daqing's history formally started four days before the National Day celebrations on 26 September 1959, when, according to official Chinese sources, oil flowed from Songji No. 3 well in Songliao Basin. In 1960, Daqing's proved oil reserves were estimated to be 400 million tons (Feng et al. 2012, 6). Production multiplied and, by the end of 1963, 46.3 percent of all oil produced in China came from Daqing (Lim 2010, 19).

The very name "Daqing" emphasizes its symbolic importance and ideological underpinning as it is derived from a combination of two words: "big" (大, *da*) and "celebration" (庆, *qing*). All spheres of the production process and daily life in Daqing were ideologized and from the outset framed as a never-ending struggle. Daqing was frequently referred to as a "battleground" (战区, *zhanqu*) or a "great battle" *(*大清会战, *daqing huizhan*).[1] The Political Department of Daqing Oilfield established a political supervisory structure similar to the one of the People's Liberation Army (Hama 1980, 190–191) and published weekly ideological updates in a newsletter entitled *Battle Report of Daqing* (大庆战报, *Daqing zhanbao*).[2] As Chu-yuan Cheng (1976, 11) points out, Daqing was deliberately designed "so as not to replicate the typical oil-boom city of the West." Yu Qiuli,[3] who was responsible for the early development of China's oil industry, instituted in Daqing a policy of self-sufficiency and frugality for oilfield workers and their dependents that subsequently has evolved into a cult of self-imposed asceticism and ideological vigor.

During the Cultural Revolution (1966–1976), Daqing played a distinct role in the Maoist ideology, when China's authorities turned oil workers into the national "labor model" (模式or 典型, *moshi* or *dianxing*) in the industrial sector.[4] Wang Jinxi, the head of a drilling crew, became the focus of the "Industry Learn from Daqing" (工业学大庆, *Gongye Xue Daqing*) national ideological campaign and gradually earned the status of a national hero.[5] He was renowned for what later came to be known as the "iron man spirit" (铁人精神, *tieren jingshen*) or "Daqing spirit" (大庆精神, *Daqing jingshen*): selflessness, unconditional loyalty to the party-state, and exceptional courage to work in hostile and harsh conditions for the sake of national prosperity. Featured on numerous propaganda posters and in newspaper articles, Wang Jinxi literally became the face of China's industrialization in the 1960s and 1970s. After Wang Jinxi died in 1970, China's authorities carefully preserved his legacy. Between 1971 and 1978, the *People's Daily* mentioned Wang Jingxi in 361 editorials (Renmin Ribao Tuwen Shujuku 2017). Wang Jinxi also became a character of many children's books and in 1973 his biography was published in 150 thousand copies. To commemorate Wang Jinxi's contribution to the development of the national oil industry, China's authorities erected elaborate monuments all around China, including a massive Iron Man Memorial in Daqing (opened in 1971, subsequently expanded).

On a broader scale, Daqing and the oil industry epitomized the success and leadership of the Communist Party of China. In the words of Zhou Enlai, Daqing symbolized "the red flag that was erected by Chairman Mao himself" (Renmin Ribao 1967a). According to the official narratives, the "red flag of Daqing" (大庆红旗, *Daqing hongqi*) made "American imperialists" and "Soviet revisionists" shiver in fear and admiration (Renmin Ribao Tuwen Shujuku 2017).

At the end of 1963, Zhou Enlai attested that "China does not need to import oil anymore and can be primarily self-sufficient" (Renmin Ribao 1963). Soon after, the idea of self-reliance[6] became a guiding principle for the energy industry development, striking deep roots into the official energy discourses and a broader discourse of national development.

In the Chinese context, the idea of self-reliance is related to the locus of control over the trajectory of national development. First and foremost, it implies an orientation on the maximum possible independence and autonomy in decision-making. Following this logic, energy self-sufficiency becomes an ultimate programmatic and policy goal and is a corollary of self-reliance. Starting from the late 1950s, the idea of self-reliance, both economically and politically, was taken to its extreme as complete non-involvement in international relations and isolation. During this time, self-reliance in the development of the energy sector was framed not as a rational and deliberate developmental choice but as a matter of survival.

Getting used to the new energy security imperatives

Between the early 1960s and the mid-1970s, China's enthusiasm and great optimism about the future of Daqing and the development of the oil industry, in general, were taken up by the West. Western imagination of China's success ran wild as a result of statements made by China's authorities (Bartke 1977, 21; Yeh 1962, 1–2) and was further ignited by reports of China-friendly foreign journalists, such as Anna Louise Strong (e.g., 1963) and Wilfred Burchett (e.g., 1974). However, as Lim Tai Wei (2010, 10–11) indicates, the exact location and size of Daqing were unknown outside China for almost a decade and up until the mid-1970s most of the available information about Daqing in the West came from a report provided by an anonymous mainland China immigrant to Taiwan.

In 1974, the chairman of the Japan-China Oil Import Council, Ryutaro Hasegawa, visited Daqing and announced on his return to Japan that soon China will become Japan's major oil supplier (Smil 2004, 8). As Vaclav Smil (2004, 9) accurately puts it, Japanese "wishful thinking was mistaken for a genuine critical forecasting" by many international observers. Some renowned Asia experts in the US concluded that by the 1980s China's oil production would have a considerable impact on the international energy market. Selig S. Harrison (1975, 4), for example, branded China as "the next oil giant," claiming that "the net effect of expanded Chinese oil exports would be to reduce global dependence on the Middle East and the Persian Gulf." In a similar vein, Park Choon-ho and Jerome Alan Cohen (1975) certified that "the oil-poor China of the past" would soon "emerge as an oil power of the future" (28) and warned that "enormous quantities of [China's oil] may be a mixed blessing" for the US (49). Arthur Jay Klinghoffer (1976, 540) believed that oil from Daqing transformed China "into a regional oil power in East Asia" and "a successful rival of the Soviet Union in the game of Asian oil politics." For their part, Soviet experts did not recognize China as a potential competitor, yet still were worried that China was becoming increasingly independent and assertive (e.g., Kulpin 1975; Kapitsa 1979). Nonetheless, while China's oil production had indeed skyrocketed from 11.31 Mtoe in 1965 to

106.15 Mtoe in 1979 (BP 2017), China was not destined to become a new Kuwait or a new Saudi Arabia.

In the 1980s, China became the world's fourth-largest oil producer outside the Middle East and started to sell its oil on the international market, signing contracts with Japan, Thailand, Philippines, Romania, and Hong Kong (Zha 2005a, 16). However, China's career as an oil exporter was soon to end. After the introduction of the "reforms and opening up" policies and the turn from Mao Zedong's "permanent revolution" to Deng Xiaoping's "socialism with Chinese characteristics" in 1978, China emerged as "the world's factory floor" and rapid economic development accelerated domestic oil demand. As early as 1993, China turned from a net oil exporter into a net oil importer. Meanwhile, the productivity of China's oilfields worsened, and the quality of domestic production declined steadily because of resource depletion. By the mid-1990s, all radical options for the development of domestic energy capacity had already been exhausted and it became clear that in the near to medium term China would be unable to overcome its foreign energy dependence on fossil fuels (Zha 2005b, 28).

China's first oil-boom town, Yumen, located in the northwest of Gansu Province, had turned into a "ghost town" by the mid-2000s when the deposits of the Laojunmiao oilfield were exhausted. Daqing has also experienced an economic downturn, yet it avoided the faith of Yumen because of its celebrity status. The central and provincial governments closely monitored the post-industrial transition and economic development of Daqing in the 2000s (Wang et al. 2014). When I visited Daqing in November 2016, the city was bearing all the typical signs of decay under a command economy. A high-speed train from Harbin, the capital of Heilongjiang Province, brought me to a newly built modern railway station that was obviously too big for a city the size of Daqing. Several hundreds of pumpjacks scattered around the city were nodding rhythmically near closed shopping malls and new residential areas unclaimed by tenants. Newly renovated roads were empty.

While Daqing's population is aging and declining, the central and provincial authorities are pouring investments not only into Daqing's infrastructure but also into its heroic heritage. Iron Man Memorial (Figure 3.1) opened in 1971 was subsequently expanded in 1991 and 2004. In 2006, the new memorial complex was built to celebrate the 47th anniversary of the discovery of Daqing oilfield. It occupies 21 square kilometers and includes a park with a 30-meter-tall granite statue of Wang Jinxi and a museum with about 2,000 exhibits.

In addition to the Iron Man Memorial, Daqing, like any other major oil city in the world, has a museum that tells the story of its oil. The main exhibition at the Museum of Daqing Oilfield funded by CNPC is divided into three parts: The Surprising Discovery of Daqing; A Difficult Start of the Great History; and The People of Daqing Oilfield Are Its Backbone. A large part of the exhibition consists of lifelike specimens and practical artifacts, including personal items of Daqing's oil workers and management (e.g., Figure 3.2). It also features works of art dedicated to the oil workers of Daqing (e.g., Figures 3.3 and 3.4). Consequently, the Museum of Daqing Oilfield is not an industrial museum but a heritage center: it is devoted almost entirely to the stories of the people who built China's oil industry rather than to the history of the industry itself. At the same time, these stories are carefully bound to the official narrative of China's development since the establishment of the PRC. In this sense, the Museum of Daqing Oilfield is a museum of China's political history and – more than anything else – showcases the ideological role that the oil industry has been playing in China since the 1950s.

In 2003, to avoid the depletion of the oilfield and to cut capital spending, CNPC (China National Petroleum Corporation) decided to bring the production down to 803.289 kbd strategically. Daqing became a "centurial oilfield," meaning that it is will operate for a century and is supposed to be China's major domestic oil production base until 2060 (CNPC 2017).[7] According to Xi Jingping (2009), the goal of Daqing in the coming decades is two-fold: "to maintain for as long as possible high and stable production to ease the tension of domestic oil demand and to protect the national energy security," and "to promote the economic development of Heilongjiang province and revitalization of the old industrial bases of the northeastern region in general to support the steady growth of the national economy." Consequently, even though Daqing is not an active center of thriving industrial development anymore, it is still a symbol of this development. Importantly, it still plays a vital role in China's quest for the maximum possible self-reliance.

Figure 3.1 Daqing Iron Man Wang Jinxi Memorial. Daqing, China, November 2016.

Figure 3.2 The Museum of Daqing Oilfield, November 2016. An oil worker studies the "two theories" of Chairman Mao after a shift.

Figure 3.3 The Museum of Daqing Oilfield, November 2016. Zheng Zhenhe (1977). The Iron Man Wang Jinxi studies the "two theories" of Chairman Mao.

Figure 3.4 The Museum of Daqing Oilfield, November 2016. Yu Daokai (1989). The birth of Daqing: Greeting the National Day with new and outstanding success.

The "going global" strategy and China's NOCs in the 2000s and the 2010s

In the 1980s, China's oil consumption increased annually by an average of 5.4 percent. In 1993, China's oil consumption surpassed its oil production, and as a result, China became a net importer of oil. In 2002, while still holding the title of the world's fourth-largest oil producer outside the Middle East, China became the world's second-largest oil consumer. Between 1993 and 2015, its net oil import dependency[8] climbed from 8 percent to 59 percent (see Table 3.1), and, so far, oil is the only source of energy for which China meets the demand by such massive net imports.

In 1997, a policy paper authored by Prime Minister Li Peng acknowledged that domestic oil production "cannot keep up with the needs of economic

Table 3.1 China's Oil Production, Consumption, and Trade: 1993–2016

	Production (Mtoe)	*Consumption (Mtoe)*	*Imports (Mtoe)*	*Exports (Mtoe)*	*Net imports (Mtoe)*	*Net import dependency (%)*
1980	105.95	86.66	8.27	−18.06	−9.79	−11
1985	124.90	89.75	9.00	−36.30	−27.30	−30
1990	138.31	112,86	7.56	−31.10	−23.55	−21
1993	144.03	145.79	36.20	−25.10	11.10	8
1994	146.08	148.12	29.00	−23.80	5.20	4
1995	149.02	160.20	36.73	−24.55	12.19	8
1996	158.52	175.67	45.40	−27.00	18.40	10
1997	160.13	192.15	67.90	−28.20	39.70	21
1998	160.18	197.08	57.40	−23.30	34.10	17
1999	160.22	209.33	64.80	−16.40	48.40	23
2000	162.62	224.22	97.49	−21.72	75.76	34
2001	164.83	229.09	91.20	−20.50	70.70	31
2002	166.87	248.10	102.70	−21.40	81.30	33
2003	169.59	276.94	131.90	−25.40	106.50	38
2004	174.05	323.41	172.90	−22.40	150.50	47
2005	181.35	328.93	171.16	−28.88	142.28	43
2006	184.77	353.15	194.50	−26.30	168.20	48
2007	186.32	370.66	211.40	−26.60	184.80	50
2008	190.44	378.06	230.16	−29.40	200.76	53
2009	189.49	392.81	256.42	−3.92	252.51	64
2010	203.01	448.49	294.37	−4.08	290.29	65
2011	202.88	465.11	315.94	−4.12	311.82	67
2012	207.48	487.07	330.89	−3.88	327.00	67
2013	209.96	508.14	281.74	−1.62	280.13	55
2014	211.43	527.96	361.80	−4.21	357.58	68
2015	214.56	561.84	335.48	−2.87	332.62	59
2016	199.69	587.66	–	–	–	–

Source: BP Energy Charting Tool and NBSC.

development" and stated that, while China is still determined to expand and diversify domestic oil production, it will also have to "go on the global level" and "invest into the development of multifaceted cooperation with foreign countries" (China Internet Information Center 2012).[9] This paper signified the official shift from "self-reliance" to "going global" (走出去, *zou chuqu*) in China's energy strategy. The three large state-owned companies – China National Offshore Oil Corporation (CNOOC), China Petrochemical Group Corporation (Sinopec), and China National Petroleum Group Corporation (CNPC) – became instruments in the implementation of this strategy.

In the process of reorganization of the ministries responsible for the energy sector, these three national oil companies (NOCs) were created in the 1980s. The ministries were repeatedly reshuffled, and eventually, ministerial authority was forwarded to three state-owned enterprises. CNOOC was created in 1982 from the offshore assets of the Ministry of Petroleum Industry and is currently responsible for the overall offshore work in cooperation with foreign enterprises. In 1983, Sinopec was created from the downstream assets of the Ministry of Petroleum Industry and the Ministry of Chemical Industry. Sinopec received full control over downstream production and took the responsibilities for all oil refining, marketing, and petrochemical manufacturing. Finally, in 1988, the CNPC was established to take control over the remaining onshore upstream oil and gas production activities. China's authorities stimulated the development and growth of CNOOC, Sinopec, and CNPC through price liberalization and the introduction of management incentives and internal market competition (Houser 2008). At the end of the 1990s, China's NOCs were ready and had a market incentive to "go global" even in the absence of a mandate by China's authorities (Downs 2006, 2007; Zhang, Z. 2012). In fact, the NOCs started to invest in developing new oil resources outside China years before the government included "going global" into the national energy strategy (Zhang, C. 2015, 280).

However, China's NOCs became visible on the international energy market and the level of their overseas investment started proliferating only after the government granted them official approval. In the 1990s, NOCs directed their investments in fields with proven reserves and focused on bringing their overseas production home (Alon et al. 2015, 298). However, by the mid-2000s, China's domestic refinery capacity expanded, and the NOCs could diversify their investment portfolio by engaging in the production and exploration of different types of crude oil (Zha 2005b, 28). At the same time, the NOCs became more ambitious by targeting exploration areas with unproven reserves and expanding the geographic scope of their business activities. Most often, the NOCs advanced their trading operations to maximize profits regardless of the oil's final destination. Between 2005 and 2006, when overseas mergers and acquisitions of China's NOCs peaked, 93 percent of their foreign production was sold on local markets, whereas equity oil[10] made up only 15 percent of China's oil imports (Chen 2011, 607, see also Houser 2008, 155). Consequently, through overseas equity investments, China's NOCs were trying to secure control over the upstream to increase their profits, rather than to advance China's national energy security. China's goals became even more apparent in the period after 2008 when China's NOCs expanded their overseas activities in the aftermath of the global financial crisis (Alon et al. 2015).

China experts report that, even though China's government does not dictate to the NOCs where, how, and when to invest, all overseas projects initiated by the NOCs have to be authorized by the National Development and Reform Commission (NDRC)[11] and the Ministry of Foreign Affairs before being implemented (Downs 2006, 2008; Andrews-Speed 2012; Zhang, C. 2015). In other words, China's party-state monitors and supports but does not run the overseas activities of the NOCs. The dynamics of China's domestic political and economic development in the 2000s led to a high degree of convergence between the interests of the state and that of the NOCs. While it is unclear whether China's NOCs consider national interests and security in their business activities abroad, they comply with and actively support the official energy security discourse (Zhang, C. 2015, 280–281).

China's "going global" energy strategy is not limited to the support of the outward investment of NOCs. It also includes merging energy security objectives with foreign policy and diplomatic efforts. As Chen Shaofeng (2008, 93), a political scientist from Peking University, points out, "securing energy resources abroad and diversifying import sources have de facto been incorporated into China's foreign strategy." In the 2000s, China advanced its bilateral relationships with oil-rich countries, such as Iran, Sudan, Libya, Myanmar, Russia, and Kazakhstan. The involvement of the Ministry of Foreign Affairs in energy deals makes it an influential stakeholder in China's energy strategy development.

A political economist of Peking University, Zha Daojiong (2005b, 28), notes that, between the 1950s and the 1970s, China had "20 years of self-reliance in a tense international environment," but, up until the early 1990s, it did not have to worry about its energy security. In the early 2000s, according to Zha (2005b, 29), it became evident that "the era of energy self-sufficiency has passed" and now China has "no alternative but to learn how to survive in the interdependent world." Nevertheless, the legacy of self-reliance and its influence on China's energy security is still strong. At the dawn of the "going out" strategy, China was still focused on maintaining its freedom from outside control and minimizing outside influence. In this sense, the "going out" strategy should be seen not as a substitute for China's energy self-reliance strategy but as its extension and evolution.

New variables in China's energy development: Sustainability and environment

Energy resources, and oil specifically, from the outset, were ideologized and securitized issues in China. As a result, up until the mid-2000s, China's energy security was limited to the supply side. China's state did not pay significant attention to control over domestic energy consumption and the advancement of a domestic clean energy agenda. China's energy security strategy focused on keeping high economic growth, and energy resources, in this framework, were viewed as strategic commodities rather than standard commercial commodities to be allocated by the free market. The initial panic over China's energy dependency started to subside gradually both inside and outside China in the mid-2000s. China's state reconciled with the fact that substantial oil imports were China's new normal and acknowledged that growing dependency on imported energy was not China's only energy problem.

China's high fossil-fuel use and carbon-intensive development also aggravated environmental degradation. By the mid-2000s, thick smog covered Beijing, Chongqing, Tianjin, Shanghai, Harbin, Ürümqi, and many other major Chinese cities, cutting visibility and causing chief disruptions in transportation and daily activities. The carbon dioxide (CO_2) footprint of China's energy consumption was far higher than that of any other single country. Coal is mostly to blame for the degradation of air quality and the increase of CO_2 emissions: it contributes about 70 percent of China's total dust, nitrogen oxide emissions, and CO_2 emissions, and up to 90 percent of China's total sulfur dioxide (SO_2). However, the growing consumption of oil by transport and industrial sectors adds their fair share to China's environmental degradation (He et al. 2005; Alam and Paramati 2015). Environmental destruction started to threaten China's economic growth, whereas rising incomes and rapid urbanization increased the demand for environmental amenities and thus political pressure for environmental protection.

In the mid-2000s, China's state shifted the focus from economic development measured in the growth of its GDP to improving the national environmental landscape and social sustainability. The "fourth generation of leaders" headed by Hu Jintao promised to evaluate China's developmental success based on "the satisfaction of the people" (Central Committee of the CPC 2003). China's new aspiration was "harmony" (和谐, *hexie*), a concept with Confucian overtones (e.g., Ge 2006, 30–42). On the domestic level, "harmony" was defined as "the development of the entire society in a sustainable and balanced manner" and "putting people first." The Chinese government operationalized it as five overarching and interdependent developmental targets (known as the "five harmonies"): (1) harmony in the development of urban and rural areas (emphasizing rural development); (2) harmony in regional development (emphasizing the gap between the coastal provinces and the rest of the country); (3) harmony in the balance between economic and social development (with emphasis on creating more jobs and providing better social services); (4) harmony in relations between people and nature (stressing resource conservation and environmental protection); (5) harmony in the balance between national development and openness to the international markets (Central Committee of the CPC 2003).

"Harmony" became the central theme of the 17th National Congress of the CPC held in 2007, and China's domestic development officially became encapsulated in the concept of a "harmonious society" (和谐社会, *hexie shehui*). After the Congress, "harmony" spilled all over China: university administrations urged students to "make the campus life harmonious," taxi companies encouraged passengers to maintain "harmonious relations with the driver," and even local farmers' markets started to promote "harmonious trade."[12] After 2007, the aspiration for harmony was omnipresent: one could find it everywhere, from the "harmonious" high-speed trains (和谐号, *Hexie Hao*) to the "harmonious family" sales promotion (和谐家庭, *Hexie Jiating*) of the American fast-food chain KFC.

"Harmony" also became the new mode and the ultimate goal of China's interactions with the international community. In 2007, Hu Jintao highlighted that China maintains "that the people of all countries should join hands and strive to build the harmonious world of lasting peace and common prosperity" (和谐世界, *hexie shijie*). Hu (2007) also promised to ensure that China's rise will be peaceful (和平发展, *heping fazhan*), calling the aspiration for peace a "strategic choice that the government and people of China have made in light of the development trend of the times and their fundamental interests" (see also Hu 2005).

Another significant contribution of the "fourth generation" to China's ideology was the concept of a "scientific outlook on development" (科学发展观, *kexue fazhan guan*)[13] that corresponded with the quest for harmony on the domestic and international levels (Wu, X. 2009). "Scientific outlook" is not about science per se but about the quality of development, as it promotes a conception of balanced and inclusive growth. On the international level, China's leaders were linking "scientific outlook" to the international "sustainability" discourse (可持续, *ke chixu* with a focus on climate change). In contrast, on the domestic level the emphasis was on the use of innovations, technology, and expertise in solving China's social and ecological problems.

Overall, the two concepts – "harmonious society/ world" and "scientific outlook on development" – defined a new developmental objective for China. In 2005, China's leaders included energy conservation and environmental protection in the national economic development framework as a part of the 11th Five-Year Plan.[14] The overarching goal was to reduce energy use per unit of GDP by 20 percent and cut national SO_2 emissions by 10 percent in the period between 2006 and 2010.

China's discursive politics of energy

What does oil mean for China?

As the first part of this chapter demonstrated, the availability of oil from the outset was ideologized and framed as a security issue in modern China. From the early 1950s to the early 2000s, China's understanding of energy security was limited to the supply side and was focused on oil. With the rapid growth of China's oil imports and even more so with the new focus on sustainable development in the mid-2000s, energy deficit has ceased to be an internal issue for China, and the concept of energy security has started to internationalize and expand.

Between 2006 and 2016, Chinese politicians often place energy on an extensive list of new non-traditional security threats. They mention it as one of the most current global developmental challenges, including terrorism, transnational cybercrimes, food insecurity, infection disease, natural disasters, and climate change (e.g., Yang 2009, 2011; Hu 2012; Xi 2015b, 2016). China's official energy discourse also emphasized the complex interconnections within the international system that make balanced and equal energy development of all states within it a universal value (e.g., State Council of the PRC 2012; Li, K. 2012; Yang 2012b).

In parallel with internationalization, the concept of energy security also started to incorporate new dimensions of energy development. In the 21st century, according to China's authorities, China's energy resources ought to be stable and secure, as well as economically efficient and clean. In this sense, "China's energy development not only guarantees domestic economic and social development but also makes significant contributions to global energy security" (State Council of the PRC 2012).

Energy security now goes beyond the supply security of fossil fuels. Over the past decade, China has emerged as both the world's largest producer and consumer of renewable energy technologies. The Renewable Energy Law of 2005 (amended in 2009) and the Energy Conservation Law of 2007 are official benchmarks for China's "green" and "sustainable" energy development (绿色发展 and 可持续发展, *luse fazhan* and *kechixu fazhan*). The Renewable Energy Law specifies measures and goals relating to mandatory grid connection, price management regulation, special funds, and tax reliefs (State Council of the PRC 2009). Importantly, this law sets the goal to increase the share of renewable resources in China's total energy mix up to 15 percent by 2020. The Energy Conservation Law (State Council of the PRC 2007) intends to strengthen energy conservation on the national level, specifically, for key energy-using entities. It also promotes efficient use of energy, the adoption of energy conservation technologies, and the application of renewable energy in various areas. Between 2009 and 2010, renewable energy resources and technological development moved to the very center of China's discursive politics of energy. As Zhang Guobao (2009, 43) summarizes, China's government realized that "if China neglects the renewable energy industry now, in the next ten years it will suddenly find itself falling behind other countries once again." As a result of this shift in thinking, "science and technology" became a new mantra of China's energy development (e.g., Jiang 2008; Hu 2012; Li, K. 2012; Liu 2012c; Wu, X. 2014a).

The shift to a broader concept of energy security is closely associated with and follows the logic of "harmonious society/ world" and "China's peaceful rise." For instance, reframing the notion of "harmonious society/ world," the authors of the 2007 China's Energy Development Report focus on "development" and "peace." In the manifesto-like introduction, they describe the availability of energy resources as a precondition of "development" and a potential obstacle to "peace," emphasizing that the global quest for energy resources leads to fierce competition between different groups of states, aggravates mistrust, and increases possible conflict between great powers. The authors of the report strongly argue in favor of "peaceful international cooperation" in the realm of energy development. In their opinion, shifting the focus from geopolitics to integrated, sustainable, and efficient development is the only solution for the global energy challenges in the

21st century. They also suggest that changing the approach to energy security on the international level will bring a noticeable change. By switching to a more inclusive and cooperative mode of international energy relations the countries of the Global North will understand that their energy security is not affected by the surge in energy demand in China, India, and other developing countries.

China's officials construct the scarcity of energy resources as producing international inequality and reinforcing the backlog in the development of the Global South in the 21st century. They see the availability of energy resources as a developmental right of all nations. In this sense, they put human development above environmental concerns. Representatives of China do not deny the negative impacts of climate change and its connection to the rising production and consumption of fossil fuels. Yet, they label the attempts to impose universal consumption limits under the umbrella of climate change as actions that hinder economic growth and poverty reduction in the Global South (e.g., Wen 2007b; Zhang, G. 2008c; Li, K. 2012).

Given their emphasis on globalization and interdependence, China's officials find the solution to the contradictory energy problems in the realm of international politics. First of all, the countries of the Global North must recognize their "historical responsibilities" toward the Global South and act accordingly, generating the political will to ensure a fairer and more equitable global energy development (State Council of the PRC 2005; Wen 2007b). It is the Global South's turn to realize its full potential and it must have an opportunity to allocate as many energy resources as it needs for its economic growth. However, China now treats economic growth as a means rather than an end. Following the logic of a "harmonious society/ world," China urges the countries of the Global South to not only prioritize their economic success but also to generate the political will for a fundamental change in the mode of energy consumption. The primary rationale here is that patterns of energy consumption developed by the Global North in the 19th and 20th centuries are unhealthy and unsustainable for the shared future of both the North and the South (Li, K. 2012).

Despite a general acknowledgment of environmental consequences of rising energy consumption of fossil fuels and the rapid expansion of solar, geothermal, wind, biofuels, and other non-traditional energy sources in the late 2000s and the 2010s, oil has kept its status as the vital energy resource for China. The leading role of oil in Chinese thinking about energy resources results in frequent terminology substitution between "energy" and "oil" in scholarly research on energy security. Many Chinese academics either explicitly or implicitly define energy security as the security of oil supply (e.g. Zhao 2006; Wu, L. 2009; Lin 2014; Zhang and Zhang 2015). Similarly, energy self-sufficiency is often understood as an ability to meet oil consumption needs from domestic supplies (e.g., Wei and Liu 2006; Wu, L. 2013; Zha 2012; Yan 2016). The overwhelming majority of academic articles published in Chinese peer-review journals between 2005 and 2016 examine China's energy development through the prism of definitions of energy security offered by American scholars. These definitions emphasize relative gains concerns, prioritize short- and medium-term security challenges, and mainly focus on the acquisition of oil. In particular, the most frequently cited unresolved issue of China's energy strategy is the reliability of the Malacca Strait as a route for China's oil imports from the Middle East and Angola, the so-called "China's Malacca dilemma" (马六甲困境, *Maliujia kunjing*).

The scholarly approach mirrors the official energy discourse that univocally describes the scarcity of oil as a security threat and a fundamental predicament for China's national development. Moreover, the official energy discourse also often defines energy security as the reliability and availability of oil supplies. China's latest white paper on energy policy (State Council of the PRC 2012) highlights "resource restraints," "low energy efficiency," and "increasing environmental pressure" as "tough challenges" of energy development. It also defines "grave challenges" to national energy security in connection to oil as follows:

> The country's dependence on foreign energy sources has been increasing in recent years. In particular, the percentage of imported petroleum in total petroleum consumption has risen from 32 percent at the beginning of the 21st century to the present 57 percent. Marine transportation of petroleum and cross-border pipeline transmission of oil and gas face ever-greater security risks. Price fluctuations in the international energy market make it more difficult to guarantee the domestic energy supply. It will not be easy for China to maintain its energy security since its energy reserves are small and its emergency response capability is weak.

The central role of oil in the definition of energy security presupposes securitization of energy development in general, implying that governance and management of energy resources is a strategic task for a state. Consequently, while energy development, in general, is framed as a global/ international challenge that should be approached as a matter of international politics rather than as a purely economic matter or a security threat, China's approach to oil is drastically different.

China's oil: Reproducing Daqing spirit under the "socialist market economy"

Daqing continues to epitomize China's aspirations for oil and inspires China's oil politics on both national and international levels, as it did six decades ago. Xi Jinping (2009) affirms that the Daqing spirit is still a crucial part of Chinese culture and Daqing, as a "modern oil city," plays a vital role in the implementation of the strategy of clean development and scientific development. The cover articles authored by Liu Tienan and Zhang Guobao, published by the *People's Daily* in 2012, offer particularly clear-cut examples of the role of Daqing in China's contemporary oil discourse. Liu's article (2012a) argues that over the past ten years China "has been carefully studying the global situation, engaging in energy diplomacy, and actively implementing the 'going global' strategy." According to him, as a result, China was able to "build an overseas Daqing" (建成了 "海外大庆," *jiancheng le "haiwai Daqing"*) by securing the four strategic transportation channels for its oil imports (North-West, North-East, South-West, and maritime routes). In a similar vein, Zhang (2012a) gives a positive assessment of the development of China's oil industry and, highlighting the success of China's offshore oil production, concludes that in the early 2000s China "has recreated a Daqing on the sea" (再造了一个海上大庆, *zaizaole yige haishang Daqing*).

China's authorities make sure that the population will be able to read those metaphors correctly. As was already mentioned in this chapter, the central and provincial governments support the fading economy of Daqing and invest in its museum infrastructure, making Daqing an attractive destination for domestic tourists. Social scientists and business management researchers study the evolution of the Daqing spirit (e.g., Li, JX. 2012; Ma 2009; Song and Wang 2013; Wang, K. 2009). North-East Petroleum University (Daqing, Heilongjiang) and Northeast Normal University (Changchun, Jilin) both have Research Centers for the Daqing Spirit that focus on building the narrative of Daqing into the curriculums of provincial and sub-provincial Party schools. Moreover, with the support of the government, Daqing spirit – rebranded as "patriotism, entrepreneurship, realism, and dedication" – is visualized in films, documentaries, and TV-shows.

An excellent example is the film *Iron Men* (铁人, *Tieren*) that was released amidst the celebrations of the 60th anniversary of the founding of the PRC in 2009. The leading actor, Wu Gang, "felt blessed to have the opportunity to represent the heroism that touched the whole country" (Renming Ribao 2009). However, the primary goal of the film is not to remind the new generation of Chinese about the glory of industrialization and fearlessness of China's oil workers of the 1960s but to help it to form a link between the heritage of Maoist China and the present China that is building a "socialist market economy."

The plot of *Iron Men* alternates between the story of a group of Daqing oil workers led by Wang Jinxi and a present-day story focused on a fictional character, Liu Sicheng, the son of one of Wang Jinxi's comrades-in-arms. Liu Sicheng continues the work of his father: he is the head of a drilling crew that struggles to find oil in the middle of an unknown desert in the early 2000s. He collects items related to Wang Jinxi and is fascinated by the early history of Daqing. The audience learns about the Daqing spirit through Liu Sicheng's recollections of conversations he had with his father. In the course of a spiritual and professional struggle, the young man ends up embracing the Daqing spirit and finds a balance between his deep feeling of patriotism and seeking commercial success for the company that he represents.

This 50-million-yuan (approximately US$7.5 million in 2009)[15] film was funded by the State Administration of Press, Publication, Radio, Film and Television, an executive branch under the State Council. The *People's Daily* reviewed *Iron Men* as a "big piece of barnstorming widescreen entertainment" (Ren 2009), yet the film still did not top the charts and did not achieve success in terms of the box office results. Daqing's iron men and their spiritual descendants had to compete for the hearts of the audience with Tony Stark, the famous American Iron Man,[16] and lost the battle. What makes *Iron Men* and other similar films (e.g., *The Founding of a Republic*, 2009, and *Aftershock*, 2010) interesting, however, is not their commercial or artistic value but their political background and agenda. *Iron Men* is a part of the effort of China's authorities to keep Daqing's brand and ideological heritage alive. Like the exposition at the Museum of Daqing Oilfield, *Iron Men* is yet another medium that communicates a whole set of official discourses, including the oil discourse.

The discourse that showcases Daqing as the model for China's oil industry is reinforced not only by the government but also through the narratives produced by China's NOCs. For example, the official website of CNPC has a page dedicated to the "Daqing spirit," summarized as "dynamic, loyal, honest, and committed." Linking its corporate history to the "miracle of China's industry," CNPC features the stories of "representative pioneers": Wang Jinxi, the old oil industry hero, and Wang Qimin, the new oil industry hero. Wang Qimin "consciously followed the example of old Iron Man Wang Jinxi" since he started to work for the Exploration and Development Research Institute of Daqing Petroleum Administration. Inspired by the legendary "iron man," Wang Qimin advanced a set of methods for oilfield development that helped "Daqing oilfield to accomplish the goal of maintaining a high and stable annual output of 50 million tons for 27 consecutive years." CNPC honors Wang Qimin as the "Iron Man of the New Era" for contributing to the "scientific research spirit of constant innovation and improvement." By emphasizing the continuity of oil workers' generations, the narrative told by the CNPC also reinforces the idea of continuity in the development of the industry.

In sum, in the 21st century, China's oil and China's ideology are as closely interconnected as they were in the early 1950s. The ability of the party-state leadership to ensure adequate and reliable supplies of oil remains one of the symbols of the enduring success of the Communist Party of China. A rebranded Daqing spirit helps to legitimize the party's ongoing rule through historical continuity. Even though China's major strategic goals in energy development have changed, when it comes to oil, China's aim is still self-reliance and maximum possible self-sufficiency.

Between 2005 and 2016, China was consistently identifying itself as a developing country that is facing a "complicated" and "grim" situation in the realm of energy security (e.g., Wen 2006; Hu 2008; Liu 2012a; Wu, X. 2014d). To support China's status as a developing country in the realm of international energy relations, China's officials often refer to BRICS, highlighting commonalities, shared interests, and challenges (Hu 2012b; Xi 2013a). The overarching idea is that the development of China and other BRICS states on the trajectory from a pre-industrialized state to a modern affluent industrialized state is unfinished. Hence, China's economic success is relative, on the one hand, to the context in which it occurs and to the living standards in the developed Western countries.

Vice Foreign Minister Fu Ying (2010) vividly articulates this idea in the keynote address at the Dinner of the Third World Policy Conference. Fu Ying univocally defines China as a developing country, facing the challenges that go beyond mere economic growth:

> China is not just a symbol or a GDP figure. It is a country that provides for 1.3 billion people, with 140 million students in schools and universities, over 20 million new job-seekers every year, including 6 million university graduates. [...] China is quickly urbanizing, and yet half of its population is still rural.

Further, Fu Ying rearticulates China's definition of energy development as a developmental right:

> Measures to mitigate the effects of climate change have a human dimension. People living in poor regions need to secure their right to proper indoor-heating. Grandmas in urban communities are debating about a fairer way to pay electricity bills. The migrant laborers demand better pay and better working conditions. Workers are laid-off when factories close due to poor energy efficiency and need to be re-employed. For China, all these rank high on the government's agenda to address human rights concerns.

Consequently, contrasting China to the developed Western countries, China's officials highlight that China's consumption per capita is still low and many Chinese still experience energy poverty. In this sense, China's official discourse on energy contraposes China to developed Western countries that must "face their historical responsibilities" (Wen 2007b, 999) and make a coordinated effort to "to achieve universal, coordinated, and balanced development" (State Council of the PRC 2005). In this sense, China's energy identity is firmly contextualized around its ongoing developmental project. As a case in point, China's Energy Policy states that "as the largest developing country in the world, China is faced with the daunting tasks of developing its economy, improving its people's livelihood, and building a moderately prosperous society" (State Council of the PRC 2012).

The quantity of China's energy consumption is as important as the quality of China's energy development for the discursive construction of China's energy identity. Zhang Guobao (2012b) argues that "China will not follow the development path of the Western countries." According to Zhang, it places greater emphasis on "scientific development, economic restructuring, and modernization of its energy structure" and "vigorously promotes energy conservation and emission reduction, as well as the development of renewable energy such as wind power, hydropower, and solar energy." Elsewhere, Zhang (2008a) points out that, at the peak of their modernization, developed Western countries accounted for only 15 percent of the total world population yet were consuming more than 60 percent of the world's energy resources. In contrast, China, according to him, "has supported the rapid development of its national economy with a relatively low rate of energy growth," and China's energy development is "healthy" when compared to the energy development of its Western counterparts (Zhang 2008a, 15). Wu Xingxiong (2014a, 5) made similar declarations, promising that, even though China's economic growth will continue in the future, "China will not repeat the traditional path of developed countries who produced uncontrolled emission of greenhouse gases during their industrialization."

At the same time, China strongly identifies itself with the Global East, as a part of "globalized Asia" (Xi 2014a) and a "member of Asia-Pacific family" (Hu 2006a). This identity reinforces China's divergence from Western developed countries. It simultaneously allies China not only with developing but also with developed Asian countries. China is making a conscious identity choice by confidently situating itself in the East (understood as East Asia and Asia-Pacific) or the Global South and distancing itself from the West or the Global North. Such self-representation allows China to claim the status of an exceptional developing country, an influential independent player, and a prospective leader of the developing world. For instance, Yang Jiechi (2012a) affirms that China is uniquely equipped to represent the Global South and promote its interests on the international stage. He further adds that China is also capable to "initiate an international reform" (促改革, *Cu gaige*) of global governance, with equitable energy development as one of the primary targets. This identity intersects with another dimension of China's official energy discourse that addresses representations of China as both consumer and producer.

China as a consumer and as a producer: The guarantor of global energy security

Pointing out that China not only tops the world's charts of the largest energy consumers but also leads the world in the production of all sorts of energy resources, Zhang Guobao (2008a and 2012b) identifies China as an "energy great power" (世界能源大国, *shijie nengyuan daguo*). Zhang constructs China as a guarantor of global energy security, pointing out that China's national energy security is (and always has been) a principal issue for global energy development rather than just a source of China's domestic concerns. For example, he argues that acting "as a responsible great power," China "for a long time has been trying its best to ensure global energy security by solving its energy security problems through maintaining self-sufficiency" (Zhang, G. 2008a, 17). Following this logic, now it is time for the international community to recognize China's heroic efforts. Importantly, these efforts, according to Zhang (2008a), should earn China not just international recognition but also the right to take part in international energy governance. The idea of China being a guarantor of global energy security corresponds well with the international ramifications of the concept of the China Dream (中国梦, *Zhongguo meng*), actively promoted by Xi Jinping after 2013.[17]

At the core of the notion of the China Dream is a negotiation of collective identity and individual aspirations. All diverse goals of the individual Chinese people are represented in the China Dream as shaped by a shared history and collective will to make China "a rich and powerful country," "revitalize the nation," and "enhance the well-being of the people'" (Xi 2014a). An essential part of the China Dream is the confidence over China's developmental achievements during the past decade and the superiority of China's development, compared with both the developed world and other countries in the developing world. This growing confidence has been transferred to international relations.

Xi Jinping's predecessor, Hu Jintao, was risk-averse and mainly focused his attention on "harmony," initiating a transition to sustainability and maintaining economic growth. While Hu was practicing a strategy of "hide capabilities and keep a low profile" (韬光养晦, *taoguang yanghui*) in foreign affairs, Xi quickly reframed China's foreign policy as "striving for achievement" (奋发有为, *fenfa you wei*) (Qian 2013).[18] In the work report presented at the 19th National Congress of the CPC, Xi Jinping highlighted that China had entered a "new era" (新时代, *Xin Shidai*). The concept is also featured in the wordy title of Xi's report: Secure a Decisive Victory in Building a Moderately Prosperous Society in All Respects and Strive for the Great Success of Socialism with Chinese Characteristics for a New Era. He specified that "it will be an era that sees China moving closer to center stage" and held out China as a model for other developing nations, emphasizing that China had developed its economy without imitating Western values. According to Xi, "the path, the theory, the system, and the culture of socialism with Chinese characteristics" provides "a new trail for other developing countries to achieve modernization" and offers "a new option" for those developing nations "who want to speed up their development while preserving their independence." Overall, Xi demonstrated extreme confidence in China's growing national power and confirmed international trends working in favor of the developmental model chosen by China. By the middle of the 21st century, Xi asserted, China will have become "a global leader in terms of comprehensive national power and international influence."

Among the other things, Xi Jinping (2017) made two commitments related to China's energy future. First, he promised that China would actively take part in the international policy response to climate change: "taking a driving seat in international cooperation to respond to climate change, China has become an important participant, contributor, and torchbearer in the global endeavor for ecological civilization." Further, Xi Jinping promised that China "will promote a revolution in energy production and consumption, and build an energy sector that is clean, low-carbon, safe, and efficient."

Consequently, in the "new era" announced by Xi, China is not only a guarantor of international energy security but also a potential model for energy development. As China is optimistically "dreaming" about a better world in which the international community will rightfully acknowledge it as a frontrunner, Xi is getting ready to take the lead in balancing common goals of the world community and China's national interests.

China's allies and adversaries in international energy politics

Since 2013, China has focused on the "correct view of morality and benefits" (正确义利观, *zhengque yi li guan*), trying to improve relations with its neighbors and developing countries at large (MFA of the PRC 2014a). This diplomatic strategy is closely associated with Xi Jinping's leadership, as it is supposed to become "a solid foundation for the smooth start of China's diplomacy in the new era" (Wang Y. 2013). China portrays its relations with the developing world as close and constructive: a "friendly cooperation" with the ASEAN countries, a "mutually beneficial partnership" with Central Asia, "people's friendship" with Latin America, and the Caribbean, and a "brotherhood" with Africa.

According to Wang Yi (2013), "African leaders and people from all walks of life speak highly of China's Africa policy and appreciated China for its selflessness in helping to Africa for a long time and solemnly refute the fallacy of China's so-called 'neocolonialism' in Africa." Wang Yi (2013) also confirmed Xi Jinping's promise to "offer the aid to Africa without any political conditions attached," helping African countries to "transform their resource advantages" into "diversified, independent, and sustainable development."

Similarly, Wang Yi's predecessor, Yang Jiechi (2010) argued that cooperation with China helps the people of Africa to convert their countries' energy resources into "the real developmental advantages." Responding to the question about Western disapproval and vocal concerns about China's investment in African oil, Yang Jiechi (2010) replied that he has noticed that "some people in the world do not want to see the development of China-African relations and often use China-African energy cooperation to 'make speculations.'" He pointed out that "the US and Europe" export more oil from Africa than China. In his opinion, since China fully supports the efforts of other countries to develop cooperation with Africa in the energy field, they also have no reason to oppose China's attempts to build a partnership with Africa. Finally, Yang Jiechi also highlighted that "Africa belongs to the African people and the African people are the owners of Africa, whereas the rest are just guests," and thus Western countries "should respect the host's right to choose partners and friends."

Along the same lines, China articulates its political and economic ambitions in Central Asia. China's officials highlight that "Shanghai spirit" (上海精神, *Shanghai Jingshen*) is an essential attribute of the SCO that makes an organization of "a new type": peace-oriented, cooperative, open, and striving toward harmony (e.g., Yang 2008; Xi 2013c). China endorses its status as the founder of SCO, as well as its major inspirer and ideologist, and offers Central Asia a partnership based on foreign policy pluralism, cosmopolitism, mutual benefits, common developmental goals, and equality. Energy resources are listed as one of many options for "pragmatic cooperation," along with socio-cultural exchanges and a joint struggle against the "three evils forces" (三股势力, *sangu shili*) that are drug-trafficking, transnational crimes, and cybercrimes (Xi 2014b, 2015a). In sum, China promotes itself as a senior yet still an equal partner in Central Asia and stresses that it will offer "no strings attached" relations.

Consequently, China is mostly surrounded by "friends," "brothers," and "friendly neighbors" in the Global South. In the 2000s and the 2010s, "win-win" (合作共赢, *hezuo gong ying*) is the most frequently repeated epithet of "cooperation" in China's discourse on South–South energy relations (e.g., Wen 2007a; Zhang, G. 2008b; Yang 2012a; Xi 2015c). According to China's officials, all China wants in the Global South is "to reduce the global imbalance, so that people of all countries share the fruits of world economic growth" (Xi 2016). In contrast, when it comes to the discursive politics of energy, China's relations with the Global North appear to be way more complicated.

China's officials describe the European Union (EU) as neither a "brother" nor a "friend" but as an "important role in the international political arena." At the same time, they still offer the EU member-states the opportunity to become China's "comprehensive strategic partners" (e.g., Song 2012) and invite them "to intensify coordination and cooperation" with China (e.g., Xi 2014a). On the narrower level of China's energy discourse, however, the EU is homogenized and treated as a single hostile entity. It becomes one of "those countries" that see China as a threat, labeling its cooperation with other developing countries as neocolonialism and questioning the possibility of its peaceful rise (e.g., Yang 2010; Ying 2010). As one of "those countries," the EU also is trying to restrict China's access to energy resources and thus prevent China from bridging the North-South gap and strengthening South–South cooperation.

Together with the homogenized EU, "those countries" also include the US. Vice Foreign Minister Fu Ying (2010), in the speech that was already cited in this chapter, urges the representatives of the developing world to "take China as [their] partner." Referring to an unspecified publication in the *New York Times*, Fu Ying encourages them to disregard the opinion of "those countries," which treat China as "the scapegoat for all problems on earth." She highlights that China is "a very convenient scapegoat" because "despite the sacred principle of freedom of speech, there is little interest among the media in those countries in informing their public the views from within China" (Fu, 2010).

Building a new Daqing overseas

At his retirement, Jiang Zemin (2008)[19] proposed the "new approach to energy development with Chinese characteristics" (中国特色的新型能源发展道路, *Zhongguo tese de xinxing nengyuan fazhan daolu*) based on six pillars: conservation of energy, energy efficiency, diversified energy development, environmental protection, technological progress, and international cooperation. He warned his successors that "the next few decades will be the crucial period for China's comprehensive socio-economic development and will mark the great rejuvenation of the Chinese nation and, [in this regard,] the task of energy development is very significant" (Jiang 2008, 351). While the term did not take root, the energy strategy formulated under Hu Jintao and further developed with the arrival of Xi Jinping fits into the framework developed by Jiang Zemin. This evolution indicates that there is a general agreement among the three latest generations of China's leaders as to how China's energy strategy should look.

Since the mid-2000s, the overall aim of China's energy development has been sustainable economic growth and social stability. China consistently chooses an "all-of-the-above" energy strategy: it plans to secure a stable supply of fossil fuels and simultaneously initiates a transition to "greener" fuels and launches a comprehensive resource conservation program.

At the symposium on China's Peaceful Development (2011), Yang Jiechi linked growing energy consumption to environmental degradation and identified these two issues as the primary "bottlenecks" of China's development. He further attested that

> Self-reliance is the foothold for development. In the final analysis, a country must rely on its strength to ensure its development. Common prosperity is the goal of development. A country can truly achieve sustainable development only when it integrates its development with the common development of the whole world.

Consequently, Yang Jiechi explicitly connects China's energy strategy to the notions of "harmonious society/world" and "China's peaceful rise." Moreover, he confirms that China firmly believes in the possibility of mutually beneficial energy cooperation and is going to focus on avoiding competition in the realm of energy development. Along similar lines, Liu Tienan (2012b, 24) argues that, by conducting "all-around international cooperation" and actively implementing its "going global" strategy, China is acting as a responsible participant in international energy relations. According to him, China's actions will balance rather than destabilize global energy markets. The white paper of energy policy (State Council of the PRC 2012) converts these ideas into the strategic aim of China's energy development and conceptualizes them as "a modern energy industry" that will "provide a solid guarantee for building a moderately prosperous society in all respects and make greater contributions to the world's economic development."

China quickly transitioned from the promise to "modernize" and "reform" its energy system (e.g., Hu 2006b, 2008; Wen 2007a) to a "revolution in energy production and consumption" (能源生产和消费改革, *nengyuan shengchan he xiaofei gaige*) (e.g., Zhang, G. 2012b; Wu, X. 2014c). According to the white paper on energy policy (State Council of the PRC 2012), China "is exploring and practicing a new way in the history of energy development to ensure its sustainable energy development." In 2014, Xi Jinping summarized China's energy strategy as "four revolutions and one cooperation" (四个革命、一个合作, *si ge geming, yige hezuo*): (1) the "revolution in energy consumption" that focuses on restraining unreasonable energy use; (2) the "energy supply revolution" that implies developing a diversified supply system; (3) the "technological revolution" that will promote modernization of energy industry; (4) the "energy system revolution" that will open a fast lane for energy development (see Xi 2015b). In addition to these four "revolutions" in China's domestic energy development, Xi also highlighted the need to strengthen international cooperation and make energy security a part of China's overall "opening up" strategy. As Wu Xingxiong (2014c, 2014b) explains Xi Jinping's plans, this final dimension of the energy strategy is "an extension" of China's new foreign policy strategy and, specifically, the Belt and Road Initiative (BRI).

As of 2016, CNOOC, Sinopec, and CNPC contributed to a combined 92 percent of the total oil industry revenue in China (IWEP ACSS 2016). They operate in more than 30 countries and have equity production in at least 20 of these countries. China maintained the principle of "China first" and "focus on domestic resources by strengthening domestic energy supply capacities and continuously improving its ability to control the dependence on external sources of oil" (Wu, X. 2014c, 4). Consequently, supporting NOCs and expanding the scope of energy diplomacy, China's government remains primarily concerned with the availability of oil and does not plan to revolutionize its approach to supply security. Following the logic of self-reliance, China is "building an overseas Daqing" (Liu 2012a). In this sense, while the dream of bringing China into a leadership position in world affairs begins to loom over the concerns about maintaining its economic growth and making it more sustainable, in China's energy politics in general, and precisely when it comes to oil, self-reliance still plays a more prominent role in structuring policies and developing relations with resource-rich countries.

China's energy paradigm: Chasing Daqing

On the international level, China's official energy discourse stresses the fundamental and persistent inequality of the current world order and, using it as a starting point, calls for reducing the gap between the Global North and the Global South. In this context, the two foremost dimensions of China's energy paradigm are the following:

- Availability of energy resources, and specifically fossil fuels, is a prerequisite for development; and
- Global distribution of energy resources is neither a purely economic issue nor a security issue but, first and foremost, a matter of international politics because energy development is a right of every nation.

In this paradigm, the focus of energy security is development. Coherently, the definition of energy security corresponds with the concept of development that in the mid-2000s was encapsulated in the aspiration for a "harmonious society/world" and "China's peaceful rise." Following the new development strategy, China's energy paradigm broadened and now includes sustainable and environmentally conscious development as a part of the concept of energy security. In addition to it, the notion of energy security started to internationalize, and, as a result, the energy deficit became more politicized. The politicization of energy deficit presupposes that binding international rules and regulations should regulate the distribution of energy resources. It also implies that international energy relations can and should be a positive-sum game.

On the domestic/ national level, however, the energy deficit is associated mainly with the reliability of the oil supply and remains securitized. As was the case 60 years ago, China treats the deficit of oil as an existential threat to its national development and a source of dangerous vulnerabilities. As a result, when it comes to oil, China's energy strategy is defined as the quest for a new Daqing.

In sum, there is a bifurcation in China's energy paradigm: while on the global/international level the energy deficit is now politicized, on the domestic/national level it remains largely securitized. China actively promotes a cooperative mode of energy development on the international level and does not call for urgent and exceptional measures to deal with the energy deficit. Nonetheless, when it comes to oil, China still does not rush to trade its self-reliance for interdependency.

An essential part of China's energy paradigm is China's energy identities. On the one hand, branding itself as a developing country, China defends its right to obtain energy resources for its growth. China also allies itself with resource-rich developing countries, framing its global quest for energy resources in terms of "win-win" South–South cooperation. Here, China presents itself as an in-group member, proposing equal partnership and "no strings attached" relations that China's representatives frame as advantageously different than relationships with the Global North. According to China's official energy discourse, the people of the Global South readily embrace the opportunities for "win-win" cooperation with China, whereas "those countries" in the Global North are still suspicious and distrustful of China's peaceful rise. On the other hand, China defines itself as a distinct case among developing countries. With the arrival of Xi Jinping, this discursive trend has intensified.

The identity of an energy producer builds on the narrative of heroic oil exploration and production in Daqing in the 1950s. While on the domestic level this narrative is perceptible, on the international level China's identity as an energy producer is supported mainly by the references to its reliable and consistent record of energy self-sufficiency. As for the identity of a consumer, China describes its energy consumption as responsible and modest relative to the Global North and showcases its recent achievements in "green" and "clean" energy development. China's official energy discourse translates the past records and current accomplishments into future promises. China's identity as the largest consumer and producer of energy merges with the identity of a developing country. As a result, not only does China become the first-choice partner for resource-rich developing countries but it can also legitimize its attempts to represent the interests of the Global South in the international energy politic. Also, by bringing these two identities together, China undermines the legitimacy of the Global North's leadership in international energy politics and, mainly, the right of the Global North to criticize China's energy choice, be that regulations of domestic energy consumptions or its energy cooperation with developing countries. The overarching idea is that China is a guarantor of global energy security, and the success of its energy development offers benefits to other participants of energy relations in both the Global South and the Global North.

China's official energy discourse details and carefully revises the story of China's "green" and "clean" energy future. It explicitly confirms that the ultimate goal of China's energy development is self-reliance and asserts that its new proactive role in global energy politics brings benefits to all other actors. Notably, Chinese representatives promise resource-rich countries to "transform their resource advantages into development advantages" and stimulate their "diversified, independent, and sustainable development" (Wang, Y. 2013). The state's financing and diplomatic backing have opened many doors for China's NOCs and helped them to bring many barrels of overseas produced oil home. Nevertheless, China's experiences in the different countries of the Global North and the Global South have varied widely. It is fair to say that all other actors have not warmly welcomed China's emergence in international energy politics.

The subsequent chapters examine China's relations with two large oil-producers, Russia and Kazakhstan. Looking at the bilateral energy relations between China and these two petrostates, I focus on two interconnected goals. First, I continue to define and deconstruct China's energy paradigm, focusing on how it is manifested and enacted in bilateral energy relations with Kazakhstan and Russia. Secondly, I address the second key question that this book puts to the fore by examining how China's emergence as a significant energy consumer influences the energy paradigms of its oil-rich counterparts, as well as how their perceptions of China have evolved.

Notes

1 The use of the term "great battle" (大会战, *dahui zhan*) is specifically noteworthy because this term was also used to describe the guerilla warfare during the Second Sino-Japanese War (1937–1945).

2 *Battle Report of Daqing* matured into a local daily newspaper, renamed in 1982 as *Daqing Daily*.

3 Yu Qiuli (余秋里) belongs to the so-called first generation leaders of the Communist Party of China. He joined the party in 1931 and took part in the Long March of 1934 as a soldier of the PLA. After 1949, he became the head of the Military Academy of China and thereafter held various posts in the central military command. In 1958, Yu Qiuli was appointed as Minister of Petroleum Industry by Mao Zedong. He occupied this post until 1964, when he became a deputy chief of the State Planning Commission. From 1977 until his retirement in 1987, he was a member the Central Politburo of the CPC.

4 For a brief period between 1966 and 1970 at the peak of the Culture Revolution, Daqing several times came under attack from the leaders of the Gang of Four; however, its celebrity status of the "model" was quickly restored (see Lim 2010, 79–106).

5 Wang Jinxi is the most famous of "five red flags" (五面红旗, *wu mian hongqi*), the group of model celebrity oil workers that also included Duan Xingzhi, Ma Deren, Xue Guobao, and Zhu Hongcha.

6 The concept of self-reliance is represented in the official discourse by two terms: "on one's own strength (自力更生, *zili gengsheng*) and "self-reliance" (自给, *zigei*).

7 In the 2000s, China not only took care of Daqing oilfield but also started to build a system of strategic petroleum reserves. The current capacity of China's strategic petroleum reserves is 36.9 Mtoe, which is equivalent to approximately 30 days of oil imports in 2016.

8 Net import dependency stands for the percentage of the amount of net oil imports over the amount of total oil consumption.

9 Originally published in 1997 as *China's Policy on Energy Resources* by Xinhua News Agency. In 2012, China Internet Information Center reprinted the document as *Li Peng: China's Energy Policy*.

10 Equity oil is that proportion of production that a concession owner has the legal and contractual right to retain.
11 NDRC is a successor to the State Development Planning Commission.
12 The author made those observations in December 2007 and March–July 2008 in Beijing and Xian'.
13 The term "scientific development" was introduced right after Hu Jintao took office as the chairman of CPC in the late 2002; however, it was fully developed into a coherent concept only by the 17th Congress of the CPC.
14 In 2005, the name of China's national developmental program was changed from "plan" (计划, *jihua*) to "guideline" or "blueprint" (规划, *guihua*). According to the official statements, the difference is not only linguistic but also conceptual. While old "five-year plans" were setting mandatory growth targets for output, the new "five-year blueprints" issues guiding developmental targets.
15 For comparison, historical drama *The Founding of a Republic* (2009) that marked the 60th anniversary of the PRC cost US$8.4 million. It was also commissioned by China's film regulator and made by the state-owned film studio. Action movie *Mulan: Rise of a Warrior* (2009) was produced without direct governmental grants and cost US$7.4 million.
16 Tony Stark, the Iron Man, is a fictional superhero portrayed by Robert Downey Jr. in the action film trilogy *Iron Man* (2008, 2010, 2013) based on comic books published by Marvel Comics. For another comparison, the first film of the trilogy (2008) costed US$140 million.
17 Xi Jinping did not invent the idea of "Chinese Dream." It was articulated first in 2006 by Li Junru, then the head of the Central Party School, and further had a life of its own, gradually achieving a wider currency in Chinese society (Ferdinand 2016).
18 Chinese officials and scholars also use other Chinese proverbs to highlight the turn to a more proactive foreign policy strategy: "take initiative" (主动进取, *zhudong jinqu*, e.g., Xi 2013b), "actively going in" (积极进取, *jiji jinqu*, e.g., MFA of the PRC 2014b), and "actively accomplish" (积极作为, *jiji zuowei*, e.g., Xi 2015d).
19 Later Jiang Zemin's article was expanded into *Research on Energy Issues in China.*

References

Adelman, I., and Sunding, D. (1987). Economic policy and income distribution in China. *Journal of Comparative Economics*, *11*(3), 444–461.

Alam, M. S., and Paramati, S. R. (2015). Do oil consumption and economic growth intensify environmental degradation? evidence from developing economies. *Applied Economics*, *47*(48), 5186–5203.

Alon, I., Leung, G. C. K., and Simpson, T. J. (2015). Outward foreign direct investment by Chinese national oil companies. *Journal of East-West Business*, *21*(4), 292–312.

Andrews-Speed, P. (2012). *The governance of energy in China: transition to a low-carbon economy*. Basingstoke: Palgrave Macmillan.

Bartke, W. (1977). *Oil in the People's Republic of China: industry structure, production, exports*. London: C. Hurst.

BP, British Petroleum (2017). *BP energy charting tool*. Retrieved 23 May 2018 from http://tools.bp.com/energy-charting-tool.

Burchett, W. (1974). Chinese tap taching potential. *Far Eastern Economic Review*, *14*(1), 45–46.

Central Committee of the CPC (2003). Zhonggong Zhongyang guanyu wanshan shehui zhuyi shichang jingji tizhi ruogan wenti de jueding (quanwen) [Resolution of the

Central Committee of the CPC on some issues of improving the socialist market economy system (full text)]. People's Network. Retrieved 18 Nov. 2017 from http://cpc.people.com.cn/GB/64162/64168/64569/65411/4429165.html.

Chen, S. (2011). Has China's foreign energy quest enhanced its energy security? *The China Quarterly*, *207*(3), 600–625.

Cheng, C-Y. (1976). *China's petroleum industry: output growth and export potential.* Westport: Praeger Publisher.

China Internet Information Center (2012). Li Peng: Zhongguo de nengyuan zhengce [Li Peng: China's energy policy]. Retrieved 19 Nov. 2017 from http://www.china.com.cn/guoqing/2012-09/10/content_26748235.htm.

CNPC, China National Petroleum Corporation (2017). History of Daqing oilfield. Retrieved 18 Nov. 2017 from http://dqyt.cnpc.com.cn/dqen/HoDO/dqen_common.shtml.

Dai, H., Masuib, T., Matsuokac, Y., and Fujimor, S. (2012). The impacts of China's household consumption expenditure patterns on energy demand and carbon emissions towards 2050. *Energy Policy*, *50*(1), 336–350.

Dikötter, F. (2011). *Mao's great famine: the history of China's most devastating catastrophe, 1958–1962*. New York: Walker and Co.

Downs, E. (2006). *The energy security series: China, the brookings foreign policy studies.* Washington, DC: Brookings Institution Press.

Downs, E. (2007). China's quest for overseas oil. *Far Eastern Economic Review*, *170*(7), 52–56.

Feng, L., Hu, Y., Hall, C. A., and Wang, J. (2012). *The Chinese oil industry: history and future*. Berlin: Springer Science & Business Media.

Feng, Z., Zou, L., and Wei, M. (2011). The impact of household consumption on energy use and CO_2 emissions in China. *Energy*, *36*(1), 656–670.

Ferdinand, P. (2016). Westward ho – the China dream and "one belt, one road": Chinese foreign policy under Xi Jinping. *International Affairs*, *92*(4), 941–957.

Fu, Y. (2010). Take China as your partner. Speech at the diner of world policy conference. Marrakech, 16 Oct. MFA of the PRC. Retrieved 16 Sept. 2017 from https://www.fmprc.gov.cn/mfa_eng/wjdt_665385/zyjh_665391/t762307.shtml.

Ge, W. (2006). *Zhongguo shidai zhengzhi sixiang shi [History of Chinese political thought]*. Tianjin: Nankai University.

Gerth, K. (2010). *As China goes, so goes the world: how Chinese consumers are transforming everything*. New York: Hill and Wang.

Harrison, S. S. (1975). China: the next oil giant. *Foreign Policy*, *20*, 3–27.

He, K., Huo, H., Zhang, Q., He, D., An, F., Wang, M., and Walsh, M. P. (2005). Oil consumption and CO_2 emissions in China's road transport: current status, future trends, and policy implications. *Energy Policy*, *33*(12), 1499–1507.

Houser, T. (2008). The roots of Chinese oil investment abroad. *Asia Policy*, *5*, 141–166.

Hu, J. (2005). Build towards a harmonious world of lasting peace and common prosperity. speech at the UN summit. New York, 15 Sept. Permanent Mission of the PRC to the UN. Retrieved 20 Sept. 2017 from http://www.china-un.org/eng/zt/shnh60/t212915.htm.

Hu, J. (2006a). Jianchi heping fazhan, cujin gongtong fanrong. Zai Yatai Jinghe Zuzhi Gongshang Lingdao ren Fenghui shang de yangjiang [Adhere to peaceful development and promote common prosperity. Speech at the APEC CEO Summit]. 17 Nov.

Hu, J. (2006b). Baoguo Jituan Tong Fazhanzhong Guojia Lingdao ren duihua huiyi bing fabiao [Meeting of the leaders of the G8 and developing countries]. 17 July.

Hu, J. (2007). Hold high the great banner of socialism with Chinese characteristics and strive for new victories in building a moderately prosperous society in all respects. Report at the 17-th National Congress of the Communist Party of China. 15 Oct. Renmin Ribao. Retrieved 20 Sept. 2017 from http://en.people.cn/90001/90776/90785/6290120.html.

Hu, J. (2008). Zai jingji daguo nengyuan anquan he qihou bianhua lingdao ren huiyi shang de jianghua [Speech at the major economies meeting on energy security and climate change]. 9 July, Hokkaido, Japan. Ministry of Foreign Affairs of the PRC. Retrieved 19 Sept. 2017 from https://www.fmprc.gov.cn/123/wjdt/zyjh/t473333.htm.

Hu, J. (2012). *Firmly march on the path of socialism with Chinese characteristics and strive to complete the building of a moderately prosperous society in all respects.* Report at the 18-th National Congress of the Communist Party of China, 27 Nov.

IWEP ACSS, Institute World Economics and Politics Chinese Academy of Social Sciences (2016). *World energy China outlook, 2015–2016 [Shijie Nengyuan Zhongguo Zhanwang, 2015–2016].* Beijing: Social Sciences Literature Publishing House.

Jacques, M. (2009). *When China rules the world: the rise of the middle kingdom and the end of the western world.* London: Penguin Books.

Jiang, Z. (2008). Dui Zhongguo nengyuan wenti de sikao [Reflections of energy issues in China]. *Shanghai Jiaotong Daxue Xuebao, 42*(3), 345–359.

Kapitsa M. S. (1979). *KNR: Tri desyatiletiya – tri politiki [The PRC: three decades and three policies].* Moscow: Politizdat.

Klinghoffer, A. J. (1976). Sino-Soviet relations and the politics of oil. *Asian Survey, 16*(6), 540–552.

Kulpin, E. S. (1975). *Tekhniko-Ekonomicheskaya Politika Rukovodstva KNR i Rabochiy Klass Kitaya [Technical and economic policy of the PRC's leaders and China's working class].* Moscow: Nauka.

Leung, G. C. K. (2010). China's oil use, 1990–2008. *Energy Policy, 38*(2), 932–944.

Li, JX. (2012). Daqing jingshen zou chuqu zhi gouxiang [The concept of Daqing spirit going out]. *Xueshu jiaoliu, 5*(10), 52–54.

Li, K. (2012). Zai Zhong-Ou gaoceng nengyuan huiyi bimu shi shang de zhici [Speech at the closing ceremony of the China-EU energy conference]. MFA of the PRC, 3 April. Retrieved 21 Sept. 2017 from https://www.fmprc.gov.cn/ce/cgosaka/chn/zgxw/t929147.htm.

Lim, T. (2010). *Oil in China: from self-reliance to internationalization.* Singapore: World Scientific.

Lin, B., and Xie, C. (2013). Estimation on oil demand and oil saving potential of China's road transport sector. *Energy Policy, 61*, 472–482.

Liu, H., Guo, J., Dong, Q., and Xi, Y. (2009). Comprehensive evaluation of household indirect energy consumption and impacts of alternative energy policies in China by input–output analysis. *Energy Policy, 37*(8), 3194–3204.

Liu, T. (2012a). Jianding bu yi de zou nengyuan kexue fazhan zhi lu [Unswervingly follow the path of energy science development]. *Remin Ribao*, 24 Sept.

Liu, T. (2012b). Nengyuan fazhan mianlin xin tiaozhan [The new challenges of energy development]. *Zhongxiao qiye guanli yu keji (Zhongxun kan), 10*, 22–24.

Liu, T. (2012c). Xin xingshi xia Zhongguo nengyuan fazhan de zhanlüe sikao [Strategic thinking on China's energy development under the new situation]. *Qiu shi, 13*, 33–35.

MacFarquhar, R., and Fairbank, J. (1991). *The Cambridge history of China: revolutions within the Chinese revolution.* Cambridge: Cambridge University Press.

Marks, R. (2012). *China: its environment and history.* Lanham, MD: Rowman and Littlefield.

Meidan, M., Sen, A., and Campbell, R. (2015). China: the "new normal." The Oxford Institute of Energy Studies. [PDF file] Retrieved 12 June 2016 from https://www.oxfordenergy.org/wpcms/wp-content/uploads/2015/02/China-the-new-normal.pdf.

MFA of the PRC, Ministry of Foreign Affairs of the People's Republic of China (2014a). Wang Yi: Zhengque yi li guan shi Zhongguo waijiao de yimian qizhi [Wang Yi: the correct view of justice and benefit is a banner of Chinese diplomacy]. 11 Jan. Retrieved 28 Oct. 2017 from https://www.fmprc.gov.cn/web/zyxw/t1117851.shtml.

MFA of the PRC, Ministry of Foreign Affairs of the People's Republic of China (2014b). Waijiao bu buzhang Wang Yi jiu Zhongguo waijiao zhengce he duiwai guanxi huida Zhong-Wai jizhe tiwen [Foreign Minister Wang Yi answers questions from Chinese and foreign journalists on China's foreign policy and foreign relations]. 8 March. Retrieved 27 Oct. 2017 from https://www.fmprc.gov.cn/chn//pds/wjb/wjbz/xghd/t1135388.shtml.

NBSC, National Bureau of Statistics of China (2017). Annual data, 2000–2017. Retrieved 17 Dec. 2017 from http://www.stats.gov.cn/english/Statisticaldata/AnnualData/.

OICA, Organisation Internationale des Constructeurs d'Automobiles (2017). Production Statistics. Retrieved 17 Dec. 2017 from http://www.oica.net/category/production-statistics/2017-statistics/.

Pan, H., Shen, Q., and Zhang, M. (2009). Influence of urban form on travel behaviour in four neighbourhoods of Shanghai. *Urban Studies*, *46*(2), 275–294.

Pan, X., Wang, L., Dai, J., Zhang, Q., Peng, T., and Chen, W. (2020). Analysis of China's oil and gas consumption under different scenarios toward 2050: an integrated modeling. *Energy*, *195*, 116991.

Park, C. H., and Cohen, J. A. (1975). The politics of China's oil weapon. *Foreign Policy*, *20*, 28–49.

Pew Research Center (2015). Car, bike or motorcycle? [PDF file] Retrieved 17 Dec. 2017 from http://assets.pewresearch.org/wp-content/uploads/sites/2/2015/04/Transportation-Topline.pdf.

Qian, T. (2013). Xi Jinping zai zhoubian waijiao gongzuo zuotanhui shang fabiao zhongyao jianghua [Xi Jinping delivering an important speech at the conference of diplomatic work toward surrounding countries]. *Renmin ribao*, 26 Oct. Retrieved 27 Sept. 2017 from http://cpc.people.com.cn/n/2013/1026/c64094-23333683.html.

Ren, X. (2009). Dianying "Tie Ren" guan hou gan [The feelings after watching "Iron Man" movie]. 18 August People's Daily Overseas Edition. Retrieved 20 Oct. 2017 from http://look.people.com.cn/GB/158820/9882250.html.

Renmin Ribao (1963). Di Er Jie Quanguo Renmin Daibiao Dahui di si ci Huiyi Xiwen Gongbao [Press release of the 4th session of the 2nd National People's Congress]. 4 Dec. 1963. Retrieved 14 Nov. 2017 from http://www.people.com.cn/zgrdxw/zlk/rd/2jie/newfiles/d1060.html.

Renmin Ribao (1967). Rang Su xiu zai Daqing hongqi mianqian fadou ba! [Let the Soviet Revisionists tremble in the face of Daqing!], 11 April 1967. Retrieved 14 Nov. 2017 from http://data.people.com.cn/rmrb/20181023/1?code=2.

Renmin Ribao (2009). "Tieren": "Chong su" yi ge Wang Jinxi? ["Iron men": "Transformation" of Wang Jinxi?]. 29 Apr. 2009. Retrieved 11 Nov. 2017 from http://paper.people.com.cn/rmrbhwb/html/2009-05/29/content_263191.htm.

Renmin Ribao Tuwen Shujuku, 1946–2018 [People's daily database, 1946–2018]. Retrieved 14 Nov. 2017 from http://data.people.com.cn/rmrb/20181023/1?code=2.

Smil, V. (2004). *China's past, China's future*. New York: Routledge.

State Council of the PRC (2005). Zhongguo de Heping Fazhan Dalu [China's path of peaceful development]. Beijing, 23 Dec.

State Council of the PRC (2007). Zhonghua Renmin Gonghe Guo Jieyue Nengyuan Fa (xiuzheng an) [Energy conservation law of the People's Republic of China (Amended)]. 28 Oct.

State Council of the PRC (2009). Zhonghua Renmin Gonghe Guo Kezaisheng Nengyuan Fa (xiuzheng an) [Renewable energy law of the People's Republic of China (Amended)]. 26 Dec.

State Council of the PRC (2012). Zhongguo de Nengyuan Zhengce 2012. Baipishu (zhongwen) [China's energy policy. White paper. Full text.] Beijing, 24 Oct.

Strong, A. L. (1963). Letters from China. Peking: New World Press. Retrieved 19 Nov. 2017 from https://www.marxists.org/reference/archive/strong-anna-louise/1963/letters_china/index.htm.

Song, C., and Wang, Y. (2013). Xin shiqi jicheng hongyang Daqing jingshen tieren jingshen de shijian yu yanjiu [Practice and research on inheriting the spirit of Daqing and the spirit of iron men in the new era]. *Daqing Shehui Kexue*, *3*, 25–29.

Song, T. (2012). A changing Europe and its relations with China. Remarks at the seminar on situation in Europe and China-Europe relations. Embassy of the PRC in the Kingdom of Denmark. 16 Aug. Retrieved 29 Oct. 2017 from https://www.fmprc.gov.cn/ce/cedk/eng/TourChina/t961116.htm.

Wang, D., Chai, Y., and Li, F. (2011). Built environment diversities and activity–travel behaviour variations in Beijing, China. *Journal of Transport Geography*, *19*(6), 1173–1186.

Wang, K. (2009). Daqing jingshen yu Tieren jingshen de jiben neihan [The basic connotation of Daqing spirit and iron man spirit]. *Daqing Shehui Kexue*, *3*, 51–53.

Wang, M., Chen, Z., Zhang, P., Tong, L., and Ma, Y. (2014). Daqing model of industrial chain extension. In Wang, Mark, Zhiming Chen, Pingyu Zhang, Lianjun Tong, and Yanji Ma (eds) *Old industrial cities seeking new road of industrialization: models of revitalizing northeast China* (pp. 107–140). Singapore: World Scientific.

Wang, Y. (2013). Jianchi zhengque yi li guan jiji fahui fu zeren daguo zuoyong – shenke linghui Xi Jiping tongzhi guanyu waijiao gongzuo de zhongyao jianghua jingshen [Adhere to the correct view of justice and interests and actively play the role of a responsible great country – profoundly understand the spirit of Comrade Xi Jinping's important speech on diplomatic work]. Renmin Ribao. 10 Nov. Retrieved 17 Oct. 2017 from http://opinion.people.com.cn/n/2013/0910/c1003-22862978.html.

Wei, L., and Liu, Q. (2006). Zhong Ya diqu de nengyuan zhengduo yu Zhongguo nengyuan anquan [Energy competition in central Asia and China's energy security]. *Shijie jingji yu zhengzhi luntan*, *6*, 73–78.

Wen, J. (2006). Quanmian luoshi kexue fazhan guan jiakuai jianshe huanjing youhao xing shehui [Fully implement the scientific development concept and accelerate the construction of an environment-friendly society]. 17 Apr. Retrieved 20 Sept. 2017 from http://www.gov.cn/gongbao/content/2006/content_303476.htm.

Wen, J. (2007a). Work in partnership to promote win–win cooperation. Speech at the 2nd East Asia Summit, 15 January 2007, Cebu, Philippines. MFA of the PRC. Retrieved 22 Sept. 2017 from https://www.fmprc.gov.cn/mfa_eng/wjdt_665385/ zyjh_665391/t290183.shtml.

Wen, J. (2007b). Xieshou hezuo gongtong chuangzao ke chixu fazhan de weilai – zai di san jie Dong-Ya fenghui shang de jianghua [Working together to create the future of sustainable development. Speech at the 3rd East Asia Summit, 21 Nov. 2007, Singapore], pp. 999–1001. In Shizheng wenxian ji lan (2007 nian 3 yue – 2008 nian 3 yue) [Current political literature collection (March 2007–March 2008)]. Beijing: Xinhua Publishing House.

Wu, L. (2009). Nengyuan an'quan tixi jiangou de lilun yu shijian [Theory and practice of energy security system construction]. Alabo shijie yanjiu, 1, 36–44. Retrieved 12

Oct. 2018 from http://mideast.shisu.edu.cn/upload/article/28/e6/d5e55c634ade9670158 edd936f7b/8af566d2-d8fa-48c5-afbc-227f04f4e2ca.pdf

Wu, L. (2013). Zhongguo nengyuan anquan mianlin de zhanlue xingshi yu duice [Strategic situations and countermeasures for China's energy security]. *Guoji Anquan Yanjiu*, *5*, 62–75.

Wu, X. (2009). Nuli zuo hao jieneng jian pai zhe pian da wenzhang: Xuexi shijian kexue fazhan guan luntan [Work hard to do a good job in energy saving and emission reduction: learning and practicing scientific development concept forum]. *Renmin Ribao*, 23 Jan.

Wu, X. (2014a). Pojie nanti zhuzhong shixiao jiji tuijin fenbu shi guangfu fadian jiankang fazhan – zai fenbu shi guangfu fadian xianchang (Zhejiang, Jiaxing) jiaoliu hui shang de jianghua [Solving the problem, paying attention to practical results, actively promoting the healthy development of solar power generation. A speech at Zhejiang, Jiaxing.] *Zhongguo jingmao dao kan*, *25*, 5–9.

Wu, X. (2014b). Zhuan fangshi diao jiegou cu gaige, qiang jianguan bao gongji hui min sheng zha: Shi zuo hao 2014 nian nengyuan gongzuo [Change model of development, regulate the structure, and stimulate reforms, strong supervision and protection to provide benefits to the people: doing a good job in energy work in 2014]. *Zhongguo meitan gongye/ China's coal industry*, *3*, 4–7.

Wu, X. (2014c). Jiji tuidong nengyuan shengchan he xiaofei geming – shenru xuexi guanche Xi Jinping tongzhi guanyu nengyuan gongzuo de zhongyao lunshu [Actively promoting the energy production and consumption revolution: an in-depth study and implementation of Comrade Xi's important discussion on energy work]. *Zhongguo jingmao dao kan*, *28*, 4–5.

Wu, X. (2014d). Tongyi sixiang mingque renwu gaige chuangxin kexue mouhua "shisanwu" nengyuan fazhan [Unified thinking, clear tasks, reforms, innovation, and scientific planning: energy development in the 13th Five-Year plan]. *Zhongguo jingmao dao kan*, *18*, 4–7.

Xi, J. (2009). Xi Jiping zai Daqing youtian faxian 50 zhounian qingzhu dahui shang de jianghua [Xi Jinping's speech at the celebration of the 50th anniversary of Daqing Oilfield]. Reming Ribao, 22 Sept. 2009. Retrieved 18 Nov. 2017 from http://energy.people.com.cn/GB/71899/152923/10110428.html.

Xi, J. (2013a). Xieshou hezuo gongtong fazhan. Zai jinzhuanguojia lingdaoren de wu ci huiwu shi de zhuzhi jianghua zhonghua renmin gongheguo zhuxi [Work hand in hand for common development. Speech at the 5th meeting of BRICS leaders], 28 March. Ministry of Foreign Affairs of the PRC. Retrieved 22 Sept. 2017 from https://www.fmprc.gov.cn/web/gjhdq_676201/gj_676203/yz_676205/1206_677220/1209_677230/t1025978.shtml.

Xi, J. (2013b). 2014 Nian Xinnian Heci [The 2014 new year's greetings]. The Central People's Government of the PRC. 31 Dec. Retrieved 26 July 2018 from http://www.gov.cn/ldhd/2013-12/31/content_2557924.htm.

Xi, J. (2013c). Hongyang "Shanghai jingshen" cujin gongtong fazhan. Zai Shanghai Hezuo Zuzhi chengyuan guo yuanshou lishi hui di 13 ci huiyi shang de jianghua, Bishenkake [Promote the "Shanghai Spirit" and promote common development. Speech at the 13th meeting of the Heads of State Council of the Shanghai Cooperation Organization, Bishkek]. Renmin Ribao, 13 Sept. Retrieved from http://cpc.people.com.cn/xuexi/n/2015/0721/c397563-27338283.html.

Xi, J. (2014a). Jiji shuli yazhou anquan guan gang chuang anquan hezuo xin jumian. Zai Yazhou xianghuxiezuo yu xinren cuoshi huiyi disici fenghui shang de jianghua [Actively establish an Asian security concept and create a new situation of security cooperation. Speech at the 4th summit meeting of the Conference on Confidence-Building Measures in Asia]. Ministry of Foreign Affairs of the PRC, 21 May. Retrieved 9 Sept. 2017 from https://www.fmprc.gov.cn/ce/cese/chn/zts/yxfh/t1158248.htm.

Xi, J. (2014b) Ning xin ju li jingcheng xiezuo tuidong Shanghai Hezuo Zuzhi zai Shang xin taijie [Concentrate on cooperation, promote the Shanghai Cooperation Organization to a new level]. Renmin Ribao. 13 Sept. Retrieved 11 Oct. 2017 from http://cpc.people.com.cn/n/2014/0913/c87228-25653522.html.

Xi, J. (2014c). *The governance of China*. Beijing: Foreign Languages Press.

Xi, J. (2015a). Towards a community of common destiny and a new future for Asia. Speech at the 2015 Boao Forum for Asia. Xinhua. March 28. Retrieved 26 July 2018 from http://www.xinhuanet.com/english/2015-03/29/c_134106145.htm.

Xi, J. (2015b). Gong hui shijie nengyuan biange de xin lantu [Drawing a new blueprint for world energy change]. *Renmin Ribao*. 9 Nov. Retrieved 11 Oct. 2017 from http://paper.people.com.cn/zgnyb/html/2015-11/09/content_1631476.htm.

Xi, J. (2015c) Mou gongtong yong xu fazhan zuo hezuo gong ying huoban. Zai Lianheguo fazhan fenghui shang de jianghua [Seeking common sustainable development and win-win partnership. Speech at the United Nations Development Summit], New York, 26 Sept.

Xi, J. (2015d). Xi Jinping zai Zhong-Ri youhao jiaoliu dahui shang de jianghua (quanwen) [Speech at the China-Japan friendship exchange conference (full text)]. MFA of the PRC. 23 Apr. Retrieved 23 Oct. 2018 from https://www.fmprc.gov.cn/ web/gjhdq_676201/gj_676203/yz_676205/1206_676836/1209_676846/t1266334.shtml.

Xi, J. (2016). Goujian chuangxin, huoli, liandong, baorong de shijie jingji. Xi Jinping zhuxi guanyu 20 guo jituan lingdao ren Hangzhou fenghui de zhongyao lunshu [Building an innovative, vigorous, linked and inclusive world economy. speech at the summit of the G20 leaders in Hangzhou]. Renmin Ribao. 17 Aug. Retrieved 2 Nov. 2017 from http://cpc.people.com.cn/n1/2016/0817/c64094-28641538.html.

Xi, J. (2017). Secure a decisive victory in building a moderately prosperous society in all respects and strive for the great success of socialism with Chinese characteristics for a new era, Oct. 18, 2017. [PDF file] Retrieved 26 July 2018 from http://www.xinhuanet.com/english/download/Xi_Jinping's_report_at_19th_CPC_National_Congress.pdf.

Yan, S. (2016). Zhongguo nengyuan anquan yu zhoubian guojia de nengyuan hezuo guanxi yanjiu [Research on energy cooperation between China's energy security and neighboring countries]. *Gaige yu Zhanlue*, *8*, 31–34.

Yang, J. (2008). "Shanghai jingshen" de yongheng meili – jinian Shanghai hezuo zuzhi chengli 7 zhounian [The eternal charm of "Shanghai Spirit." commemorating the 7th anniversary of the establishment of Shanghai cooperation organization]. Renmin Ribao, 16 June. Retrieved 12 Sept. 2017 from http://world.people.com.cn/GB/1030/7383613.html.

Yang, J. (2009). Hongyang xin Zhongguo waijiao youxiu chuantong zuo hao xin xingshi xia de waijiao gongzuo [Carry forward the outstanding tradition of China's diplomacy and do a good job in the diplomatic work under the new situation]. Renmin Ribao, 5 Sept. Retrieved from http://world.people.com.cn/GB/8212/9491/142315/9992496.html.

Yang, J. (2010). Yang Jiechi da Zhongwai jìzhe wen (2010 nian) [Yang Jiechi's press conference with Chinese and foreign journalists, 2010]. 6 March.

Yang, J. (2011). Heping Fazhan: Zaofu Zhongguo, Zaofu Shijie. [Peaceful development: benefit China, benefit the world]. "Zhongguo de Heping Fazhan" Baipishu Zuotanhui

Fayan Zhaibian [Lecture at the symposium on "China's Peaceful Rise" white paper]. *Renmin Ribao*, 16 Sept.

Yang, J. (2012a). Yang Jiechi jiu woguo duiwai zhengce he duiwai guanxi wenti da jizhe wen [Yang Jiechi's remarks on China's foreign policy and foreign relations, press conference]. 31 March.

Yang, J. (2012b). Shizhong bu yu zou heping fazhan daolu (xuexi guanche shiba da jingshen) [Always follow the path of peaceful development. Learning and implementing the spirit of the 18th National Congress]. *Reming Ribao*, 14 Dec.

Yeh, K. C. (1962). *Communist China's petroleum situation*. Santa Monica, CA: Rand Corporation.

Zha, D. (2005a) Xianghu yilai yu Zhongguo de shiyou gongying an'quan [Interdependence and China's oil supply security]. *Shijie Jingji yu Zhengzhi*, 15–20.

Zha, D. (2005b). Cong guoji guanxi jiaodu kan Zhongguo de nengyuan an'quan [China's energy security from the perspective of international relations]. *Guoji Jingji Pinglun*, 28–32.

Zhang, C. (2015). *The domestic dynamics of China's energy diplomacy*. Singapore: World Scientific Publishing Co.

Zhang, G. (2008a). Kaizhan nengyuan hezuo cujin jingji fazhan [Carry out energy cooperation and promote economic development]. *Zhongguo shiyou qiye / China Petroleum Enterprise*, *8*, 15–17.

Zhang, G. (2008b). Zhongguo de nengyuan guanli he nengyuan jiegou tiaozheng [China's energy management and energy structure adjustment]. *Zhongguo fazhan guancha*, *4*, 26–28.

Zhang, G. (2008c). Jieyue nengyuan tigao nengxiao [Save energy, improve energy efficiency]. *Zhongguo keji touzi*, *8*, 7.

Zhang, G. (2009). Zhongshi xin nengyuan fazhan [Paying attention to the development of new energy]. *Shidai Qiche / Auto Time*, *4*, 43.

Zhang, G. (2012a). Wei Zuguo jingji tengfei tigong nengyuan baozhang [Providing energy security for the motherland's economic take-off]. *Remin Ribao*, 13 June.

Zhang, G. (2012b). Woguo nengyuan jiegou tiaozheng yao xia da juexin [Transformation of China's energy structure]. *Zhongguo he gongye/ China Nuclear Industry*, *11*, 10–13.

Zhang, N., and Zhang, B. (2015). Zhong-E nengyuan hezuo de chan rong jiehe moshi yanjiu – yi shiyou gongye wei li [Research on the combination of industry and finance in Sino-Russian energy cooperation. Taking the petroleum industry as an example]. *Dongbei ya xue kan*, *6*, 53–58.

Zhang, Z. (2012). The overseas acquisitions and equity oil shares of Chinese national oil companies: a threat to the West but a boost to China's energy security?. *Energy Policy*, *48*, 698–701.

Zhao, H. (2006). Guanyu Zhong-Mei nengyuan hezuo de ji dian sikao [Reflections on Sino-US energy cooperation]. *Xiandai guoji guanxi*, *1*, 47–53.

Zhou, X. (2013). *Forgotten voices of Mao's great famine, 1958–1962: an oral history*. New Haven: Yale University Press.

4 China–Russia energy relations

The year 2019 marked the 70th anniversary of China-Russian diplomatic relations. The relations between these two close neighbors have been nothing short of turbulent, being marked by the waves of friendship and confrontation (Garver 1998; Datsyshen 2014). Since the early 2000s, formal statements of friendship proclaimed in 1996 started to transform into practical cooperation agenda. Chinese and Russian representatives in unison declared that the relations between the two states are more developed than at any time in their history. While some of Russia's experts support this rapprochement with China (e.g., Lukin 2019, Karaganov 2016), whereas others are anxious about the increasing asymmetries of the bilateral relations and the extent to which Russia depends on China both economically and politically (e.g., Voskresenski 2015; Trenin 2012). Many experts also worry about China's growing assertiveness in Eurasia, typically considered Russia's backyard (e.g., Tsomaya 2014; Savvidi and Voloshin 2016). Others are concerned about the emergence of a bipolar economic world order in which Russia would have a subordinate role vis-à-vis China and the US (e.g., Dynkin and Pantin 2012; Portyakov 2013). For their part, Chinese experts note that Vladimir Putin's regime develops an explicitly aggressive approach toward the West. With rare exceptions (e.g. Yan 2013), they argue that China should avoid this new geopolitical rivalry (e.g., Zheng 2008; Tian 2007; Li, JM. 2012). Recognizing the constraints that hinder the creation of a stronger alliance between the two states, virtually all experts, nevertheless, agree that in terms of forging energy cooperation China and Russia are a perfect match (Lukin 2009; Portyakov 2013; Luzyanin and Semenova 2016; Voskresenski 2015; Lang and Wang 2007; Trenin 2012; Li, Y. 2013; Li, JJ. 2014; Yan 2016; Wang and Wan 2013 to name just a few studies in Russia and China).

As was noted in the previous chapter, the Soviet Union provided China with the technology, equipment, and expertise required to develop a modern oil industry. This assistance was abruptly withdrawn in 1958 as China-Soviet relations deteriorated. Over the following three decades, the two countries developed their energy sectors independently from each other. In the mid-1990s, Russia was recovering after the collapse of the Soviet Union, and its economic, commercial, diplomatic, and political priorities had changed. In contrast, China was becoming a net importer of oil. As a result, the governments and NOCs of both Russia and China started to develop an interest in each other. The Treaty of Friendship signed in 2001 specifically identified energy as the crucial sphere of cooperation. However, real energy cooperation between Russia and China started to emerge only after 2005, and despite the undeniable logic for the construction of a direct oil pipeline from Russia to China, NOCs did not complete it until 2011. Against the background of sharply deteriorating relations between Russia and the West in the mid-2010s, the China–Russia energy relations have picked up momentum. By 2016, Russia became China's second-largest supplier of oil, whereas China surpassed Germany as the top importer of Russian oil. The contracts signed by Russia's and China's NOCs in the late 2010s anticipate a further increase in exports of oil over the next decade.

The first part of this chapter is devoted to the discussion of Russia and its discursive politics of energy. It interrogates two mutually constitutive discourses – the discourse of energy superpower and the discourse of raw-material appendage – and explains how they shape Russia's energy politics. Further, the chapter returns to China. I start with an overview of the development of China–Russia energy relations with a focus on oil-related deals between 2005 and 2016. Further, I explain how and with what effect China's and Russia's energy paradigms are manifested and enacted in their bilateral energy relations.

Russia's discursive politics of energy

Putin's discursive politics of energy: Russia as the energy superpower

Since Vladimir Putin rose to power in 1999, Russia has been explicitly asserting itself as a great power and "geopolitical subject" (Putin 2012) and behaving accordingly. "Greatpowerness" (*великодержавность*, *velikoderzhavnost'*) is perceived as an inherited property that belongs to Russia by virtue of its enormous size, resources, culture, and history (Laruelle 2007; Urnov 2014). Constructed as a property, this "greatpowerness" becomes Russia's concomitant characteristic and fundamental quality rather than a position or a condition that is subject to change. In other words, in this framework, Russia's great power status is a matter of fact. There is a broad agreement among political elites that Russia's "greatpowerness" must be reaffirmed on the international level. However, only when Putin updated the underlying foundations of Russia's claim for the status of great power with a new focus on control over energy resources during the oil price surge of the mid-2000s that it became clear how Russia might accomplish this goal.[1]

In December 2005, at a meeting of the Security Council of the Russian Federation, Putin proclaimed that Russia would become one of the leaders and "trendsetters" of the global energy sector. According to him, in the 21st century, energy resource wealth is Russia's "natural competitive advantage" that will not only be a "locomotive" that pulls Russia's economy forward but also help Russia to improve its position in the international arena (Putin 2005a). Vladislav Surkov (2006), the deputy chief of Putin's administration at that time, was even more direct about Russia's future: "If you have strong legs, you should be doing the long jump rather than playing chess." Putin himself emphatically avoided using the term "superpower" (e.g., Putin 2006c). In contrast, Surkov (2006) explained that while "adherents of the liberal obscurantism" think that market liberalization is the driving force of Russia's economic development, Putin offers a "realistic model" which is "the concept of Russia as the energy superpower." In July 2006, during the G8 summit in Saint-Petersburg, Putin presented the concept of Russia's energy leadership to the international public through the discussion of global energy security (Putin 2006a and 2006b). By the end of his second term as president (2004–2008), Putin successfully regained full state control over the national energy complex and "discovered the value of 'securitizing' the energy business," actively and explicitly using energy resources as a tool or lever to promote Russia's foreign policies (Baev 2012, 178). As a result, in the mid-2000s for Russia to be a great power meant to be the energy superpower.

Over the following decade, Russia's domestic politics was full of internal contradictions, yet ad hoc opportunism is an endogenous variable rather than an invariable feature of Russian politics (Orttung 2009, Orttung and Overland 2011). As Robert W. Orttung explains, Russia's political development in the mid-2000s was not driven by growing energy rents alone. Instead, it echoed Putin's awareness of the 1990s and represented his endeavor to "correct what he considered to be some of the mistakes of that era" (Orttung 2009, 54).[2] In this sense, while the new Russian authoritarianism and Putin's project of restoring Russia's imperial prerogative[3] lost over the 1990s benefited significantly from the dramatic rise of oil rents, they were not caused by it. Importantly, as Anne Applebaum (2012, 4) argues, the ideas that are associated with Putin's political leadership constitute "a carefully worked out system, with carefully designed institutions," and thus should be approached as an ideology. Constructing Russia as an energy superpower is one of the central themes of this ideology.

In the mid-2000s, introducing the discourse of energy superpower into the narrative of Russia's "greatpowerness," Putin's regime was making a conscious identity choice. The discourse of energy superpower continues to influence the development of the hierarchy of domestic and foreign policy objectives, even though after 2011 Putin's regime shifted the gravity of identity-building project onto "religion, patriotic values, military achievements, and defending the rights of ethnic Russians" (Rutland 2015, 84).

One illustrative example of the ideological value of the discourse of energy superpower in the mid-2010s is the attempt to merge it with the narrative of Russia's victory in World War II. As a case in point, during the 2015 annual celebration of the victory of the Soviet Union over Nazi Germany in the Great Patriotic War (Victory Day), the square in front of the Gorky Central Park of Culture and Leisure in Moscow was decorated with a massive multimedia art installation entitled *Energy of the Great Victory*. The installation featured symbols of gas, electrical, and oil energy: a gas drilling rig, a transmission tower, and an oil horse (see Figures 4.1 and 4.2). According to the Park administration's press release, the installation was commemorating "the role of the energy sector in the development of the national economy in the wartime and heroic deeds of the

Figure 4.1 Multimedia art installation *Energy of the Great Victory*. May 2015. Gorky Central Park of Culture and Leisure, Moscow, Russia.

Figure 4.2 Outline of the multimedia art installation *Energy of the Great Victory*. © Museon.ru. Courtesy of Museon.ru.

Soviet power engineers, who together with all other Soviet people were victorious over fascism." A documentary with an identical title that was broadcasted by the state-owned television channel Russia-1 (Terner and Yevsyukov 2015) also presents ample energy supplies of the Soviet Union as one of the major causes of its victory over fascism. The central idea of the documentary is that the Soviet energy sector not only helped to save the country from fascism but also kick-started its economic development after the hardship years of the war and eventually made it one of the world's two superpowers.

In the realm of international relations, Russia's authorities construct energy wealth as one of Russia's key competitive advantages. Dominant official discourses define energy cooperation between Russia and the major energy consumers as a "dialogue." Specifically, Russia's representatives use the concept "energy dialogue" (*энергодиалог, energodialog*) to describe Russia's relations with the European Union and China. They highlight mutual vulnerabilities to portray these relations as being based on a set of symmetrical interdependencies (e.g., Medvedev 2010a, Lavrov 2007a) and describe them as "cooperative" (Putin 2005b, Lavrov 2007b, Novak 2013a), "pragmatic" and "mutually beneficial" (Medvedev 2010b), "dynamic" (Shmatko 2010), "partnership-based" (Novak 2014b), "stable" (Novak 2015a), and "positive" (Denisov 2016).

A raw-materials appendage and a victim of a resource curse

The Russian public accepts the broad discourse of "greatpowerness" as it resonates well with popular perceptions of Russia. As the most recent surveys of Levada Center[4] (2016, 31–34) show, 64 percent of Russians believe that Russia is a "great power" and 76 percent think that it must maintain this role in the future. Moreover, 43 percent expressed nostalgia for the Soviet Union because of "the lost sense of belonging to a great power" (Levada Center 2016, 257). However, only 17 percent of Russians think that possessing vast natural resources qualifies a country as a great power (Levada Center 2016, 35–36) and only 18 percent believe that Russia's international respect is based on its resource wealth. Consequently, Russians want Russia to be a great power, yet they do not associate the "greatpowerness" with natural resources and do not see a great power as an energy superpower.

The survey conducted as a part of the NEORUS project (2013)[5] adds another layer to the findings of Levada Center. This survey reveals that 64 percent of respondents agree that Russia is an energy superpower. At the same time, however, the survey also shows that the Russian public not only approves of the discourse of energy superpower but also is markedly influenced by a conflicting discourse that identifies Russia as a "raw-materials appendage" (*сырьевой придаток, syr'yevoy pridatok*). Specifically, the survey found that 63 percent of respondents think that "Russia should not be a raw-material appendage" (NEORUS 2013).

The metaphor of "appendage" and the discourse that goes with it have a long history in Russian politics, going back to the early years of the Soviet Union. In 1925, Joseph Stalin (1952, 297) encouraged the building of the Soviet economy "in such a way as to prevent our country from becoming an appendage of the world capitalist system" and "not as a subsidiary enterprise of world capitalism, but as an independent economic unit." Later Soviet authorities used the metaphor of "appendage" to describe the position of the decolonized countries of the Third World in the global capitalist system. In the early 1990s, opponents of economic and political liberalization claimed that Michael Gorbachev's reforms were transforming Russia into a "raw-material appendage of the West" (*сырьевой придаток Запада, syr'yevoy pridatok Zapada*) (e.g., Andreyeva 1990; Kol'ev 1995). Since then, the discourse of raw-material appendage has become more complex and developed three interrelated expressions. In the 2000s, at the core of it is the idea that extraction and export of resources are primitive and unsustainable economic activities, appropriate only for underdeveloped and weak countries. Secondly, following the update of the raw-material appendage discourse, dependence on resource exports constrains Russia's economic development and inevitably consigns it to a low place in the international hierarchy. Finally, only a corrupted and traitorous government can condemn Russia to such a humiliating and miserable position. In its original version, the discourse of raw-material appendage focused on the West as Russia's negative Other, yet over the past decade it has expanded to include China as the second negative Other (e.g., Khramchikhin 2013; Grek 2015; Pestsov 2015).

In sum, the discourse of raw-material appendage presents Russia's vast energy resources not as a foundation of extraordinary national power but as a source of tremendous vulnerability. In this sense, the popularity of this discourse indicates that an energy superpower in the popular imagination has a definition by contradiction: being an energy superpower means not being a raw-material appendage.

The power of the discourse of raw-material appendage is particularly evident in the experts' debates on the role of energy resources in Russia's development. Only a few Russian experts speak with enthusiasm of using energy resources as the foundation of Russia's economic growth and rise in the international arena (e.g., Simonov 2006, 2007; Inozemtsev 2015). In a widely discussed book with a revealing title, *Energy Superpower* (2006, 7), Konstantin Simonov argues that "creating a sovereign system for extracting and selling energy resources, which will allow Russia to determine independently the directions of its export flows, is not a matter of imperial ambitions but a matter of the country's survival." However, despite his passionate support of the concept of an energy superpower, Simonov is not satisfied with how Putin utilizes Russia's energy wealth.

Other experts openly call Putin's attempts to turn Russia into an energy superpower a strategic failure (e.g., Denisov and Grivach 2008; Evstafiev 2014; Trenin 2016). In this critique, the discourse of raw-material appendage coincides with the broader discourse of resource curse that holds that resource wealth might impact negatively economic growth and cause so-called Dutch Disease (e.g., Roland 2006; Tabata 2006, 2009; Gaddy and Ickes 2010, 2013). Fyodor Lukyanov (2016), for example, claims that in the mid-2000s the discourse of energy superpower was perceived by Russia's political elites as a strategy of "smart downshifting." The initial goal was not to rest on the laurels of an energy superpower but to use energy resources as a tool to encourage Russia's economic development and strengthen its international political ties. However, in Lukyanov's opinion, in the 2010s this strategy has proven itself unsuccessful and even harmful because it slowed down the evolution of post-Soviet economic and political systems. For their part, Vladimir Mau (e.g., 2008), Aleksey Kudrin (e.g., 2015), German Greff (e.g., 2016), and other Russian liberal economists compare Russia's dependence on energy exports with heavy drug addiction and frequently use the metaphor of "sitting on the oil needle" (*сидеть на игле, sidet' na igle*) to describe Russia's economic development.

The overlaps between the broader discourse of resource curse and the discourse of raw-material appendage, however, are limited to the economic rationalities. The concept of the political resource curse that suggests that resource wealth weakens the quality of institutions and erodes democracy and is often applied to Russia by Western political scientists (e.g., Fish 2005; Ross 2001, 2012), is dismissed by most Russian scholars. They claim that this concept is ideologically biased (e.g., Popova 2015) or consider it only a "partly justified opinion" (Mezhuyev 2010, 19, see also Kuyan, 2016). Overall, Russian academics and think-tank experts not only rarely explicitly link Russia's authoritarianism with resource revenues but also generally avoid an open discussion of corruption and political bribery in the state-run oil and gas companies. Journalistic investigations (e.g., Konstantinov 2006; Mukhin 2006; Panyushkin and Mikhail 2008) and reports of oppositional NGOs, such as Alexey Navalny's Anti-Corruption Foundation (e.g., Kulachenkov 2015), fill this gap. However, the most vivid and unapologetic expressions of all spectrum of ideas that constitute the discourse of raw-material appendage are found outside of conventional political forums.

Contesting Putin's energy superpower

Russian contemporary art and literature became a locus of critiques of Russia's oil-driven development. Similarly, Russia's popular culture is a vehicle not only for legitimating Putin's ideology but also a conduit through which counter-discourses find a voice. The official constructions of energy resources as Russia's primary competitive advantage are confronted by critical discourses that evolve around the struggles over values and over who is in control over the vital national assets. The current authoritarian regime constrains the dissemination of these discourses in the domain of public politics, but artists, musicians, and writers can unsilence and activate them.

Andrei Molodkin literally fills democracy with crude oil (Figure 4.3). His installation consists of nine separate three-dimensional letters arranged to form the word "DEMOCRACY" that are filled with crude oil through a system of interconnected pipes. According to Molodkin, he wanted to show that democracy is "not an idea" anymore but "just a souvenir," and thus it is only useful as "an empty canister" to carry oil (Moscow House of Photography 2008). Vasya Lozhkin, a renowned representative of Russian "punk trash" art, turns the oil into life-giving water and vodka. On his stylized icons, a grim Mother-oil (*матушка-нефть, matushka neft'*) is nursing a man dressed in the grey suit, a uniform of an official in Russia (Figure 4.4). Lozhkin's other painting – *The Black Vodka* – presents a group of identical grey-suited men feasting on oil that is coming from a pipeline (Figure 4.5). In a similar vein but with different visual images, emerging artist Alexandra Zheleznova (Poletaeva) depicts relations between statesmen and

Figure 4.3 Molodkin, A. (2013). *Democracy* [mixed media installation, crude oil, neon]. © Andrei Molodkin. Courtesy of Gregory R. Staley, American University Museum at the Katzen Arts Center.

Figure 4.4 Vasya Lozhkin (2012). *The Pagan Deities* [acrylic on paper]. © Vasya Lozhkin. Courtesy of the artist. Inscriptions on the painting: "Father-Gas" (left) and "Mother-Oil" (right).

Figure 4.5 Vasya Lozhkin (2012). *The Black Vodka* [acrylic on paper]. © Vasya Lozhkin. Courtesy of the artist.

oil as a destructive love affair. In her pictures, oil is not a mother but a dominatrix "madame Oil." This femme fatale wears a revealing dress, and her makeup is evocative and dramatic. She is insidious, greedy, and seductive. She corrupts and unmans top-energy officials, subordinating them to her evil will. The message of these works is rather straightforward: Russia's relations with oil are not healthy, as they take a form of destructive and violent addiction and thereby sustain corruption, malpractice, and abuse of power.

A popular song, "I Love Oil," focuses on another aspect of Russia's oil-driven modernity, ridiculing the prosperity generated by oil revenues. A spouse of an oilman sings: "If there is oil in Russia, I am in Milan." The music video presents the most essential symbols of the so-called "well-fed 2000s" (*сытые нулевые, sytyye nulevyye*): lavish parties, luxury shopping in Europe, expensive cars, and skyscrapers of Moscow's business district. The video also features women in folk costumes dancing against the backdrop of oil rigs. Eventually, the main character's love for oil and gas transforms into love for Russia. Brought together, the lyrics and images construct oil as a part of Russia's national identity and link oil to the timely and timeless Russianness.

A more striking and straightforward example of the critique of Russia's dependency on oil revenues in popular culture is Semyon Slepakov's "Song about Oil" that appeared on social media in 2015, amidst a new upsurge of the economic crisis. The comedian Slepakov speaks on behalf of "a simple worker of a tractor factory," who grumbles that he recently started to notice that he "does not have enough money to live his bad life." In an ironic and satirical monologue, the "simple worker" comments on the TV news reports that explain the current economic downfall by blaming the US and promise that "soon the prices on the mother-oil will go up again." Complaining that he might not survive while waiting for the oil prices to go up, he blames the authorities:

> Dear all who are at the helm of
> Our immense oil ship,
> I don't get it. How did it all go like this?
> You said it's going to be all right!
>
> You have been pumping the oil all these years,
> You did know limits, grief, and sorrows.
> You worked day and night, serving your fatherland.
> And you earned enough money for ten thousand lives.
>
> But how am I supposed to live [through this], guys?
> I'm a simple worker. My only savings are my kidney stones [and]
> Very little flesh on the surface of my bones.
> I might not live to see the oil prices going up!

In a similar humorous fashion, Yury Shevchuk, a renowned rock musician, poet, and ardent critic of Putin's regime, links oil and political power in a tender but grim romance. Speaking directly to Russia, Shevchuk promises her that "when oil runs out, our president will die" and "the world will be a bit freer." The last verses of his song go:

> We will learn once again to love and to be wise,
> There will be no handouts and eternal arguments,
> All mermaids and fairies will pray for us,
> Once we will drink all the oil, once we will smoke all the gas.

Even though Shevchuk's song was censored on TV (Vinogradov 2009) and has never been played on the radio since its release in 2007, it instantly became popular and regained its popularity again during the political protests of 2012 and 2013.

No less striking and vivid actualizations of the discourse of raw-material appendage emerge in Russian fiction writing. In the 2000s and the 2010s, an entire corpus of Russian "petro-fiction" has evolved, including travelogues (e.g., Golovanov 2014), detective novels (e.g., Yudenich 2007), and dystopias (e.g.,

Sorokin 2006, 2008, 2013; Pelevin 2003, 2006; Bykov 2006; Khazin 2017). Summarizing the main trends in this literature, Ilya Kalinin (2015, 143) argues that oil is "transformed into a systematic motif of contemporary Russian literature (and of culture as a whole)" and "acts as one of the central symbolic figures through which the post-Soviet unconscious finds a language." Indeed, Russian authors utilize this language to criticize the oil-driven capitalism of post-Soviet Russia, as well as the nationalistic ideology and new consumer culture that arise around it. In addition to it, they construct the moral, intellectual, cultural, and social progress as a function of Russia's oil-dependent development. The early writings of Victor Pelevin (2003, 124) exemplify this idea:

> Our whole culture is just a mold on the pipe that exists only because the oil in the pipe is heated. And the oil is heated not to blossom the mold but because it is just faster to pump.

The presence of oil in Russia's contemporary high and popular culture vividly demonstrates that the discursive politics of energy spills into and onto all areas of life in Russia. Artists, musicians, comedians, and writers become increasingly bold in their political protest. They condemn oil as a source of Putin's regime resilience, chronicle socioeconomic inequality, and political corruption. Representations of Russia's oil-driven modernity in Vasya Lozhkin's grotesque paintings and Vladimir Pelevin's dystopian novels are as aggressive and vivid as in Yury Shevchuk's rock ballads and Semyon Slepakov's comedy.

These variations of the raw-material appendage discourse explicitly challenge Putin's ideology, as well as the legitimacy and credibility of Putin's regime. Being obsessed with political corruption, these diverse expressions of the raw-material appendage discourse do not capture environmental concerns associated with direct and measurable negative consequences of the oil industry expansion. They also do not intersect with discourses that aim at constructing an understanding of energy security with climate as an integral consideration. In this sense, Russia's critical oil discourses are not "anti-oil" but "anti-Putin."

"We" and "they" in Russia's discursive politics of energy

The analysis of Russia's discursive politics of energy makes apparent two overarching constructions of Russia: the energy superpower and a raw-material appendage. It also uncovers one prominent discursive silence. Being obsessed with its energy wealth, Russia does not identify itself as a petrostate (for a detailed analysis see Rutland 2008, 2015). Both official and critical discourses avoid comparisons of Russia with other energy-rich states. Russian representatives never measure Russia's economic successes and failures against the experience of Iraq, Kuwait, Saudi Arabia, Kazakhstan, Venezuela, Nigeria, Norway, and other prominent petrostates.

The discourse of energy superpower constructs Russia as a one-of-a-kind actor of international energy politics. It frames Russia as an indispensable and irreplaceable energy exporter and emphasizes Russia's exceptional role in global energy security, implying that energy importers need Russia as much as, if not more than, Russia needs them. Defending, reinforcing, and justifying the claim for Russia's special status in international energy relations, Putin's regime responds to the raw-material appendage discourse that portrays Russia as addicted to the revenues generated by energy exports and thus weak and vulnerable. While being the mirror opposite of each other, the two discourses construct the West (mainly, the European Union) and the East (mainly, China) as Russia's most important Others.

While Russia belongs to a broader European intellectual and cultural history, it never identified itself and was never recognized by others as a Western country without a stipulation for some uniquely Russian qualities. This complex and contradictory identity creates a gap of alterity between post-Soviet Russia and the countries that are traditionally designated as the West. The Western version of modernity is simultaneously perceived as "a developmental or civilizational model to emulate" and "as a degenerate and dehumanized foil for what Russia should never become" (Clunan 2009, 79; see also Malinova 2012).

The discourse of raw-material appendage identifies Russia as a potential or actual victim of Western expansionism. In this discursive framework, Russia's energy cooperation, as well as general economic and political rapprochement with the West, is perceived as a threat. In contrast, the discourse of energy superpower presents Russia as an equal among equals in relations with the West. In this regard, the discourse of energy superpower forces Russia's representatives to seek from the West the recognition of Russia's unique status in international energy relations. More specifically, Russia's role in European energy security becomes a cornerstone of Russia's claim for energy superpower status (Kuteleva 2020).

At the same time, the concept of "the West versus the Rest" (Huntington 1996) assists Putin's regime in promoting the idea of Russian cultural aversion to the "Western" notion of democracy and categories related to it. Russia's "sovereign democracy" (*суверенная демократия*, *suverennaya demokratiya*) is based on supposedly unique Russian cultural values and thus is immune to international criticism. Ekaterina Shulman (2010) describes this as a "reverse cargo cult":[6] even though de jure Russia is building a Western-type liberal democracy, Russian elites refuse to adopt the Western norms and follow recommendations of international organizations because the West allegedly deviates from its proclaimed principles or does not adequately follow its own advice. A case in point is Russia's energy relations with the EU.

Identifying itself as an energy superpower, Russia claims the "right for an independent viewpoint" (Shmatko, 2008). It rejects asymmetrical definitions of energy relations, which recognizes the "normative power" (Manners 2002) of the EU, as well as its general political superiority. These articulations of Russia's normative sovereignty are particularly evident in the evolution of Russia's primary strategic energy policy document. The first Energy strategy (2003) contains references to "European norms" and expresses a commitment to adopt "European regulations." In contrast, its newest additions (2009 and 2015) appeal to "international norms" and "international regulations."

By reaffirming Russia's political autonomy and normative independence from the EU and the West more generally, Russian politicians elevate Russia's role in international energy security and construct Russia as a sovereign and powerful actor of international energy politics. In addition to this, Russia's rejection of European norms in the realm of energy politics is an expression of the "cargo cult." For example, in the mid-2000s, Russian representatives started to accuse their European counterparts of establishing a double standard approach in relations with Russia:

> Certainly, we can give access to our partners [to our resource extraction and transportation infrastructure]. However, we have a question: will they give us access to anything? [...] We do not mind working on the principles of [the European Energy Charter]. But we need to understand what we will receive in exchange.
>
> (Putin 2006b)

Following this logic, the principal regulations of the EU's Third Energy Package were labeled by Russian politicians as "unwise" (Lavrov 2012), "indiscreet" (Lavrov 2013), "short-sighted" (Novak 2014b; Putin 2013a), "ineffective" (Novak 2015b), and "unfair" (Putin 2013b). In Putin's Munich speech of 2007, this criticism is particularly tangible, when Putin claims that the European Energy Charter "is not so acceptable" for Russia because neither Russia nor the EU member-states want to follow it (Putin 2007).

By and large, in the mid-2000s Russia adopted a defensive position in relations to the West. Notably, Russia's representatives wanted the EU member-states to respect Russia's interests in international energy politics and accept Russian claims for the status of an energy superpower. Instead, Russia's European counterparts allegedly "follow the old habit, treating Russia as the Soviet Union" (Khristenko 2006a) and have "complexes" that do not allow them to "reconcile themselves to their dependence on external sources of energy" (Lavrov 2007b). Following the logic of Russia's defensive discursive strategy, Russia can be a reliable partner for the EU member-states, but only if they treat it as an energy superpower.

Similar trends are apparent in Russia's construction of the East. In the context of Russian energy politics, the East is understood as Asia. Russia's representatives describe Asia as "promising," "dynamic," and "energetic" yet paint it with a wide brush. For example, discussing the new trends in international development, Lavrov (2006) notes that globalization has "an Asian face" but does not specify to whom precisely this face belongs. Most often, Russia's representatives designate Japan, South Korea, China, and India as Asia. According to Lavrov (2006), these countries are "interested in a prosperous Russia" because without Russia's energy resources they will not be able to achieve "the goals of economic growth." In a similar vein, other Russia's representatives claim that Asian countries recognize it as a "natural partner" (Khristenko 2006b) and an "infallible guarantor of energy security" (Shmatko 2009).

Conflicts with the major Western powers, on the other hand, evert Russia's identity and accentuate its non-Western self-representations that Elizabeth Wishnick (2017) has termed the "Asian state" identity. However, while Asia is increasingly more important in Russia's energy politics, the historical, cultural, and political gulf separating Russia from the East is considerably more profound than that separating it from the West. Russia constructs other non-Western societies as premodern or even anti-modern and thus inferior relatively to itself (Bassin 1991; Clunan 2009). Both real and perceived differences between Russia and its non-Western Others, specifically those in Asia, reinforce Russia's understanding of self as a part of the West (Curanović 2012; Morozov 2015).

At the same time, in a quantitative sense, post-Soviet Russia is currently a "normal developing country" (Schleifer and Treisman 2005). In terms of income inequalities, macroeconomic instability, corruption, crime, and other typical problems of the developing world Russia is far from the worst (better than Nigeria) but still not at the top (worse than China). The apparent rise of East Asian and Southeast Asian nations at the end of the 20th century and their newly found economic clout contradicts traditional perceptions of the East as lower in status and subordinate in relation to Russia. Specifically, it is increasingly difficult for Putin's regime to construct Russia as an energy superpower vis-à-vis rising China, and, as a result, its rapprochement with China triggers the raw-material appendage discourse (e.g., Grek 2015; Pestsov 2015).

In sum, the discourse of energy superpower presents Russia as an equal among equals in relations with the West and as superior in relations with the non-Western powers. At the same time, however, the discourse of raw-material appendage identifies Russia as a potential or actual victim of Western and Chinese expansionism. In this discursive framework, Russia's energy cooperation, as well as general economic and political rapprochement with the West and China, is perceived as a threat. The discourse of energy superpower forces Russia's representatives to seek from the West and China the recognition of Russia's unique status in international energy relations. More specifically, Russia's role in Eurasian energy security becomes a cornerstone of Russia's claim for energy superpower status. This discursive framework sustains the construction of Russia as located in the midst of an infinite dialogue between the East and the West. Consequently, Putin's regime carved for Russia a distinctive and prominent yet lonely position in international energy politics. Inasmuch as Russia's "We" is with neither the West nor the East, Putin's regime is doomed to protect its energy sector – in Putin's own words (2006c), "the holy of holies of Russia's economy" – from everyone.

Russia's energy paradigm: A discursive bipolar disorder

In the mid-2000s, control over energy resources became the ends and means of political power at the domestic level and a center of gravity in Putin's project of restoring Russia's international status that was lost during the 1990s. As oil prices rose, the multifaceted and contradictory ambitions of Russia's political elites for the national future in the international arena became encapsulated in the discourse of energy superpower. In this discursive framework, the possession of abundant energy resources and control over energy streams automatically make Russia a player of consequence on the international stage. Accordingly, Russian representatives socially instrumentalize energy resources as one of the primary sources of national economic growth, pride, power, and independence, as well as a sustainable foundation for mutually beneficial relations with its partners in both Europe and Asia.

Introducing the discourse of energy superpower into the narrative of Russia's "greatpowerness," Putin's regime made a long-term identity choice. The discourse of energy superpower has outlived the oil price boom of the mid-2000s and occupies a prominent place in Putin's ideology in the 2010s. The discourse of energy superpower, being one of the integral parts of Putin's ideology, is produced and reproduced by Russia's authorities. This discourse was replicated even under the presidency of Dmitry Medvedev (2008–2012) who was promoting political and economic modernization, openly urging Russia away from "humiliating dependence on raw-materials" (Medvedev 2009).

The presence and the strong influence of the critical discourse of raw-material appendage reinforce the production and reproduction of the discourse of energy superpower. This counter-discourse recognizes Russia's energy wealth as a function of multiple vulnerabilities. In this sense, the discourse of raw-materials appendage challenges Putin's ideology, as well as the legitimacy and credibility of Putin's rule. In this sense, the discourses of energy superpower and raw-material appendage are mutually constitutive, meaning that the two discourses simultaneously exclude and reinforce one another. The discourse of raw-material appendage forces Putin's regime to sustain the discourse of energy superpower by replicating it on both national and international levels. In other words, Putin's regime must present Russia as an energy superpower and frame its interactions with other international actors accordingly because rejecting the discourse of energy superpower will entail accepting its antithesis, the discourse of raw-material appendage. As a result, Russia's energy diplomacy becomes a hostage of the conflict between the discourse of energy superpower and the discourse of raw-material appendage.

China–Russia energy relations

Loans-for-oil and new pipelines

Since Vladimir Putin rose to power in 1999, one of his primary goals has been to reestablish full state control over the energy sector. The culmination of Putin's efforts was the nationalization of the rebellious Yukos.[7] In 2003, one of the most valuable assets of Yukos – Yuganskneftegaz – was sold by a controversial closed-room auction (Sixsmith 2010) and was eventually acquired by Rosneft for US$9.3 billion. Rosneft was not able to raise the full amount of cash from domestic sources. Western banks refused to offer it a loan because of the controversies that surrounded the Yukos affair. CNPC, on the contrary, agreed to lend Rosneft US$6 billion as an advance payment for five-year deliveries of oil, passing the credit through China's Export-Import Bank of China (Exim Bank). Even though Russia's exports to China increased, Russian authorities again suspended plans to build a direct pipeline from Eastern Siberia to Northern China.

In 2006, against the background of sharply deteriorating relations between Russia and European consumers of its energy, Putin announced that in the nearest decade Russia would increase its oil exports to Asia tenfold, from 3 percent to 30 percent. Transneft, the state-owned operator of the oil pipeline networks, initiated the construction of a new pipeline system to transport oil from Eastern Siberia to the Pacific coast at Nakhodka. However, the new project did not include a direct branch to China. Between 2006 and 2008, more than 60 percent of Russian oil was delivered to China by the East Siberian railway, whereas the rest was delivered through Kazakhstan via the Atasu-Alashankou pipeline and by tankers from Sakhalin (Eder et al. 2009, 229–231). The breakthrough in pipeline negotiations happened only after the 2008 global economic crises hit the Russian economy hard.

As oil prices were collapsing from the July 2008 high of US$147 to the December 2008 low of US$32, Russia's NOCs were eager to sign new deals with the Chinese. In February 2009, Chinese and Russian officials announced the China Development Bank (CDB) would lend Rosneft and Transneft US$15 billion and US$10 billion, respectively, with an interest rate of 5.69 percent. China had already used loan-for-oil and loan-for-gas deals to secure long-term supplies before and amidst the economic crises in 2009 it offered generous loans to many energy-rich states but not at this scale and in such quantity.[8] Chinese and Russian governments played an active role in facilitating these deals. Russian government and Rosneft initiated the negotiations by approaching China's government in 2008 (Goncharov, interview, November 2016, Beijing). As a result, Russia's NOCs covered the holes in their budget, whereas CNPC was supposed to get 15 Mtoe of crude oil yearly at market price over the next 20 years. The loans were also contingent upon the construction of a spur from Russia's newly launched ESPO pipeline to China. In 2011, the 1,030-kilometer-long pipeline linked the ESPO to the Daqing refinery complex via Skovorodino. Transneft built the 65-kilometer-long section of this pipeline on Russian territory using CDB's loan, whereas the CNPC completed the 965 kilometers located inside China.

In 2010, Russia became one of the top five oil suppliers to China and its exports to China have grown steadily since then. Even though a significant price dispute quickly arose between Rosneft and CNPC,[9] in 2013 Russia's and China's NOCs signed new multiple energy deals. Notably, Rosneft signed a 25-year oil deal worth US$270 billion with CNPC and another ten-year oil deal worth US$85 billion with Sinopec. As a result, Rosneft's export deals with China jumped to over 25 Mtoe per year. Also, CNPC and Rosneft signed a memorandum of understanding to form a joint venture to develop Russkoye and Yurubcheno-Tokhomskoye oilfields in Eastern Siberia that will supply local demand, as well as Chinese and other Asian markets.

At the end of 2014, Transneft added three more oil pumping stations to the ESPO System, increasing the oil pumping capacity of the stations built in 2011. A year later, the initial pipeline was joined by a parallel one. Once China's spur of the ESPO expanded its capacity, China received more than 50 Mtoe from Russia, which constituted 14 percent of the total China's imports and 18 percent of Russia's total exports. In 2016, this allowed Russia to compete with Saudi Arabia for the status of China's second-largest supplier of oil, whereas China surpassed Germany as the top buyer of Russian oil. The existing China–Russia contracts anticipate a further increase in exports of oil over the remainder of the 2010s and well into the 2020s.

Discursive politics of energy in Russia's China policy

Framing the relations with China as an "energy dialogue," Russia's representatives claim that this dialogue is motivated and sustained by market incentives rather than a desire to form a new political coalition against the West. They describe it as "pragmatic" (Denisov 2014a) and "clearly defined" along the lines of economic development (Lavrov 2012). The frame of market rationalism highlights Russia's extraordinary and enduring capacity to satisfy China's growing energy demand. It also connotes that Russia is interested in China as a market and desires to strengthen its relations with it. Importantly, by using this frame, Russia's officials discursively instrumentalize Russia's ample resource wealth as a significant competitive advantage rather than a curse or a source of vulnerabilities. Russia's energy exports to China have become not a consequence of an unhealthy addiction to resource revenues and a necessity to diversify energy exports in the face of deteriorating relations with the West but a rational economic choice stipulated by the development of the global energy market.

Another part of the official discourse on China–Russia energy relations is the frame of regionalism. It foregrounds geographic proximity as a foundation for China–Russia mutually beneficial energy cooperation. This frame, however, has several serious limitations. As the discussion of Russia's constructions of "we" and "they" in the previous section points out, Russia does not perceive itself as an Asian state. As Russia's current ambassador to China Andrey Denisov (2014a) puts it, China and Russia "are neighbors, but [they] are different." In other words, Russia is in Asia but Russia is not Asia. Hence the references to shared past and cultural affinity with China support the frame of regionalism. Moreover, whereas in the case of Russia's relations with the EU, official discourses temporally harken back to the past (e.g., World War II, Cold War), the discursive construction of China–Russia energy relations is framed in terms of the future (e.g., expected future economic growth).

For example, framing Russia's relations with the EU, Victor Khristenko (2006a) argues that "Russia had never cut off supplies to Europe – neither during the Cold War nor during the financial crises of 1998 – because [Russia] historically sees itself as a part of Europe" (also Lavrov 2012; Novak 2014b). In contrast, discussing Russia's energy cooperation with Asia, Khristenko (2006b) focuses on geoeconomic rather than geopolitical or geocultural links:

> We view the eastern direction as a strategic one, since here – on the outer contour – Russia has such countries as Japan and Korea, the leaders of the world economy, China and India, with their huge markets and industrialization potentials, and dynamic and ambitious Southeast Asian states. The internal contour is East Siberia and the Far East. [...] There is a situation when there is a real opportunity to realize Mikhail Lomonosov's famous prediction that "the power of Russia shall be increased by Siberia."

Consequently, the frame of regionalism does not create another dimension within the construction of China–Russia energy cooperation but reinforces its reading as a rational choice based purely on the matching economic interests of the two countries.

Alexander Gabuev, a China expert and a senior associate at the Carnegie Moscow Center, argues that, despite the recent progress in China–Russia energy relations, China is still not "a priority partner for Russia" (interview, October 2016, Moscow). According to Gabuev, the Russian elite identifies itself as "Europeans" and sees its future "in Europe":

> Russian business and high-ranking officials – everyone – want to return to business with the West. No one ever wanted any serious partnership with Asia. [The Russians] are a little culturally limited, racists, often not well informed [about Asia], and not pragmatic, and thus a partnership with China is still a cultural choice. If you sell more oil to the West, then you are a European country, you are striving for capitalism, a market democracy, and high Western standards of consumption. If you sell more oil to China, then you become a more authoritarian country, in which human rights are violated, and so on.
>
> (Interview, October 2016, Moscow)

Indeed, discussing the diversification of energy exports toward the East, Russian representatives stress that China is not going to replace Europe in Russia's energy diplomacy. For example, Putin (2006d) declares confidently that even though Russia wants to have "access to the developing Asian markets," its European partners "need not fear" that Russia will reduce their energy supplies. Similarly, in all his public statements, especially those aimed at the Western audience, Alexandr Novak insistently rejects the notion that enhanced cooperation between Russia and the countries of the Asia-Pacific region marks a turn to "the East" in Russia's energy politics (e.g. Novak 2015a, 2015c). Besides, Novak, on multiple occasions, emphasizes that Russia will not favor the interests of its new partners over those of current ones. Consequently, Russia's rapprochement with China and other Asian nations is constructed not as a redirection of Russia's energy politics but as its globalization. As the First Deputy Minister of Energy Alexey Texler (2015) puts it, in the 2010s Russia like a "double-headed eagle looks in both directions."

Nevertheless, in the mid-2000s and even more so after Putin's regime officially admitted its "turn to the East" (*разворот на Восток, razvorot na Vostok*) in 2014, China started to represent the major (if not only) counterbalance to the West in Russia's energy diplomacy. On the discursive level, Putin's regime uses energy relations with China to maintain Russia's status as the unique provider of continental energy security and reinforce the discourse of energy superpower. In this context, the frame of strategic partnership becomes critical for the construction of China–Russia energy relations.

This third frame is based on the notion of national interests (e.g., Denisov 2014a, 2016; Putin 2012, 2013b). Denisov (2014b) describes Russia–China energy cooperation as "a product of the political will of the leaders of the two countries." Similarly, Lavrov (2012) argues that "the main secret" of steady development of the China–Russia relations is "a systemic approach" that includes yearly meetings at the highest level and "sets the necessary political tone for practical projects." In addition, China–Russia energy cooperation is elevated to the global level, and its development is presented not only as a part of the bilateral relations but also as an essential factor in the development of international energy politics. For example, in an article for *People's Daily* (2012), Putin argues that

> The energy-sector dialogue between our two countries has a strategic dimension. Our joint projects have a big impact on shaping the global energy market's entire configuration. They offer China more reliable and diversified energy supplies for its domestic needs and offer Russia the chance to open up new export routes to the fast-growing Asia-Pacific region.

While Putin (2014) recognizes that "Chinese friends drive a hard bargain as negotiators," the more aggressive expressions of the discourse of energy superpower (see Kuteleva 2020, 86-87) are absent in Russia's official discourse about China–Russia energy relations. There is evidence, however, to suggest that the assertiveness of the energy superpower marks Russia's relations with China on an unofficial level. Sergey Goncharov, the former director of the Representative Office of Rosneft in China (2006–2013), characterizes Russia's senior officials responsible for negotiations with China as "mobsters" with "the mentality of drug dealers" (interview, November 2016, Beijing). According to him, in internal communications, they formulated the goal of China–Russia negotiations over oil exports in the late 2000s as "to put China on the needle" (*посадить на иглу, posadit' na iglu*) thereby comparing Russia's oil to heroin. A current employee of Rosneft in China also confirmed that his supervisors believed that the ESPO pipeline would "fasten the Chinese to Russia" and, subsequently, China will accept the oil-linked gas pricing mechanism offered by Russia (interview, November 2016, Beijing). The fact that Russia's representatives never made statements like these in public indicates that the energy superpower discourse has a vindictive and protective nature. In the realm of energy diplomacy, Russia's representatives evoke its aggressive expressions only when they consider that their foreign counterparts threaten Russia without due respect and question its unique status in international energy relations.

The discourse of raw-material appendage and China–Russia relations

Generally, Russians like China but are hesitant about the Chinese. In 2016, 36 percent of Russians believed that China is Russia's friend (Levada Center 2017, 194 and 205). A decade ago, only 12 percent of Russian thought so. Public opinion about China is steadily improving. However, many Russians still believe that there is a danger of "Chinese expansion" which will be caused by China's overpopulation and, accordingly, will lead to the loss of eastern Russian territories (for a detailed analysis of Russian fears about "Chinese expansion" see Larin 2009; Yankov 2010; Curanović 2012). According to the surveys, 46 percent in 2005 and 24 percent in 2016 agreed that the authorities need to limit the residence of the Chinese on the territory of Russia (Levada Center 2017, 174).

As it was already pointed out through this chapter, the discourse of raw-material appendage initially focused on the West as Russia's negative Other and has expanded to include China as the second negative Other only relatively recently (e.g., Khramchikhin 2013; Yanitskiy 2010). However, the contradictory attitudes toward China and the Chinese do not transform into a coherent China threat discourse in the realm of energy politics.

Alexander Gabuev notes that Russia is often portrayed as China's raw-material appendage because of the unbalanced trade turnover between the two countries and frames this opinion as a "widespread liberal discourse" (interview, October 2016, Moscow). According to him, the formula "our raw materials in exchange for your cars and consumer goods" is a product of Russia's economic structure rather than a result of China's attempts to conquer Russia. This opinion is widely shared by most of Russia's China experts. Ksenia Kushkina, a project specialist at the Energy Systems Center of the Skolkovo Institute of Science and Technology, points out that China is often perceived as an "Oriental mystery" and a "'black box' in which something enters but what comes out of is not clear" (interview, October 2016). According to her, the Chinese are "quite pragmatic and truthful" because "they always honestly define their long-term goals, albeit in vague phrases." Like Gabuev, she describes the critique of China–Russia energy cooperation and the perceptions of China as a threat as an opinion of the "radical liberals." She attributes it to the ignorance of China and its intentions. Importantly, Russia's China experts believe that as a buyer of energy resources China is the ultimate choice for Russia. As Raisa Epikhina of Moscow State University puts it, "China has no equals" because "China is a huge market, and, from this point of view, China will always be attractive for everyone" (interview, October 2016).

The opinion described by China experts as "liberal" indeed is often held by adherent critics of Putin's regime who stand up for liberal economic reforms and comprehensive political reforms. For example, Yulia Latinina, a well-known journalist, public intellectual, and to a certain extent a symbol of Russian liberalism, criticizes China–Russia energy deals as unprofitable for Russia (e.g., 2014a, 2014b). However, her criticism targets corruption in Russia's energy sector rather than perpetuates the perceptions of China as a threat. Similar representations of China–Russia relations appear in fiction writing (e.g., Sorokin 2006; Chizhova

2017), where China takes advantage of the greed of corrupt Russian officials to gain control over Russian energy resources.

In sum, the raw-material appendage discourse labels as a threat not China but Russia's unhealthy addiction to the energy rent in general. In this sense, Sinophobia that exists in Russian society is not a challenge for the development of China–Russia energy relations because it exists in another discursive space. The discourse of raw-material appendage, however, forces Putin's regime to reproduce the discursive logic of energy superpower in its constructions of China–Russia energy relations. Consequently, the expressions of the energy superpower discourse in Russia's discursive politics of China–Russia energy cooperation can be attributed to two factors. First, it is a part of the discursive structure that legitimizes Putin's regime. Second, it sustains the discursive construction of Russia as an influential actor in international energy politics.

China's construction of Russia as a partner in energy relations

China's leaders and senior officials at the end of the 2000s and the early 2010s described China–Russia relations as "healthy" and "dynamic" (Hu 2012a), praising Russia as a trusted partner and a good neighbor (Liu 2005; Li 2016a). Energy cooperation was always a priority for the Chinese side. At the dawn of China–Russia energy relations, Liu Guchang (2005), China's ambassador to Russia at that time (2003–2009), bluntly formulated the Chinese approach to the energy dialogue with Russia: "China needs oil and gas, Russia needs a market, and the Chinese market is the most convenient and stable." He also noted that successful energy cooperation would elevate China–Russia relations to a new level.

The 2007 China's Energy Development Report argues that in the mid-2000s "the highly politicized nature" of international energy relations exposes Russia to "enormous pressure." According to it, the decision of Russia's authorities to increase oil exports to Asia in 2006 is a logical step in creating a "multipolar" energy strategy. Importantly, the authors of the report unite Russia and China by portraying them both as victims of unfounded criticism of the West. Their concluding remarks are worth quoting in length:

> Since the beginning of 2006, Russia has switched to a diversified strategy of energy exports. This strategy turned the international public opinion against Russia: some argued that Russia "uses energy resources as a foreign policy tool," "manages geopolitics through energy exports," and "tries to manipulate the West with energy resources." On the other hand, the energy needs of some major energy consumers were also criticized. For example, China's and India's rapid economic development caused a rapid increase in energy demand. The countries were labeled as "the world's energy black holes," "energy-hungry dragons," and even as the chief culprits of the oil prices rise. As a result, China's and India's contribution to global economic development was diluted, whereas their energy demand was placed under the spotlight and

> examined with a magnifying glass. In this framework, the United States and Western European countries emerged as "threatened" because their energy security is jeopardized by Russia's intentions to explore Asian markets, and their energy supply is affected by the surge in demand in China, India, and other developing countries.

In this discursive framework, Russia is explicitly constructed as an antipode to the West and thus as China's potential ally, even though it does not appear as a part of China's "we" (because the "we" is "developing countries"). Other experts of state-affiliated think tanks and research institutions sketch a similar portrait of Russia. Li Zhonghai (2009, 5–6) of the Chinese Academy of Social Sciences defines Russia as an "independent energy producer" and claims that "China's government, business, and people have always had high hopes to meet China's growing energy demand through the development of China-Russia relations." Along similar lines, Zhang Hongxia (2007, 38), also a researcher at the Chinese Academy of Social Sciences, claims that the energy wealth became "the 'golden key' to Russia's economic development and the 'tool' for the rise of Russia as a great power" in the 2000s. Some Chinese scholars point out that Russia's economic overdependence on the energy sector is not sustainable in the long run (e.g., Zhang 2007; Wu 2006). However, overall the rich body of literature on Russia's energy strategy and energy diplomacy that emerged in China between 2006 and 2009 presents Russia as a promising energy supplier and provides a positive outlook for the development of China–Russia cooperation (e.g., Wang 2006; Li, ZH. 2009).

China's officials, on the contrary, between 2006 and 2009 bypassed the topic of China–Russia energy cooperation in silence. Against the background of the 2005 loan-for-oil, China's representatives had high hopes for the pipeline project (Liu 2005; MFA of the PRC 2005). When Russian authorities suspended the plans to build a direct pipeline from Eastern Siberia to Northern China, their Chinese counterparts removed the development of energy cooperation with Russia from their agenda. The language of the public statements made by China's officials during this period is vague, and it seems that they struggle to find practical examples to illustrate the "strategic" nature of China–Russia relations. For instance, calling 2006 and 2007 "extraordinary years in the history of China-Russia relations," Liu Guchang (2007) describes the strategic component of these relations as follows:

> China and Russia exchange their opinions in a timely manner and maintain close cooperation on the major global and regional issues, which contributes to strengthening the influence and effectiveness of the two countries in the international arena and contributes to the peaceful development of the planet.

China's officials start to talk about strengthening energy relations with Russia again only after 2009. Their construction of China–Russia energy relations is structurally similar to the Russian one, but the emphasis falls differently.

Like their Russian counterparts, China's representatives define China–Russia energy relations as a "dialogue" based on "the principle of mutual benefit and complementing each other with advantages" (MFA of the PRC 2010). The frame of market rationalism occupies a central place; however, while the idea of interdependence plays a crucial role in Russian discourse, China's representatives put the accent on the absence of geopolitics and link China–Russia relations with the concepts of "peaceful rise" and "harmonious world." They frame China–Russia energy cooperation in terms of the desire of the two countries to use their development potential and ensure dynamic economic growth rather than to form an anti-Western coalition. Reinforcing the logic of the "peaceful rise," Hu Jintao (2012b) argued that "the whole world" will benefit from a closer interaction between China and Russia. China's representatives often describe China–Russia energy relations as "business cooperation" (e.g., Hu 2012a; Li 2012b).

The frame of regionalism is also present in China's construction of China–Russia energy relations. A common metaphor for China–Russia relations evoked by both China's officials and foreign policy experts is a popular proverb "a close neighbor is better than a distant relative" (远亲不如近邻, *yuan qin bu ru jin lin*) (e.g., Liu 2008; Ma 2008; Wang H. 2009). Unlike their Russian partners, China's representatives present China–Russia energy cooperation not as a novelty but as an opportunity to revitalize the historical economic, social, and cultural networks connecting the two countries. As a case in point, Xi Jinping (2013) compared oil and natural gas pipelines to the Thousands-miles Tea Route (万里茶道, *wanli chadao*).[10] According to him, the new pipelines will become "arteries" that connect China and Russia in the 21st century, like the route over which traders exchanged Chinese tea for Russian furs two centuries ago. Reinforcing the narrative of "win-win" cooperation, Xi Jinping argued that in the case of China and Russia "one plus one is more than two" because of their complementary interests.

Finally, China's official discourse of China–Russia relations also frames energy cooperation between the two countries as a part of the strategic partnership. However, China's officials emphasize the "comprehensiveness" of China–Russia diplomatic rapprochement and broaden the content of energy cooperation. Whereas for the Russian side energy cooperation means first and foremost exports of fossil fuels and the construction of the transportation infrastructure to facilitate these exports, Chinese representatives focus on expanding the portfolio of China–Russia energy relations and moving beyond "traditional oil and gas" (e.g., MFA of the PRC 2010; Li, H. 2012a, 2012b).

The construction of the energy cooperation as a part of China–Russia's "comprehensive strategic partnership" did not change once Xi Jinping replaced Hu Jintao. Starting from 2014, however, Xi and other China's senior officials highlight that energy relations are based on "practical cooperation" (e.g., MFA of the PRC 2014; Xi 2015; Li, H. 2016a, 2016b). By 2017, "practical" (务实, *wushi hezuo*) became the most recurring epithet for China–Russia relations in China's official discourse. Accordingly, China's representatives feature energy in their recent public statements not as a central strategic priority but just as another item in the long list of items on the cooperation agenda (e.g., Xi 2017; Li, H. 2017). Notably, the discussion of the further expansion of energy infrastructure was incorporated into the discourse of BRI and framed as one of the "connectivity" issues (e.g., Xi 2015; Huangpu and Wang 2015). This shift means that the Chinese side wants to include the negotiations on future pipelines in the broader theme of regional integration, as well as potentially "linking up" the Eurasian Economic Union and BRI.[11] In this framework, the pipelines are not a matter of bilateral relations but a part of the integration package.

Xi's "China dream" and Putin's "energy superpower"

Despite the undeniable logic for the rapprochement between Russia and China, their "energy dialogue" has been complicated. Despite the steadily rising growth of demand for and of imports of oil on China's part, Russia hesitated to enter long-term agreements with China until the end of the 2000s. In the late 2000s, some scholars argued that a convergence of outlook between Russia and China in regard to their preferences for the state controlling the vital sectors of the economy will create a stronger foundation for the cooperation (e.g., Ferdinand 2007; Williams 2009). However, the direct pipeline to China was not completed until 2011 and relatively stable energy cooperation between Russian and China started to emerge only after 2013.

While Russia separates itself from the West, the historical, cultural, and political gulf separating it from China is substantially deeper. The pattern of China–Russia energy relations between 2005 and 2017 indicates that Russia turns to the East only when it faces challenges in the West: the need to find the cash to finance the controversial nationalization of Yukos' assets in 2005, the decline in Western demand for Russian oil following the 2008 global financial crises, and, finally, the recent alienation between the West and Russia following the Ukrainian crises in the mid-2010s. Russia's energy identities and discursive politics of energy appear to be driving it away from China. Putin's regime must present Russia as an energy superpower and frame its interactions with China accordingly because rejecting the discourse of energy superpower will entail accepting its antithesis, the discourse of raw-material appendage. As a result, Russia's energy diplomacy toward China becomes a hostage of the conflict between the discourse of energy superpower and the discourse of raw-material appendage.

While the Soviet Union was China's "big brother" (老大哥, *laodage*), modern Russia is not a member of China's family but merely a business partner. In the 2010s, China can buy as much Russian oil as its economic development requires and recognizes that Russia needs China's money much as China needs Russia's energy resources. For the Chinese side, a partnership with Russia is a matter of convenience and a rational choice determined by its current economic interests. Xi Jinping's China Dream does not include a geopolitical coalition with Putin's energy superpower. Russia is losing (or already has lost) its competitive advantages in relations with China because in the 2010s oil supplies can buy China's friendship but cannot turn it into a geopolitical ally.

Notes

1 See Bouzarovski and Bassin (2011) and Rutland (2015) for a general discussion of the role of energy resources in debates over Russian national identity.
2 As Thane Gustafson (2012, 101) puts it, in the energy sector "the market reforms went irretrievably wrong." Market liberalization of oil industry was a child of the 1990s, a period that is commonly referred to in Russia as "the reckless and evil 1990s" (*лихие д евяностые*) or "the time of confusion" (*смутное время*). On privatization of Russia's oil industry in the 1990s see Freeland (2000), Dixon (2008), Gustafson (2012), and Sakwa (2014).
3 Imperial prerogative is a concept developed by Partha Chatterjee (2005, 2012). It is understood as a self-claimed right of an empire to declare the colonial exception within its spheres of influence, such as proclaiming other political entities as in need of intervention because they are unable to manage their own affairs.
4 Levada Center is a Russian independent non-governmental polling and sociological research organization.
5 The survey was conducted by the firm Russian Public Opinion and Market Research (ROMIR) as a part of the NEORUS (Nation-building and nationalism in today's Russia) project of the Department of Literature, Area Studies and European Languages at the University of Oslo.
6 Initially, the term "cargo cult" chiefly, but not solely, referred to diverse Melanesian religious practices characterized by the belief that material wealth could be obtained through ritual worship. Later, the term was used metaphorically to describe attempts to achieve successful outcomes by replicating a set of conditions associated with those outcomes, although those conditions are either not related to the causes of the outcomes or not sufficient enough to reproduce them by themselves (e.g., "cargo cult science" or "cargo cult programming"). According to Shulman (2010), in Russia's case "all forms of social organization and public administration are almost entirely borrowed and implanted with more or less violence, in the course of repetitive [...] waves of westernization," yet "many of these forms have a purely decorative character of window dressing" because there is a belief that this state of affairs is the same in the West but "they are just better than we are at pretending."
7 For a detailed analysis of the Yukos affair see Sixsmith, 2010.
8 In 2009, China signed similar deals with Bolivia, Brazil, Ecuador, Venezuela, and Turkmenistan, but none of these loans exceeded US$10 billion. By the end of 2010 the total value of loans extended by China to energy-rich countries is estimated to be about US$77 billion (Jiang and Sinton, 2011); however, not all these loans were directly backed by energy supply contracts (e.g., the US$10 loan to Kazakhstan in 2009 and US$13 billion loan to Ghana in 2010).
9 In 2012, following the disagreement over the terms of the contract related to pipeline fees, CNPC reduced its payments for Russian oil. The dispute settled with a compromise.
10 This historic route connected European Russia to China through Siberia in the 18th and the 19th centuries. It is better known as the Siberian Route (*Сибирский тракт, Sibirsky trakt*).
11 The energy cooperation, nevertheless, was not mentioned in the Joint Declaration on the Connection of the Silk Road Economic Belt and the Eurasian Economic Union signed in 2015 by Putin and Xi (Joint Declaration 2015).

References

Andreyeva, N. (1990). Ostanovit' spolzaniye k katastrofe! K otvetu likvidatorov i mogil'shchikov nashego sotsialisticheskogo Otechestva! [Stop the slipping to the disaster! Call to account the gravediggers of our socialist Motherland!]. In A. Byelicki (Ed.), *Kratkiy Kurs Istorii Perestroyki* [A short history of perestroika] (pp. 66–76). Leningrad: Krasny Octyabr.

Applebaum, A. (2012). *Putinism: the ideology*. The London School of Economics and Political Science. Strategic update 13.2. [PDF file] Retrieved from http://www.lse.ac.uk /ideas/Assets/Documents/updates/LSE-IDEAS-Putinism-The-Ideology.pdf [Accessed 12 Jan. 2017].

Baev, P. K. (2012). From European to Eurasian energy security: Russia needs and energy perestroika. *Journal of Eurasian Studies* 3, 177–184.

Bassin, M. (1991). Russia between Europe and Asia: the ideological construction of geographical space. *Slavic Review*, 50(1), 1–17.

Bouzarovski, S., and Bassin, M. (2011). Energy and identity: imagining Russia as a hydrocarbon superpower. *Annals of the Association of American Geographers*, 101(4), 783–794.

Bykov, D. (2006). *ZhD* [The railway]. Moscow: Vagrius.

Chatterjee, P. (2005). Empire and nation revisited: 50 Years after Bandung. *Inter-Asia Cultural Studies*, 6 (4): 487–496.

Chatterjee, P. (2012). *The black hole of empire: history of a global practice of power*. Princeton, NJ: Princeton University Press.

Chizhova, Ye. (2017). *Kitaist* [Sinologist]. Moscow: AST.

Clunan, A. L. (2009). *The social construction of Russia's resurgence: aspirations, identity, and security interests*. Baltimore: Johns Hopkins University Press.

Curanović, A. (2012). Why don't Russians fear the Chinese? The Chinese factor in the self-identification process of Russia. *Nationalities Papers*, 40(2), 221–239.

Datsyshen, V. G. (2014). *Istoriya rossiysko-kitayskikh otnosheniy v kontse 19–nachale 20 vv*. [The history of Russian-Chinese relations in the late 19th and early 20th centuries]. Moscow: Directmedia.

Denisov, A. I. (2014a). Interv'yu agentstvu "Interfaks," 17 noyabrya 2014 goda [Interview for interfax news agency, 17 Nov. 2014]. Ministery of Foreign Affairs of the RF. 18 Nov. Retrieved from http://www.mid.ru/ru/maps/cn/-/asset_publisher/ WhKWb5DVBqKA/ content/id/790826. [Accessed 3 Sept. 2018].

Denisov, A. I. (2014b). Interv'yu informagentstvu TASS, 1 oktyabrya 2014 goda [Interview for TASS news agency, 1 October 2014]. Ministery of Foreign Affairs of the RF. 2 Oct. Retrieved from http://www.mid.ru/nb_NO/publikacii/-/asset_publisher / nTzOQTrrCFd0/content/id/668403. [Accessed 3 Sept. 2018].

Denisov, A. I. (2016). Interv'yu Posla Rossii v KNR A. I. Denisova informagentstvam «Rossiya segodnya» i TASS [Interview of the Ambassador of Russia in the PRC A. I. Denisov to the news agencies, Russia Today and TASS]. June 21.

Denisov, A., and Grivach, A. (2008). Uspekhi i neudachi "energeticheskoy sverkhderzhavy" [The gains and failures of the energy superpower]. June 15. Retrieved from http://www .globalaffairs.ru/number/n_10633. [Accessed 10 Nov. 2017].

Dixon, S. (2008). *Organisational transformation in the Russian oil industry*. Cheltenham: Edward Elgar Publishing.

Dynkin, A., and Pantin, V. (2012). A peaceful clash: the US and China: which model holds out promise for the future? *World Futures*, 68(7), 506–517.

Eder, L., Andrews-Speed, P., and Korzhubaev, A. (2009). Russia's evolving energy policy for its eastern regions, and implications for oil and gas cooperation between Russia and China. *Journal of World Energy Law & Business*, 2(3), 219–242.

Evstafiev, D. (2014). Strategiya Neudobnogo Partnerstva [The strategy of uncomfortable partnership]. *Russia in Global Affairs*. March 10. Retrieved from http://www.globalaffairs.ru/global-processes/Strategiya-neudobnogo-partnerstva-16470. [Accessed 10 Nov. 2017].

Ferdinand, P. (2007). Russia and China: converging responses to globalization. *International Affairs*, 83(4), 655–680.

Fish, M. S. (2005). *Democracy derailed in Russia: the failure of open politics*. New York: Cambridge University Press.

Freeland, C. (2000). *Sale of the century: Russia's wild ride from communism to capitalism*. New York: Crown Business.

Grek, Yu. (2015). Itogi i zadachi povorota Rossii na Vostok. [Results and goals of Russia's "turn to the East"]. *Questions of Social Sciences: Sociology, Political Science, Philosophy, and History*, 9(49), 5–9.

Gaddy, C. G., and Ickes, B. W. (2010). Russia after the global financial crisis. *Eurasian Geography and Economics*, 51(3), 281–311.

Gaddy, C. G., and Ickes, B. (2013). *Bear traps on Russia's road to modernization*. New York: Routledge.

Garver, J. W. (1998). Sino-Russian relations. In S. Kim (Eds.) *China and the world: Chinese foreign policy faces the new millennium* (pp. 114–132). New York: Routledge.

Greff, G. (2016). *Russia and the world: Russia and the world: looking into the future*. Presentation at the 7th Gaidar forum, Moscow, Russia. Jan. 14.

Golovanov, V. (2014). *Kaspiyskaya kniga. Priglasheniye k puteshestviyu*. [The Caspian book. A travel invitation.] Moscow: Novoye Literaturnoye Obozreniye.

Gustafson, T. (2012). *Wheel of fortune*. Cambridge, MA: Harvard University Press.

Hu, J. (2012a). Most cherez tri okeana. Interv'yu "Rossiyskoy gazete" [A bridge across three oceans. Interview with "Rossiyskaya Gazeta"]. *Rossiyskaya Gazeta – Stolichnyy Vypusk*, 5740(67). 28 March. Retrieved from https://rg.ru/2012/03/28/knr.html. [Accessed 7 Sept. 2018].

Hu, J. (2012b). Razvivat' sotrudnichestvo i partnerstvo. Interv'yu "Rossiyskoy gazete" [Develop cooperation and partnership. Interview with "Rossiyskaya Gazeta"]. *Rossiyskaya Gazeta – Stolichnyy Vypusk*, 5800 (127). 6 June. Retrieved from https://rg.ru/2012/06/05/czintao.html. [Accessed 7 Sept. 2018].

Huangpu, P., and Wang, J. (2015). Ruhe zou hao yidai yilu jiaoxiangyue [How to play the belt and road symphony]. *Liao Wang /Outlook Weekly*, 24 March. Retrieved from http://www.ciis.org.cn/chinese/2015-03/24/content_7772711.htm. [Accessed 26 July 2018].

Huntington, S. P. (1996). *The clash of civilizations and the remaking of world order*. New York: Simon & Schuster.

Inozemtsev, V. (2015). Vybor Rossii: energeticheskaya sverkhderzhava ili strana-luzer [Russia's choice: an energy superpower or a looser-state]. July 2. Retrieved from Slon.ru: https://slon.ru/posts/53541. [Accessed 5 Oct. 2017].

Jiang, J., and Sinton, J. (2011). Overseas investments by Chinese national oil companies: assessing the drivers and impacts. *IEA Energy Papers*. 1 Feb. 2011.

Kalinin, I. (2015). Petropoetics: the oil text in post-Soviet Russia. In *Russian literature since 1991* (pp. 120–145). Cambridge: Cambridge University Press.

Karaganov, S. 2016. From East to West, or Greater Eurasia. *Russia in Global Affairs*. October 25. http://eng.globalaffairs.ru/pubcol/From-East-to-West-or-Greater-Eurasia-18440.

Khazin, V. (2017). *Truba i drugie labirinty* [The pipe and other labyrinths]. Moscow: LitRes.

Khramchikhin, A. A. (2013). *Drakon Prosnulsya? Vnutrenniye Problemy Kitaya kak istochnik kitayskoy ugrozy Rossii* [Is the dragon awake? China's internal problems as a source of Chinese threat to Russia.]. Moscow: Klyuch-S.

Khristenko, V. (2006a). *Doveriye k Rossii* [Trust in Russia]. July 11.

Khristenko, V. (2006b). *Energeticheskaya Strategiya: Proryv na Vostok* [Energy strategy: a breakthrough to the East]. Feb. 2.

Kol'ev, A. (1995). *Myatezh Nomenklatury: Moskva 1990–1993* [The revolt of the nomenclature: Moscow, 1990–1993]. Moscow: Saveliev.

Konstantinov, A. (2006). *Korumpirovannaya Rossiya* [Corrupt Russia]. Moscow: OLMA-Press.

Kudrin, A. (2015). *Stenogramma: Otkrytaya beseda Aleksandra Mamuta i Alekseya Kudrina* [Transcript: an open discussion between Alexander Mamut and Alexei Kudrin]. 9 Sept. Retrieved from http://strelka.com/ru/magazine/2015/09/09/discussion-mamut-kudrin. [Accessed 10 Nov. 2017].

Kulachenkov, A. (2015). *Natsional'noye dostoyaniye v opasnosti* [The national treasure at risk]. August 20. Retrieved from https://fbk.info/investigations/post/89/. [Accessed 17 Nov. 2017].

Kuteleva, A. (2020). Discursive politics of energy in EU–Russia relations: Russia as an "Energy Superpower" and a "Raw-Material Appendage". *Problems of Post-Communism*, 67(1), 78–92.

Kuyan, M. (2016). Resursnoye proklyatiye Rossii: Mif ili real'nost'? [Resource curse of Russia: myth or reality?] *Bulletin of Omsk University. Historical Sciences*, 1 (9), 140–143.

Lang, Y., and Wang, L. (2007). Eluosi nengyuan di yuan zhengzhi zhanlüe ji Zhong-E nengyuan hezuo qianjing [Russia's energy geopolitical strategy and prospects of sino-Russian energy cooperation]. *Ziyuan kexue*, 29(5), 201–206.

Larin, A. G. (2009). *Kitayskiye migranty v Rossii. Istoriya i sovremennost'* [Chinese migrants in Russia: history and modernity]. Moscow: Vostochnaya Kniga.

Laruelle, M. (2007). *La quête d'une identité impériale: le néo-eurasisme dans la Russie contemporaine*. Paris: Editions Pétra.

Latinina, Yu. (2014a). Za "vygodnyy" kontrakt s Kitayem pridetsya yeshche i priplachivat' [For the "profitable" contract with China we will have to pay extra]. *Russkiy Dom*. Retrieved from http://russiahousenews.info/economics-news/yuliya-latinina-kontrakt-kitay. [Accessed 2 Oct. 2018].

Latinina, Yu. (2014b). Kak zastrelit'sya iz gazovoy truby [How to shoot yourself from a gas pipe]. *Novaya Gazeta*, 23 May. Retrieved from https://www.novayagazeta.ru/articles/2014/05/21/59655-kak-zastrelitsya-iz-gazovoy-truby. [Accessed 2 Oct. 2018].

Lavrov, S. (2006). Pod"yem Azii i vostochnyy vektor vneshney politiki Rossii [The rise of Asia, and the eastern vector of Russia's foreign policy.] *Russia in Global Affairs*, 4(3), 68–80.

Lavrov, S. (2007a). Nastoiashchee i budushchee global'noi Politiki [The present and the future of global politics]. *Rossiya v Global'noy Politike*. Retrieved from http://www.globalaffairs.ru/number/n_8385. [Accessed 23 Sept. 2018].

Lavrov, S. (2007b). Sderzhivanie Rossii: nazad v budushchee? [Containing Russia: back to the future?]. *Rossiya v Global'noy Politike*. Retrieved from http://www.globalaffairs.ru/number/n_9236. [Accessed 23 Sept. 2018].

Lavrov, S. (2012). *Vystuplenie v khode vstrechi s predstaviteliami Assotsiatsii evropeiskogo biznesa v Rossiiskoi Federatsii* [Speech at the meeting with representatives of the association of European businesses in the Russian federation]. Oct. 8.

Lavrov, S. (2013). State of the Union Russia–EU: prospects for partnership in the changing world. *JCMS: Journal of Common Market Studies*, 51(S1), 6–12.

Levada Center (2016). *Obshchestvennoye mneniye-2016* [Public Oppinion-2016]. Moscow: Levada Center. Retrieved from https://www.levada.ru/cp/wp-content/uploads/2017/02/OM-2016.pdf. [Accessed 12 June 2016].

Levada Center (2017). *Obshchestvennoye mneniye-2017* [Public oppinion-2017]. Moscow: Levada Center. Retrieved from https://www.levada.ru/cp/wp-content/uploads/2018/05/OM-2017.pdf. [Accessed 12 June 2016].

Li, H. (2012a). Interv'yu nakanune ofitsial'nogo vizita Vitse-prem'yera Gossoveta KNR Li Ke Tsyana v RF [Interview the day before the official visit of Vice-Premier Li Keqiang to the Russian Federation]. *Embassy of the PRC in the RF*. 26 Apr. Retrieved from http://ru.china-embassy.org/rus/sghd/t926347.htm. [Accessed 9 Aug. 2018].

Li, H. (2012b). Interv'yu rossiyskim i kitayskim SMI [Interview to Russian and Chinese media]. *Embassy of the PRC in the RF*. 30 Nov. Retrieved from http://ru.china-embassy.org/rus/sghd/t994261.htm. [Accessed 9 Aug. 2018].

Li, H. (2016a). Eluosi guoji wen chuan dianxun she caifang [Interview with interfax]. *Ministery of Foreign Affairs of PRC*. 20 Dec. Retrieved from https://www.fmprc.gov.cn/web/dszlsjt_673036/t1425689.shtml. [Accessed 9 Aug. 2018].

Li, H. (2016b). Miqie Zhong-E zhanlue xiezuo, zaofu liang guo he liang guo renmin – zai Eluosi Guoli Guanli Daxue Yanjiang. [Close Sino-Russian strategic cooperation for the benefit of the two countries and the two peoples – speech at the Russian national management university]. *Ministery of Foreign Affairs of PRC*. 15 June. Retrieved from https://www.fmprc.gov.cn/web/dszlsjt_673036/t1372384.shtml. [Accessed 9 Aug. 2018].

Li, J. J. (2014). Zhong-E zhanlue xiezuo he Zhong-Mei-E "sanjiao guanxi" [Sino-Russian strategic cooperation and China-US-Russia "triangular relationship"]. *Eluosi Dong-Ou Zhongya yanjiu*, 4, 7.

Li, J. M. (2012). Xin Pujing shidai de jiben zhengce zouxiang [Policy directions of the new Putin era.]. *Zhongguo dang zheng ganbu lun tan*, 7, 49–52.

Li, Y. (2013). Zuxiang quanmian zhanlue hezuo de Zhong-E guanxi [Sino-Russian relations towards comprehensive strategic cooperation]. *Dongbei Ya luntan*, 4, 3–9.

Li, Z. H. (2009). Zhang-E nengyuan hezuo: cong shanchong shuifu dao jianru jiajing [Sino-Russian energy cooperation: from challenges to a gradual improvement]. *Lingdao zhi you*, 1, 51–53.

Liu, G. (2005). Interv'yu "Nezavisimoy gazete" [Interview with Nezavisimaya Gazeta]. *Renmin Ribao*. 22 June. Retrieved from http://russian.people.com.cn/31519/2589533.html. [Accessed 9 Aug. 2018].

Liu, G. (2007). Eksklyuzivnoye interv'yu gazete Zhen'min' zhibao on-layn [An exclusive interview with the people's daily on-line]. *Renmin Ribao*. Retrieved from http://russian.people.com.cn/31857/92877/6328528.html. [Accessed 9 Aug. 2018].

Liu, G. (2008). *O Vneshney Politike Kitaya i Kitaysko-Rossiyskikh Otnosheniyakh* [On China's foreign policy and Chinese-Russian relations]. St. Petersburg: St. Petersburg University Publishing. [PDF file] Retrieved from http://www.lihachev.ru/pic/site/files/Dip_Programma/030_luguchan.pdf. [Accessed 9 Aug. 2018].

Lukin, A. V. (2009). Rossiysko-kitayskiye otnosheniya: ne oslablyat' usiliy [Russian-Chinese relations: do not relax efforts]. *Mezhdunarodnaya zhizn'*, 11, 89–105.

Lukin, A. (2019). Russian–Chinese cooperation in Central Asia and the idea of greater Eurasia. *India Quarterly*, 75(1), 1–14.
Lukyanov, F. (2016). Umnyy daunshifting: kak Rossii dognat' promyshlennuyu revolyutsiyu [Smart downshifting: how can Russia catch up with the industrial revolution]. 1 March. Retrieved from http://www.forbes.ru/mneniya/mir/313863-umnyi-daunshifting-kak-rossii-dognat-promyshlennuyu-revolyutsiyu. [Accessed 2 April 2017].
Luzyanin, S. G., and Semonova, N. K. (2016). Rossiya-Kitay-Tsentral'naya Aziya: transportnyye i energeticheskiye interesy [Russia-China-Central Asia: transport and energy interests]. *Nauchno-analiticheskiy zhurnal Obozrevatel'*, 2, 56–66.
Ma, F. (2008). Bijiao wenhua yujing zhong de Zhong-E guanxi [Sino-Russian relations in a comparative cultural context]. *Waijiao Pinglun: Waijiao Xueyuan Xuebao*, 2, 32–41.
Malinova, O. (2012). Russia and "the West" in the 2000s: redefining Russian identity in official political discourse. In R. Taras (Ed.) *Russia's identity in international relations: images, perceptions, misperceptions* (pp. 73–91). London: Routledge.
Manners, I. (2002). Normative power Europe: a contradiction in terms? *JCMS: Journal of Common Market Studies*, 40(2), 235–258.
Mau, V. (2008). Logika rossiyskoy modernizatsii: Istoricheskiye trendy i sovremennyye vyzovy [The logic of Russia's modernization: historical trends and modern challenges]. In L. Borodkin et al (Eds.), *Ekonomicheskaya istoriya: Yezhegodnik 2008* [Economic history yearbook 2008] (pp. 359–420). Moscow: Institut Rossiyskoy Istorii RAN.
Medvedev, D. (2009) *Rossiya, vperod!* [Go, Russia!]. 10 Sept. 2010.
Medvedev, D. (2010a) *Interv'yu datskoy radioveshchatel'noy korporatsii* [Interview to Danish broadcasting corporation]. 26 April.
Medvedev, D. (2010b) *Press-konferentsiya po itogam vstrechi na vysshem urovne Rossiya – Yevropeyskiy soyuz* [Press statements following EU-Russia summit]. 7 Dec.
Mezhuyev, B. (2010). Perspektivy politicheskoy modernizatsii Rossii [Prospects for Russia's political modernization]. *Polis: Political Studies*, 6, 6–22.
MFA of the PRC, Ministery of Foreign Affairs of the PRC (2005). Waijiao Bu fayan ren Qin Gang zai li xing jizhe hui shang da jizhe wen [Foreign Ministry Spokesperson Qin Gang's remarks at the regular press conference]. 8 Sept. 2005. Retrieved from https://www.fmprc.gov. cn/web/gjhdq_676201/gj_676203/yz_676205/1206_677148/fyrygth_677156/t210899.shtml. [Accessed 12 Aug. 2018].
MFA of the PRC, Ministry of Foreign Affairs of the People's Republic of China (2010). Foreign ministry holds briefing on premier Wen Jiabao's official visit to Russia and Tajikistan and attendance at the 15th regular meeting between Chinese and Russian Prime Ministers and the 9th Prime Ministers' meeting of the SCO member countries. 11 Nov. Retrieved from https://www.fmprc.gov.cn/mfa_eng/ topics_665678/wenjiabaozonglifangwenelshetjkst_665774/t770940.shtml. [Accessed 25 Aug. 2018].
MFA of the PRC, Ministery of Foreign Affairs of the People's Republic of China (2014). Xi Jinping huijian Eluosi zongtong Pujing [Xi Jinping meets with Russian president Putin]. 9 Nov. Retrieved from https://www.fmprc.gov.cn/ce/cenp/chn/zgwj/t1208880.htm. [Accessed 7 Nov. 2017].
Ministry of Energy of the Russian Federation (2009). Energy strategy of Russia for the period until 2030. Adopted by the Decision of the Government of Russian Federation No. 1715-r, dated 13 Nov.
Ministry of Energy of the Russian Federation (2015). Energy strategy of Russia for the period until 2035. Revisions, dated 24 June.
Ministry of Fuel and Energy of the Russian Federation (2003). Energy strategy of Russia for the period until 2020. Adopted by the decision of the government of Russian Federation No. 1234-r, dated 28 Aug.

Morozov, V. (2015). *Russia's postcolonial identity: a subaltern empire in a eurocentric world.* London: Palgrave Macmillan.
Moscow House of Photography (2008). *Russian dreams*. Press release. 27 Nov. Retrieved from http://www.russiandreams.info. [Accessed 3 March 2017].
Mukhin, A. 2006. *Kremlevskiye vertikaly: Neftegazovyy control* [The Kremlin verticals: oil and gas control]. Moscow: Tsentr Politicheskoy Informatsii.
NEORUS (2013). *National survey 2013.* University of Oslo, Retrieved from http://www.hf.uio.no/ilos/english/research/projects/neoruss/national-survey-2013.xls. [Accessed 11 Nov. 2017].
Novak, A. (2013a). Prioritety rossiyskoy energeticheskoy politiki [Priorities of Russian energy politics"]. Presentation at brookings, USA, 6 Dec.
Novak, A. (2013b). Interv'yu gazete RBK [Interview to the RBC daily]. Dec. 24.
Novak, A. (2014a). *Interv'yu gazete Rossiyskaya Gazeta* [Interview to the Russian Gazeta]. 26 May.
Novak, A. (2014b). Razvitiye mirovoy energetiki i geopolitika. 10-ya plenarnaya sessia 21-go Vsemirnogo Neftyanogo Kongressa, Moskva [Development of global energy sector and geopolitics. Presentation at the 21st world petroleum congress, Moscow]. 19 June.
Novak, A. (2015a). Energetika Yevrazii: put' v budushcheye. Presentation in Berlin. [Eurasian energy sector: the way to the future]. 13 Apr.
Novak, A. (2015b). Interv'yu Vesti Economica: importozavisimost' ot gaza v Yevrope rastet [Interview to the Vesti Economics: Europe's import dependency on gas is increasing]. 15 Apr.
Novak, A. (2015c). Interv'yu nemetskoy Gazete Handlsblatt [Interview to the German].
Orttung, R. W. (2009). Energy and state-society relations: socio-political aspects of Russia's energy wealth. In J. Perovic, R. W. Orttung, and A. Wenger (Eds.), *Russian energy power and foreign relations: implications for conflict and cooperation* (pp. 51–71). London: Routledge.
Orttung, R. W., and Overland, I. (2011). A limited toolbox: explaining the constraints on Russia's foreign energy policy. *Journal of Eurasian Studies*, 2 (1), 274–285.
Panyushkin, V., and Mikhail, Z. (2008). *Gazprom: novoye russkoye oruzhiye* [Gazprom: New Russian Weapon]. Moscow: Zakharov.
Pelevin, V. (2003). *Svyashchennaya Kniga Oborotnya* [The sacred book of the werewolf]. Moscow: Eksmo.
Pelevin, V. (2006). *Empire "V."* Moscow: Eksmo.
Pestsov, S. K. (2015). Vneshnepoliticheskiy povorot Rossii: kuda vedot novaya doroga? [Russia's foreign policy turn: where does the new road lead?] In *Vostochnyy vektor rossiyskoy politiki i yego politicheskoye i ekonomicheskiye posledstviya: materials of the round table* [Eastern vector of Russian politics and its political and economic consequences: the round table proceedings] (pp. 9–14).
Popova, O. (2015). Politicheskiye aspekty "resursnogo proklyatiya" [Political aspects of the "resource curse"]. Bulletin of St. Petersburg university. *Political Science and International Relations*, 6(2), 26–28.
Portyakov, V. Ya. (2013). Rossiysko-kitayskiye otnosheniya: sovremennoye sostoyaniye i perspektivy razvitiya [Sino-Russian relations: current state and development prospects]. *China in the World and Regional Politics. Past and Present*, 18(18), 6–15.
Putin, V. (2005a). *Sovmestnaia press-konferentsiia po itogam peregovorov s Prem'er-ministrom Bel'gii Gi Verkhofstadtom* [Joint press conference following talks with the Prime Minister of Belgium, Guy Verhofstadt]. Oct. 3.
Putin, V. (2005b). Vstupitel'noe slovo na zasedanii Soveta Bezopasnosti po voprosu o roli Rossii v obespechenii mezhdunarodnoi energeticheskoi bezopasnosti [Opening remark

at the security council of the Russian Federation on the role of Russia in international energy security]. 22 Dec.

Putin, V. (2006a). Sovmestnaia press-konferentsiia s Federal'nym kantslerom FRG Angeloi Merkel' [Press conference following talks with the federal chancellor of Germany, Angela Merkel]. Moscow, 16 Jan.

Putin, V. (2006b). Press-konferentsiia po itogam vstrechi glav gosudarstv i pravitel'stv "Gruppy vos'mi," [Press conference following the working meeting of the heads of state and government of the G8 members]. St. Petersburg: Strelna, 17 July.

Putin, V. (2006c). Stenograficheskii otchet o vstreche s uchastnikami tret'ego zasedaniia Mezhdunarodnogo diskussionnogo kluba "Valdai" [Transcript of meeting with participants in the third meeting of the valdai discussion club]. *Novo-Ogarevo*, 9 Sept.

Putin, V. (2006d). *Stenograficheskii otchet o vstreche s predstaviteliami delovykh krugov Bavarii* [Speech at the meeting with representatives of the business circles of Bavaria]. Oct. 11.

Putin, V. (2007). Presentation and discussion at the Munich conference on security policy, Feb. 10.

Putin, V. (2010). Rech' i otvety na voprosy na IV yezhegodnom ekonomicheskom Forume rukovoditeley i top-menedzherov vedushchikh germanskikh kompaniy [Speech and answers to questions at the IV annual econmic forum of CEOs and top managers of leading German Companies]. Nov. 10.

Putin, V. (2012). Rossiya sosredotachivayetsya – vyzovy, na kotoryye my dolzhny otvetit' [Russia muscles up: the challenges that we have to answer]. *Izvestia*, 16 Jan. Retrieved from http://izvestia.ru/news/511884. [Accessed 12 June 2016].

Putin, V. (2013a). Press-konferentsiia po itogam rabochego zasedaniia glav gosudarstv i pravitel'stv stran-uchastnits Foruma stran-eksportorov gaza [News conference following the working meeting of the gas exporting countries forum]. 1 July.

Putin, V. (2013b). Poslanie Prezidenta Federal'nomu Sobraniiu [Presidential Address to the Federal Assembly]. Dec. 12.

Putin, V. (2014). Otvety na voprosy zhurnalistov po itogam vizita v Kitay [Answers to journalists' questions following a visit to China]. May 14, Shanghai.

Roland, G. (2006). The Russian economy in the year 2005. *Post-Soviet Affairs*, 22(1), 90–98.

Ross, M. (2001). Does oil hinder democracy? *World Politics*, 53(3), 325–361.

Ross, M. (2012). *The oil curse: how petroleum wealth shapes the development of nations*. Princeton, NJ: Princeton University Press.

Rutland, P. (2008). Russia as an energy superpower. *New Political Economy*, 13(2), 203–210.

Rutland, P. (2015). Petronation? Oil, gas, and national identity in Russia. *Post-Soviet Affairs*, 31(1), 66–89.

Sakwa, R. (2014). *Putin and the oligarchs: the Khodorkovsky–Yukos affair*. New York: I.B. Tauris.

Savvidi, S. M., and Voloshin, A. I. (2016). Pereoriyentatsiya Rossii na Vostok: problemy i riski [Russia's reorientation to the East: problems and risks]. *Ekonomika: teoriya i praktika*, 1, 23–26.

Schleifer, A., and Treisman, D. (2005). A normal country: Russia after communism. *Journal of Economic Perspectives*, 19(1), 151–174.

Shmatko, S., (2008). Svet v okne i gaz za oknom [Light in the window and gas outside the window]. *Interview to Rossiyskaya Gazeta*. 25 Dec.

Shmatko, S. (2009). Interv'yu Corriere della Sera [Interview to Corriere della Sera]. 24 May.

Shmatko, S. (2010). Vstupitel'noye slovo na Yubileynoy konferentsii Energodialoga Rossii-EU g. Bryussel' [Opening address at the jubilee conference of the Russia-EU, Brussels]. 22 Nov.

Shulman, E. (2010). Solomennyi samolet [Straw Plane]. 22 Jan. Retrieved from http://users.livejournal.com/-niece/126963.html?page=3.

Simonov, K. V. (2006). *Energeticheskaya Sverkhderzhava* [Energy superpower]. Moscow: Algorythm.

Simonov, K. V. (2007). *Global'naya Energeticheskaya Voina* [The global energy war]. Moscow: Algorythm.

Sixsmith, M. (2010). *Putin's oil: the Yukos affair and the struggle for Russia*. New York: Bloomsbury Publishing.

Sorokin, V. (2006). *Den' oprichnika* [Day of the oprichnik]. Moscow: Litres.

Sorokin, V. (2008). *Sakharnyi Kreml'* [The sugar kremlin]. Moscow: AST.

Sorokin, V. (2013). *Telluria* [Telluria]. Moscow: AST.

Stalin, I. (1952). Politicheskiy otchet Tsentral'nogo Komiteta XIV s'yezdu VKP(b) [Political report of the central committee at the 14th congress of the all-union communist party]. In I. Stalin (Ed.), *Sochineyniya* [Works] (pp. 261–352). Retrieved from http://grachev62.narod.ru/stalin/t7/t7_32.htm. [Accessed 11 Nov. 2017].

Surkov, V. (2006). Suverenitet – eto politicheskiy sinonim konkurentosposobnosti. [Sovereignty is a political synonym for competitiveness]. *Politnauka*. 7 Feb. Retrieved from http://www.politnauka.org/library/public/surkov.php. [Accessed 14 June 2016].

Tabata, S. (2006). *Dependent on oil and gas: Russia's integration into the world economy*, Vol. 11. Hokkaido: Slavic Research Center, Hokkaido University.

Tabata, S. (2009). The influence of high oil prices on the Russian economy: a comparison with Saudi Arabia. *Post-Soviet Geography and Economics*, 50(1), 75–92.

Terner, S. (Author) and Yevsyukov, A. (Director). (2015). *Energiya Velikoy Pobedy* [Energy of the great victory]. [Motion picture]. Moscow: All-Russia State Television and Radio Broadcasting Company.

Texler, A. (2015). Nerazmennyy barrel'. Rossii ne nado snizhat' dobychu i eksport nefti. Interv'yu Rossiyskoy Gazete. [Unredeemable barrel. Russia does not need to reduce the production and export of oil. Interview Rossiyskaya Gazeta]. *Rossiyskaya Gazeta*. 21 Jan. Retrieved from https://rg.ru/2015/01/22/texler.html. [Accessed 12 Sept. 2018].

Tian, Y. (2007). Zhong-E guanxi de xianzhuang, tedian ji qianjing [The status quo of Sino-Russian relations: characteristics and prospects]. *Eluosi yanjiu*, 3, 40–41.

Trenin, D. (2012). *Vernyye druz'ya? Kak Rossiya i Kitay vosprinimayut drug druga*. [True partners? How Russia and China see each other]. Moscow: Center for European Reforms.

Trenin, D. (2016). Vneshnyaya politika Rossii v blizhaishie pyat let: tceli, stimuli, orientiry. [Russia's foreign policy in the next five years: goals, incentives, guidelines]. Apr. 29. Retrieved from http://www.globalaffairs.ru/global-processes/Vneshnyaya-politika-Rossii-v-blizhaishie-pyat-let-tceli-stimuly-orientiry-18128. [Accessed 11 Nov. 2017].

Tsomaya, M. A. (2014). Kitay: partner ili konkurent? [China: partner or competitor?]. *Vestnik RGGU. Seriya «Politologiya. Istoriya. Mezhdunarodnyye otnosheniya. Zarubezhnoye regionovedeniye. Vostokovedeniye»*, 7(129), 217–222.

Urnov, M. (2014). ‘Greatpowerness’ as the key element of Russian self-consciousness under Erosion. *Communist and Post-Communist Studies*, 47(3–4), 305–322.

Vinogradov, Ye. (2009). Neft' zakonchit'sya mozhet, a prezident net [Oil can end, but the president does not]. *Deutsche Welle*. 4 July. Retrieved from https://www.dw.com/ru/блогозрение-нефть-закончиться-может-а-президент-нет/а-4456242.

Voskresenski, A. D. (2015). Rossiysko-kitayskiye otnosheniya v kontekste aziatskogo vektora rossiyskoy diplomatii (1990–2015) [Russian-Chinese relations in the context of the Asian vector of Russian diplomacy (1990–2015)]. *Sravnitel'naya Politika/Comparative Policy*, 1(18), 32–52.

Wang, H. (2009). Zhong-E guanxi: Zhanlüe jichu yu fazhan qushi [Sino-Russian relations: strategic basis and trends]. *Eluosi yanjiu*, 156(2), 3–9.

Wang, L. (2006). Eluosi Dongfang nengyuan waijiao yu Zhong-E nengyuan hezuo [Russian far eastern energy diplomacy and sino-Russian energy cooperation]. *Xiandai Guoji Guanxi*, 8, 8–13. Retrieved from http://www.cssn.cn/gj/gj_gjwtyj/ gj_elsdozy/201311/t20131101_819700.shtml. [Accessed 23 Oct. 2018].

Wang, S., and Wan, Q. (2013). Lun xinxing Zhong-E guanxi de weilai zouxiang: Jieban haishi jiemeng? [On the future direction of the new Sino-Russian relationship: companions or allies?] *Dangdai yatai*, 4, 4–22.

Williams, C. (2009). Russia’s closer ties with China: the geo-politics of energy and the implications for the European Union. *European Studies*, 27, 151.

Wishnick, E. (2017). In search of the ‘Other’in Asia: Russia–China relations revisited. *The Pacific Review*, 30(1), 114–132.

Wu, D. (2006). Zhong-E zhanlue xiezuo huoban guanxi: Shi nian shijian de lishi kaocha [Sino-Russian strategic partnership of cooperation: a historical study of ten years of practice]. *Eluosi Zhong Ya Dong Ou Yanjiu*, 3, 1–9. Retrieved from http://www.cssn.cn/gj/gj_gjwtyj/gj_elsdozy/201311/t20131101_819676.shtml. [Accessed 23 Oct. 2018].

Xi, J. (2013). Shunying shidai, qianjin chaoliu, cujin shijie heping fazhan – zai Mosike Guoji Guanxi Xueyuan de yanjiang (Mosike) [Conform with the trends of the times and promote the peaceful development of the world. Speech at MGIMO University, Moscow]. *Renmin Ribao*, 23 March. Retrieved from http://cpc.people.com.cn/xuexi/n/2015/0721/c397563-27337993.html [Accessed 21 Oct. 2017].

Xi, J. (2015). Zayavleniya dlya pressy po itogam rossiysko-kitayskikh peregovorov [Press statements following Russian-Chinese talks]. *Kremlin.ru*. 8 May. Retrieved from http://kremlin.ru/events/president/transcripts/49433. [Accessed 2 Nov. 2017].

Xi, J. (2017). Ukreplyat' obshchnost' interesov. Interv'yu Rossiyskoy Gazete. [Strengthen community of interest. Interview with Rossiyskaya Gazeta]. *Rossiyskaya Gazeta*. 2 July. Retrieved from https://rg.ru/2017/07/02/si-czinpin-kitaj-i-rossiia-dolzhny-ukrepliat-obshchnost-interesov.html. [Accessed 12 Aug. 2018].

Yan, S. (2016). Zhongguo nengyuan anquan yu zhoubian guojia de nengyuan hezuo guanxi yanjiu [Research on energy cooperation between China’s energy security and neighboring countries]. *Gaige yu Zhanlue*, 8, 31–34.

Yan, X. (2013). For a new bipolarity: China and Russia vs. America. *New Perspectives Quarterly*, 30(2): 12–15.

Yanitskiy, O. N. (2010). Izmenyayushchiysya mir Rossii: resursy, seti, mesta [The changing world of Russia: resources, networks, places]. *Mir Rossii. Sotsiologiya. Etnologiya*, 19(3), 3–22.

Yankov, A. G. (2010). Sinofobiya-rusofobiya: real'nost' i illyuzii [Sinophobia-Russophobia: reality and illusions]. *Sotsiologicheskiye issledovaniya*, 3, 65–71.
Yudenich, M. (2007). *Neft'* [Oil]. Moscow: Populyarnaya Literatura.
Zhang, H. (2007). Eluosi nengyuan zhuangkuang yu nengyuan zhanlue tan wei. [Russia's energy situation and energy strategy]. *Eluosi, Zhong Ya, Dong Ou yanjia*, 5, 38–43. Retrieved from http://www.cssn.cn/gj/gj_gjwtyj/gj_elsdozy/201311/ t20131101 _818576.shtml. [Accessed 9 Aug. 2018].
Zheng, Y. (2008). *Pujing shidai* [Putin's era]. Beijing: Beijing jingji guanli chubanshe.

5 China–Kazakhstan energy relations

After the collapse of the Soviet Union, China received new opportunities to intensify its geopolitical presence and influence in Central Asia (Laruelle and Peyrouse 2010). China recognized the five Central Asian states – Kazakhstan, Kyrgyzstan, Tajikistan, Turkmenistan, and Uzbekistan – in December 1991 and as early as January 1992 began diplomatic exchanges with them. One of China's core interests in the region is securing energy supplies: maximizing access to Central Asia's energy resources and expanding the overland energy supply lines. In 2007, CNPC received its first license to explore and extract onshore gas in Turkmenistan and built a new 3,666-kilometer-long pipeline to bring Turkmen gas home. By the end of the 2010s, Turkmenistan became fully dependent on China for its gas sales. Uzbekistan also supplies gas to China through the pipeline network upgraded between 2007 and 2009. In Kyrgyzstan, China built two refineries, near the cities of Kara-Balta and Tomok. The refineries, financed by CNPC and supplied by CNPC-run oilfields in Kazakhstan, produce 1.2 million tons of refined products annually (Azattyq 2012). China's key energy partner in Central Asia is Kazakhstan, the second-biggest oil exporter in the former Soviet space behind Russia.

The record time in which China constructed the Kazakhstan–China pipeline illustrates well the high priority China attaches to energy cooperation with Kazakhstan. The landmark project – the Atasu-Alashankou section of the first direct oil import pipeline between China and Central Asia – was completed in just ten months. It began to pump oil in December 2005 and its capacity as of 2018 is at 14 Mtoe of crude oil per year (KCP LLP 2018). Kazakhstan is also the largest recipient of Chinese investment in Central Asia. According to the Eurasian Development Bank (2017, 6), between 2009 and 2016 Chinese investment in Kazakhstan increased from US$9.5 billion to US$21.5 billion; 89 percent of this investment was in oil and gas (Eurasian Development Bank 2017, 46). In 2013, Xi Jinping choose Kazakhstan's Nazarbayev University to announce China's plans to build the Silk Road Economic Belt, clearly signaling that he recognizes Kazakhstan as China's key ally and Central Asia's potential sub-hegemon. This elevates the status of Kazakhstan in China's international strategy, including both China's ongoing quest for energy resources and its attempts to reframe energy relations with resource-rich countries of the Global South as a positive-sum game.

The first part of this chapter focuses on Kazakhstan and its discursive politics of energy. I examine the dominant discursive constructions that shape Kazakhstan's energy paradigm and how Kazakhstan constructs China as its Other. From there, the focus shifts back to China. First, I examine how China constructs Kazakhstan as its Other in international energy politics. Further, I explain how and with what effect China's and Kazakhstan's energy paradigms are manifested and enacted in their bilateral energy relations. The closing section summarizes the findings.

Kazakhstan's discursive politics of oil

Nazarbayev's discursive hegemony

Kazakhstan's oil industry counts its history from 1899 when the first oil gusher fountained occurred in Karashungul (Cherdayev 2012, 12). In the mid-1910s, British investors started to produce oil in the northeast of the Caspian Sea (now Atyrau Region of Kazakhstan), receiving concessions from the Russian Empire. After West Turkestan[1] became a part of the Soviet Union in the early 1920s, the oil industry was nationalized. The Soviet state offered the people of West Turkestan a paternalistic social welfare system, mass education, a robust public health system, socialist justice, and security. It also invested heavily in the industrialization of the region and especially in the development of resource sectors. In exchange, the region was assigned the role of a commodity supplier. For 70 years its economy was subordinated to the needs of the European part of the Soviet Union (Loring 2014).

After the collapse of the Soviet Union in 1991, Kazakhstan became an independent state and found itself holding 3.2 percent of the world's total proven oil reserves. Nursultan Nazarbayev – the first and until March 2019 the only president of Kazakhstan – turned the extraction of energy resources into the foundation of Kazakhstan's national prosperity. In 1997, Kazakhstan became the proud leader among the post-Soviet states in per capita foreign direct investment, and in 1999, it registered the first budget surplus. Throughout the 2000s, Kazakhstan's growth performance averaged almost 8 percent annually in real terms (World Bank 2018). Since 2006, riding largely on high oil prices, Kazakhstan has transitioned from lower-middle-income to upper-middle-income status. To the credit of Nazarbayev and his allies, Kazakhstan's government invested generously and consistently not only in the poverty eradication but also in the new middle class, and as a result, Kazakhstan became one of the most socially and politically stable post-Soviet states (Kalyuzhnova and Patterson 2016; Azam and Ahmed, 2015).

Nazarbayev's regime also had ambitious plans to diversify the economy away from natural resource extraction, but little progress was made in this direction in the 2000s and the 2010s. In 2017, the manufacturing sector accounted for 11 percent of GDP, while the agricultural sector constituted only 5 percent. Both sectors are inefficient and fail to compete successfully with foreign producers (World Bank 2018). In contrast, rents derived directly and indirectly from the sale of energy resources constitute about 25 percent of Kazakhstan's GDP (World Bank 2018). Consequently, after independence, Kazakhstan became a classic rentier state (Ostrowski 2011; Franke et al. 2009), and its fragile economy is extremely vulnerable to downward global oil demand and price shocks.

Nazarbayev has steadily centralized the power in his own hands. The 1995 referendum extended Nazarbayev's term in office to 2000. However, in the aftermath of the 1998 Ruble crisis, Nazarbayev called for elections ahead of schedule and was re-elected as president in 1999. In 2005, he got 91.2 percent of the vote and won another seven-year term. In 2007, a constitutional amendment exempted Nazarbayev personally from the two-term limit on the presidency. In 2010, the parliament of Kazakhstan awarded Nazarbayev an honorary title of the Leader of Nation (*Елбасы, Elbasi*), which uniquely empowered Nazarbayev to secure a lifetime role in domestic and foreign policy decision-making. Darkhan Kaletayev, the first deputy chairman of the ruling pro-presidential party Nur Otan (2008–2009), provides the most precise summary of the dominant vision of Nazarbayev's leadership:

> Nazarbayev is not just the president of Kazakhstan but is the leader of the nation, like Atatürk for the Turks, Mahathir for the Malayans, Lee Kuan Yew for the Singaporeans, and Roosevelt for the Americans. He is a kind of personality that comes precisely in the period of the demand and need for serious progress in the development and growth of the nation. Supporters and opponents of Nazarbayev are united in one thing: without him, there would be no present-day Republic of Kazakhstan in the modern state system.
>
> (Suleev 2009)

Nazarbayev's decision to retire in March 2019 took many observers by surprise. Over the past decades, an increasing amount of scholarship is dedicated to understanding the discursive mechanisms employed by Nazarbayev's regime to legitimize and strengthen its power in Kazakhstan. Marlene Laruelle (2014) argues that "Nazarbayevism" is closely bound to the civic nationalism (Kazakhtanness) and ethnic nationalism (Kazakhness)[2] and intimately connected to transnationalism, that is the idea of Kazakhstan as a modern nation-state integrated into the world community and benefiting from economic globalization. Rico Isaacs (2010, 448) demonstrates that discourses that construct Nazarbayev as "the father of independence" and the single person capable of resolving the challenges of post-Soviet nation-building are not only "projected from above at the elite level" but also shared and accepted by most of the citizens. Similarly, Mariya Y. Omelicheva (2016), exploring the legitimacy discourses produced by Nazarbayev's regime and evaluating the effectiveness of these discourses, based on data from the 2011 World Values Survey, concludes that the Nazarbayev's discursive politics echo the beliefs about socioeconomic and political development widely held in Kazakhstani society. Elsewhere, Omelicheva (2013, 84–85) argues that the concept of a presidential democracy became popular among the Kazakhstani because it resonates well with the widely shared idea of a strong visionary leader responsible for the national success. Other scholars (e.g., Kudaibergenova 2015; Alff 2015; Sullivan 2017) point out that Nazarbayev's regime also monopolizes discourses of development and uses them to legitimize Nazarbayev's everlasting rule.

In sum, Nazarbayev established himself as an authoritarian ruler and an authoritarian discourse-maker that enjoys broad popular support. Even though the discursive politics of Nazarbayev's regime is contested in some realms (e.g., Kudaibergenova 2016), its discursive dominance has remained unchallenged for the past three decades. Nazarbayev has successfully monopolized all formal discursive domains, including public communication of Kazakhstani officials, academic discussions, and media. His speeches and articles are compiled into edited volumes, including four collections of quotations. Besides, Nazarbayev is a prolific writer, authoring 22 books between 1985 and 2017 on the political and socioeconomic development and history of Kazakhstan.

Given Nazarbayev's discursive hegemony, my analysis of Kazakhstan's discursive politics of energy largely focuses on the texts produced by Nazarbayev. Kazakhstan's official discourses (Model 1) are represented by a set of 77 texts, including key policy and programmatic documents and public statements of Kazakhstani officials; 33 out of 77 texts are authored by Nazarbayev. In Kazakhstan's case, cultural representations (Model 3A) and marginal political discourses that are produced by NGOs, academics, and public intellectuals (Model 3B) often replicate, entrench, and even intensify the official discourses. Notably, my survey of Kazakhstani academic literature on energy politics revealed that an overwhelming majority of scholarly works contain at least one quotation from Nazarbayev's treatises.[3] Nazarbayev's discursive dominance is reinforced through the creation of numerous symbolic references that construct him as a protector and encourager of the development of science and education in Kazakhstan. Almost all major initiatives of the last decade related to enhancing Kazakhstan's intellectual and research potential – new schools, universities, research centers, museums, libraries, scholarships, and special bursaries – have been named after Nazarbayev. Nazarbayev dominates even the physical discursive spaces. In Nur-Sultan and Almaty, Nazarbayev's quotations can be found everywhere: facades and entrances of public buildings, billboards, freeway overpasses, benches, and public art. Consequently, the position of the highly centralized and personified regime of Nazarbayev enjoys a full political and discursive hegemony in Kazakhstan. With only sporadic and isolated exceptions, wider political debates in Kazakhstan are shrunk to the point of being barely significant for the analysis of Kazakhstan's dominant energy paradigm and China–Kazakhstan relations. Following Nazarbayev's resignation in March 2019, the Senate speaker Kassym-Jomart Tokayev took office as the president. In the interim, Tokayev made a generous gift to Nazarbayev by pushing through the parliament a law renaming the capital of Kazakhstan in his honor to Nur-Sultan. This symbolic move indicates that Nazarbayev's legacy will endure and the leadership transition is not going to bring significant ideological changes in the nearest future.

Kazakhstan's oil: A blessing and a threat

Control over national oil resources occupies a distinct place in Kazakhstan's official narrative of national independence and sovereignty. Narrating the modern history of Kazakhstan, Nazarbayev (2006, 107) emphasizes that, being a part of the Soviet Union, Kazakhstan never felt like a "real master" of "the great treasures hidden in its bowels." Only as a sovereign state, Kazakhstan was able to use oil as the "foundation of [its] economic independence" (108). Nazarbayev starts the story of Kazakhstan's sovereignty by calling oil "the blood of the Kazakhstani economy" and "the black gold of Kazakhstani lands" that helped the government to kick-start the growth in the early 1990s (99). Developing this story further, he argues that the vast resource wealth is "an object of envy and claims [of other states] because of which Kazakhstan could indeed lose its independence" (100). According, in the middle of the very same paragraph, oil transforms from Kazakhstan's "blood" and "black gold" into a "beast" that Nazarbayev and his team "managed to tame," while "always remembering that for a minute we cannot relax and deceive ourselves by the fact that we control it" (100). Consequently, there are two competing narratives about oil in the official energy discourse: oil as a blessing and oil as a threat.

Like Russia, Kazakhstan struggles with the identity of the victim of the resource curse and seeks to reposition itself. However, while Putin's Russia reframes itself as an energy superpower, Nazarbayev's Kazakhstan consistently and emphatically declares the "economy first" principle. Besides, Nazarbayev's regime has developed a complex construction that rationalizes and reframes Kazakhstan's dependence on energy revenues as a transitional phase in its development, neutralizing the negative connotations of the resource curse discourses.

Portraying Kazakhstan as a sovereign owner of its energy resources and as a modern state that is aspiring to join the "international energy resources club" (130), Nazarbayev (2006) claims that the focus on the oil sector and the quest for foreign investments was the only rational developmental choice for Kazakhstan after it became independent:

> Each country enters the process of [international economic] integration with luggage. This luggage is different for each country: intellect and labor, industrial and technological, cultural, and resource potentials or a combination of these potentials. And, based on the capabilities of a country, the world market sets conditions for this country's integration into it. Each country must pay a kind of "membership fee," offering the world market whatever it can contribute to the integrated economy at the moment.
>
> (128)

Kazakhstan, according to Nazarbayev, paid its "membership fee" in the late 1990s by giving access to its natural resources to large international companies. Foreign investments in the oil sector must "smoothen the difficulties of the transition period" during the first decades of independence and help Kazakhstan become a part of the global economy; however, this developmental choice does not determine Kazakhstan's long-term future and its "fate" in international politics (Nazarbayev 2006, 128–129). Consequently, Nazarbayev constructs Kazakhstan's dependence on oil revenues as a conscious choice and an inevitable side effect of its successful integration into the global economy. As a Kazakhstani expert summarized it, "the president explained to us that we need to sell our oil, if want to become Kuwait" (interview, February 2017, Almaty).

Nazarbayev also highlights that by bringing home foreign investment and inviting international companies to develop oil reserves, Kazakhstan did not surrender its newfound independence but, on the contrary, was able to strengthen its sovereignty by revitalizing the economy (Nazarbayev 2009, 2010a). Also, according to the official discourse, Kazakhstan will eventually outgrow its petrostate status and obtain the recognition of the international community in the realm of technological innovations, particularly by developing "green" sectors. When addressing Kazakhstani citizens between 2005 and 2016, Nazarbayev yearly repeated like a mantra that the government is determined to develop the non-primary sectors of the economy and will use oil revenues to create the "new economy of the future" (*новая экономика будущего, novaya ekonomika budushchego*).

Consequently, while Russia's energy discourses construct the dependency on oil revenues as a humiliating "downshifting," Nazarbayev's regime presents Kazakhstan as a proud petrostate that perceives oil as a purely economic commodity and does not take its oil-based prosperity for granted. A case in point is Nazarbayev's (2017, 221) framing of the oil-boost of the mid-2000s as a unique "respite" that allowed the government to "take a comprehensive look at the emerging model of the national economy." He also stresses that even in the early 1990s he "clearly realized" that Kazakhstan needed "a model of balanced, sustainable development" (221) and was determined to diversify Kazakhstan's economy away from oil.

Kazakhstani experts and scholars reproduce Nazarbayev's official discourse, solidifying its legitimacy. They diagnose Kazakhstan with certain symptoms of the Dutch Disease and address the risks related to its dependence on volatile commodity markets (e.g., Nurmaganbyetov 2011; Karyenov 2014; Ondash 2012, 2013; Yelyubayev 2016). With only rare exceptions (Temirkhanov 2014a, 2014b, 2015), experts agree that the state is the only actor that can protect Kazakhstan from the resource curse and present Nazarbayev's developmental programs as effective preventive measures for mitigating it. The metaphor of raw-material appendage appears in the popular discourse but is absent in experts' vocabulary. Overall, the general attitude of the expert community toward the economic consequences of Kazakhstan's dependence on oil income is most vividly summarized by Murat Temirkhanov (2014a), the Head of Research at the investment bank Halyk Finance: "The resource curse is the evil, but it makes happy both the ordinary Kazakhstanis and the officials."

Like their Russian colleagues, Kazakhstani experts rarely discuss the political side of the resource curse and avoid references to the studies that focus on possible antidemocratic effects of resource wealth. Quite notably, none of the Kazakhstani experts cites quasi-canonical works of Michael Ross (e.g., 2001, 2012) or mention the popular "no taxation, no representation" axiom that inspired many studies of the resource curse. On the contrary, some of them reframe the political implications of the resource curse as an external sovereignty threat, echoing Nazarbayev's concerns about Kazakhstan's oil causing the envy of other nations. For instance, Jumageldi Yelyubayev of the Al-Farabi Kazakh National

University (2016, 83) argues that one of the major expressions of the resource curse is "the increasing pressure on the national governments from transnational energy corporations and countries where [these corporations] are registered" that "undermines the basis of the state sovereignty." This brings us to the broader energy discourse that constructs oil as a heavily sought-after resource and follows Nazarbayev's alarming narrative of energy and environmental crises.

When writing about sustainable development and the future of human civilizations, Nazarbayev is rather pessimistic about the role of oil in social, political, and economic progress. In *Radical Renewal of Global Society and Partnership of Civilizations* (2010b, 6), Nazarbayev identifies the energy and environmental crisis as one of the three "most urgent and topical problems for all mankind," along with food shortages and income inequality. He characterizes these as a contradiction between energy security and environmental protection. According to him, the crises are provoked by the depletion of world oil reserves and are further deteriorated with the expansive growth of China, India, and other developing countries. As the prices for oil and costs of its transportation are growing, oil becomes a "geopolitical factor":

> Whether we like it or not, oil becomes a geopolitical factor and an effective lever of political pressure. We are now forced to talk about energy blackmail, energy threat, and energy terrorism. Sources and supply routes of energy became potential and very vulnerable targets for attacks by international terrorists. *We have crossed the line from the civilization that controls oil to the civilization that is controlled by oil!* We are ready to pay for it more and more literally and figuratively.
>
> (Nazarbayev 2010b, 43, emphasis added)

Consequently, according to Nazarbayev, oil is the energy resource of the 21st century. His concept of energy security is focused on the availability of oil supplies. At its core is the idea of oil scarcity and global oil dependence. In this context, oil becomes extremely securitized and appears on the "panic politics" agenda. To complete the picture, Nazarbayev presents the environmental side of the crisis as an unfolding "ecological catastrophe" (Nazarbayev 2010b, 44). Without going into details, he argues that it is a result of "ecological violence" and "irrational use of hydrocarbons as an energy carrier" (43).[4]

Following Nazarbayev's logic, Kazakhstan's vast oil reserves expose it to potential (but unspecified) geopolitical threats in the present, whereas the inevitable depletion of these reserves in the future is constructed as a structural problem for its long-term development. Nazarbayev (2010b, 49) concludes that "one thing is clear":

> We need to take urgent measures to implement the global energy imperative and ecological imperative, which commands us to actively – that is daily – engage in innovative development of existing energy technologies: optimizing consumption, conserving natural resources, energy-saving, developing renewable energy, and promoting alternative energy.

In sum, the dominant energy discourses construct the vast oil reserves simultaneously as a blessing and as a source of multiple vulnerabilities. Oil is the foundation of Kazakhstan's independence and the greatest threat to its sovereignty after the collapse of the Soviet Union. Kazakhstan's dependence on oil incomes is framed as a temporary phase in its economic development. Accordingly, Kazakhstan is portrayed as a modern and dynamic petrostate that will not lie on its oars but will use its oil money to transition to new modernity and elevate itself onto a new development level. In this framework, Nazarbayev's regime secures for itself the role of the only guarantor of the post-oil bright future.

Constructing Kazakhstan as a petrostate: Oil rent and Nazarbayevism

In the early 2000s, Kazakhstan reshaped the relationship between the political authorities and the economy, building a structure similar to Putin's "power vertical" in Russia. As Wojciech Ostrowski's research (2010) reveals, the security of the Nazarbayev regime's control over the oil sector is founded on managing and rotating cadres according to various considerations, the foremost of which is loyalty to Nazarbayev. Successfully securing control over the rent from the country's oil resources, Nazarbayev gained access to enough political and economic resources to impose and maintain a regime that Ostrowski defines as "quasi-corporatist" (Ostrowski 2010, 139). One of the major features of Nazarbayev's domestic energy politics in the early 2000s was "Kazakhization" of the oil industry and its sub-contractors: a company is "only granted access to the oil industry because it is at least partly owned by the regime's client, who is also an ethnic Kazakh" (Ostrowski 2009, 36). In addition, Nazarbayev's regime staffed KazMunayGas with ethnic Kazakhs, creating barriers for other non-Kazakh specialists to join it. This policy elevated the status of ethnic Kazakh oil men and, as a result, they "not only owe their patron Nazarbayev the high positions they are handed but are also indebted to him for their special, privileged positions in post-Soviet Kazakhstan that go beyond measurable benefits" (Ostrowski 2009, 36). Consequently, the Kazakhization of the oil sector allowed Nazarbayev to build complex, modern, and mediated patron–client ties that determine relationships of loyalty over ethnicity or clan affiliation.

On the discursive level, however, oil is instrumentalized by Nazarbayev's regime not as a source of the political power of ethnic Kazakhs but as a source of collective prosperity of all people of Kazakhstan. Nazarbayev's government encourages among the population a sense of national pride in valuing oil as a national asset and, as a result, the rising national consciousness of the population is tightly bound to Kazakhstan's resource wealth. In other words, the sovereign control over the national natural resources and, specifically, oil became one of the cornerstones of the self-determination of the multi-ethnic Kazakhstani nation.

It is important to highlight one significant contradiction here. While the official nation-building discourses are concentrated around the idea of the Kazakhstani as the symbolic owners of their own house, the people of Kazakhstan were never designated as the holders of natural resources. All official texts, starting with the 1995 Constitution (Article 3, Section 6), emphasize that the state owns natural resources. The 2010 Law on Subsoil and Subsoil Use explicates this constitutional norm further, defining state ownership of natural resources as "one of the constituent basic elements of state sovereignty of the Republic of Kazakhstan" (Chapter 10, Article 1). While Nazarbayev can be fairly called the most secular president in the post-Soviet space, he turns to religion, rationalizing the state ownership of natural resources enshrined in the Constitution and other laws of the country:

> The subsoil, water, flora, and fauna remained exclusively in the state ownership. Not everyone who participated in drafting the [1995] Constitution supported this view. The enthusiastic proponents of private property offered to allow the possibility of private ownership for everything. At the same time, most of the members of the working group considered it unsubstantiated to allow private ownership for what was not created by human labor. *The wealth of our land was given to us by God and was preserved by our ancestors, this is what existed before us, and will exist after, and therefore belongs not only to us but also to our future generations.*
>
> (Nazarbayev 2006, 80, emphasis added)

In this discursive framework, the state is presented as the sole, authentic, and only legitimate owner of natural resources. Since the regime and the state in Kazakhstan are purposefully conflated, Nazarbayev, acting as the "guarantor of the inviolability of Kazakhstan's special path of development" (Suleev 2009), takes personal responsibility for governing the natural resources and redistributing resource revenues.

This discursive construction is reinforced further by references to the ability of Nazarbayev's regime to satisfy citizens' socioeconomic needs. Namely, Nazarbayev on multiple occasions praised himself for spending the oil money wisely during the period of high commodity prices by redirecting substantial portions of it into the main sovereign wealth fund, the National Fund of the Republic of Kazakhstan (NFRK). In 2006, Nazarbayev warned his nation that if Kazakhstan boosted the social welfare and incomes of its citizens with the "easy oil money," it will only "get hocked up" to oil revenue (Nazarbayev 2006, 139). Instead, he proposed to save this money "for a rainy day" (139) or to direct it to "supporting and developing the priority things for the country" (261). While "the priority things" remain hidden in the black box of Nazarbayev's regime, the "rainy day" came with a broad-based economic slowdown twice, in 2008 and 2014. In the 2014 address to the nation, Nazarbayev pointed out that because he did not let the Kazakhstani people "spend the oil money on their daily needs"[5] when oil prices were on the rise but "saved and multiplied it," now Kazakhstan has the reserves that will help its people to "overcome grim times and to stimulate the growth of the national economy."

Another discursive construction that legitimizes the Nazarbayev regime's new strategy of resource nationalism and its model of state capitalism is the narrative that problematizes the privatization of the early 1990s. In the mid-2000s,

Nazarbayev (2006, 183) called privatization "the most controversial page in the history of Kazakhstan." He further described it as being vital to economic progress yet also a chaotic and disorderly process, which nourished a class of business elite with nothing but contempt for national interests. Later, he also frequently emphasized the stark contrast between the Kazakhstan of the early 1990s and the Kazakhstan of the mid-2000s (e.g., Nazarbayev 2010c, 2011a, 2013). In this framework, reestablishing state control over the strategic oil sector becomes another nation-building exercise, whereas Nazarbayev's regime becomes the only power that can ensure the fairness and rightfulness of this process.

Many discourses produced by Nazarbayev's regime are materialized in the literal sense in Nur-Sultan, the first capital of independent Kazakhstan.[6] As many studies point out, Nur-Sultan's new cityscape is purposefully designed to stimulate feelings of national pride and to support a particular construction of national identity (e.g., Anacker 2004; Dave 2007; Schatz 2010; Koch 2010). The city became a focal point of the omnipresent nationalist propaganda and plays an important role in the nation-building project of Nazarbayev's regime. It is symbolic that even Nur-Sultan's urban geography reflects the intimate relationship between oil and the state in Kazakhstan: in the bureaucratic district (known as the Left Bank) the grandiose headquarters of KazMunayGas (KMG) neighbors the Ak Orda Presidential Palace, the Supreme Court, and various state ministries.

The headquarters of KMG (Figure 5.1) is a part of Nur-Sultan's Round Square, a 70.000-square-meter architectural composition. The building that holds KMG's headquarters is a massive construction serving as the main entrance of Round Square. The building reflects multiple inspirations in its architectural structure. With an archway located between two high towers and slightly lower rectangular buildings, the KMG's headquarters is reminiscent of a triumphal arch. The 18-storey building is almost entirely made from golden-pink glass windows separated by white and grey concrete ribs that emphasize the vertical lines on the facade imitating Greek columns. With its multiple references to world architecture, the KMG's headquarters reflects both the traditional (e.g., triumphal arches) and the modern (glass and concrete). To access the Round Square, a pedestrian walks on the esplanade that passes under the arch of KMG's headquarters. This pathway forms one of the main axes of Nur-Sultan because it connects the building with three other key landmarks: the Khan Shatyr Entertainment Center, the Bayterek Tower, and the Ak Orda Presidential Palace (Figure 5.2).

Climbing the stairs to enter the Round Square from the north, a pedestrian observes the shape of the Bayterek Tower located outside it (see Figures 5.3 and 5.4). The tower is a popular observatory and a symbol of Kazakhstan (e.g., the 10.000 Kazakhstani tenge note features the image of the Bayterek Tower). Like the KMG's headquarters, the Bayterek Tower merges linear and circular shapes. It constitutes the main steel base that slowly opens in see-through metal points like flower petals. A massive golden ball is located at the center of these steel petals. The Baiterek Tower is meant to embody a Kazakh folktale about a mythical tree of life and a magic bird of happiness, and, in this sense, it links the new Kazakhstani modernity to the Kazakh traditions. The observation deck is 97 meters above ground level, corresponding to the year 1997 when Nur-Sultan (back then called Astana) officially became the capital of Kazakhstan. Inside the top level of the observatory, one can find a gilded handprint of the right hand of Nazarbayev mounted on an ornate pedestal. A plaque invites the visitors to place their hand in the imprint and make a wish. Visitors of the Bayterek Tower's observatory see the Ak Orda Presidential Palace, where the KMG's headquarters' pathway also leads.

The Ak Orda Presidential Palace (see Figure 5.5) is the official workplace of the president of Kazakhstan and has been Nazarbayev's residence since 2004. Like the other buildings I described earlier, the Palace is of mixed inspiration. Its facade has a semi-circular portico supported by massive pillars that were inspired by the White House, the official residence and workplace of the president of the US. The Palace's general structure is rectangular and supports a sky-blue and gold dome (national colors of Kazakhstan) that is topped with a gold spire with a golden sphere at its apex. The Palace remains connected to the other two buildings – the KMG's headquarters and the Bayterek Tower – by the pedestrian esplanade that leads from one building to another.

Finally, the same esplanade also leads to the Khan Shatyr (Royal Marquee) Entertainment Center. Climbing the stairs to the south to exit the Round Square through the KMG's headquarters' arch, one can see the shape of the Khan Shatyr slowly emerging in the space of the arch (see Figures 5.6 and 5.7). Designed in 2006 by British techno-architect Norman Foster, the Khan Shatyr is a neo-futurist building and one of the key architecture landmarks of Nur-Sultan. It is a metallic see-through leaning structure shaped like a pointed tent on an elliptical base. From the birds-eye view, the building looks like the traditional Kazakh dwelling, the yurt. The Khan Shatyr is one of the elite buildings in Nur-Sultan and is consistently framed in the official discourses as a symbol of the new Kazakh modernity and prosperity (for more on the Khan Shatyr's role in the nation- and city-building see Koch 2013).

Overall, the four landmarks described above constitute an urban composition that purposefully links symbols of the personified state power (the Ak Orda Presidential Palace), the independence and nation-building narratives (the Bayterek Tower), oil incomes (the headquarters of KMG), and the new Kazakh modernity (the entertainment center Khan Shatyr). They all play with shapes and materials to mix the idea of traditions and innovations into a single authoritative ideological message of power.

Overall, the whole city is a large-scale commemoration of Kazakhstan's oil-driven modernity. According to its citizens, Nur-Sultan is nourished by the oil companies that generously and supposedly voluntarily donate funds for various infrastructure projects (interview, Jan. 2017, Nur-Sultan). Edward Schatz (2005, 126) also highlights this popular narrative, adding that "foreign states whose extractive industries sought a foothold in the lucrative Kazakhstani market found themselves 'donating' to the construction of the capital city, in a clear bid for preferential allocation of contracts." In this framework, oil becomes an ultimate blessing for Kazakhstan and a source of national pride, whereas Nazarbayev yet again is portrayed as the only guarantor of the fair redistribution of oil incomes in the best interests of the people of Kazakhstan.

Figure 5.1 The headquarters of KMG in Nur-Sultan. © Peter Korolev. Courtesy of the photographer.

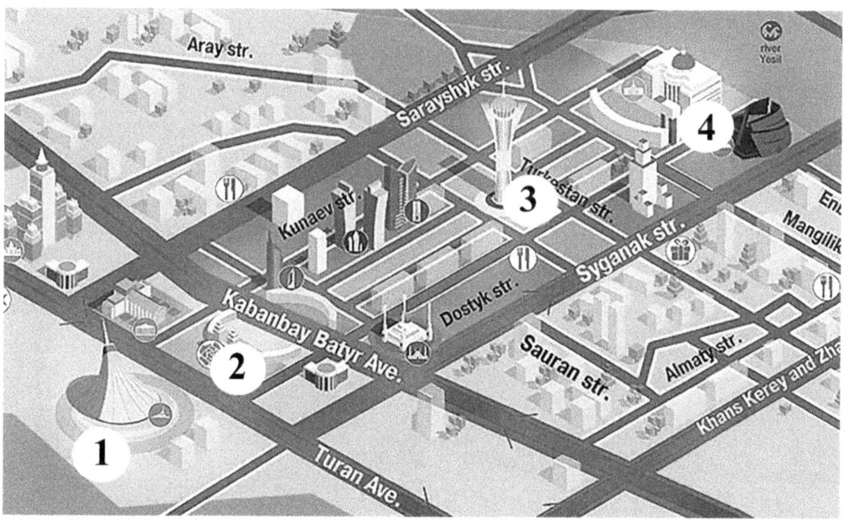

Figure 5.2 Map of Nur-Sultan. The main urban axis of Nur-Sultan: the Khan Shatyr Entertainment Center (1), the KMG's headquarters and the Round Square (2), the Bayterek Tower (3), and the Ak Orda Presidential Palace (4).

Figure 5.3 The headquarters of KMG, the view on the Baiterek Tower from the Round Square (North). © Peter Korolev. Courtesy of the photographer.

Figure 5.4 The Baiterek Tower and the Ak Orda Presidential Palace. © Peter Korolev. Courtesy of the photographer.

Figure 5.5 The Ak Orda Presidential Palace, the view from the Baiterek Tower. © Peter Korolev. Courtesy of the photographer.

Figure 5.6 The headquarters of KMG, the view on the entertainment center Khan Shatyr from the Round Square (South). © Peter Korolev. Courtesy of the photographer.

Figure 5.7 The entertainment center Khan Shatyr. © Peter Korolev. Courtesy of the photographer.

Petro-multiculturalism and internationalism

In the early 1990s, Kazakhstan's deep political, economic, and social crisis was coupled with the ideological and ideational vacuum produced by the collapse of the Soviet ideology. The Kazakhstani people had to reinvent not only their statehood but also themselves. After independence, many Muslims in Kazakhstan felt great reverence for the religion of their forefathers (Jessa 2006; Khalid 2014; Yemelianova 2014). However, Nazarbayev's regime has failed to translate Islam into a source of political legitimacy and thus has started to frame Islam as a threat to national unity and political stability.

According to the official nation-building discourses of Nazarbayev's regime, the major political project for Kazakhstan is to create the Kazakhstani nation, perceived not as an ethnic category but as one of civil collective solidarity (Isaacs 2010; Laruelle 2014; Omelicheva 2015). In this framework, Islam becomes one of many symbols of the local culture, whereas Nazarbayev's petrostate wants very strongly to remain secular. As Galina M. Yemelianova (2014, 9–10) argues, Kazakhstan's political elites remain "extraordinarily ignorant about Islam in any form" and, as a result, view Islam as fanatical and anti-progressive. Since the mid-1990s, Nazarbayev's regime has imposed authoritarian and repressive secularism from the top down. It is vigilant in its determination to keep "Islamic fanaticism" and "Islamic extremism" from taking root in the country and initiates all-out campaigns against any Muslim political activities. Public manifestations of religiosity became securitized.[7]

According to the official discourses, Kazakhstan's internal unity and openness to Western modernity are supposed to strengthen its international prestige and, therefore, secure a steady inflow of foreign investment. This logic allows Nazarbayev's regime to put secularism at the service of protecting its interests in the energy sector, constructing the consolidation of Islamic sentiment not only as a threat to political stability but also as an imminent threat to the country's oil incomes. The same discourses are enacted on the international level. As Bahva Dave (2007, 136) puts it, Nazarbayev's regime has "skillfully learned to cultivate and exploit" an image of "a Muslim-dominated oil-rich state, which is politically stable, devoid of ethnic or religious conflict or a threat of 'terrorism,' under strong leadership with a pro-Western outlook" to attract Western and Asian investors.

At both domestic and international levels, Nazarbayev actively publicizes the idea of national unity based on Kazakhstan's distinctive brand of secular multiculturalism that is presented as the utmost value and a prerequisite for sustainable economic development. Nazarbayev's *The Way of Kazakhstan* (2006, 5) opens with the following claim:

> If we talk about the Kazakhstan way, of course, this way is not limited only to the choice of an economic model. This is also a political model, which includes not only general constitutional provisions but also the political regime and inter-confessional relations. This is the richest array, and in this regard, Kazakhstan emerged as a model state in the modern world. This realm [of Kazakhstan's development] received a high international and domestic recognition. The preservation of the ethnic and religious consensus in such a fragile region of the planet for a decade and a half largely determines the Kazakhstan way.

Along the same line, in his latest book about Kazakhstan's history, *The Era of Independence* (2017, 155), Nazarbayev concludes that Kazakhstan "found the optimal golden mean in the relationship between the state and religion, which allowed the state and religious denominations to fruitfully work together to strengthen the national accord." Securitizing cultural and religious differences, Kazakhstan 2050 Strategy released in 2012 defines "the clash of civilizations" as one of the ten key challenges for Kazakhstan in the 21st century and outlines the following as a response to it:

> We must learn to live in the co-existence of cultures and religions. We must be committed to a dialogue between cultures and civilizations. Only in dialogue with other nations our country will be able to succeed and gain influence in the future. In the 21st century, Kazakhstan must strengthen its position as a

> regional leader and become the bridge for dialogue and interaction between East and West.
>
> (Nazarbayev 2012)

The secular multiculturalism discourse intersects and overlaps with Nazarbayev's aspirations to make Kazakhstan a part of the international community as an equal and contributing member. In this context, both Kazakhstan's multiculturalism and secularism are celebrated not in the name of liberal tolerance and universal humanity, beyond cultural, national, and religious differences, but as a sign of Kazakhstan's openness to globalization and readiness to cooperate with whoever is willing to invest in its economy.

Finally, the second pillar of Nazarbayev's construction of Kazakhstan as a modern petrostate is internationalism that becomes the foundation of a pronouncedly non-confrontational and multi-vector foreign policy. Locating Kazakhstan "at the heart of Eurasia," Nazarbayev (e.g., 2005, 2006, 2017) presents it as an indispensable and natural ally of Russia, China, the European Union, Turkey, Iran, India, Japan, South Korea, and so on. In every presidential address, Nazarbayev reminds the Kazakhstani people about the importance of international economic integration. He wants them to "think globally" (2011b) and be ready to "take part in the global decision-making," contributing to "the formation of a new architecture of international relations" (2010c). At the same time, Nazarbayev (2010b) highlights that Kazakhstan needs to accept the logic of globalization and learn to act according to it:

> The global economic system is a well-built and well-functioning mechanism that operates according to its own rules. And we must work by these rules. We are not expected at the world markets, but we need to make ourselves in demand there and gain a foothold.

This idea of internationalism is firmly tied to the discourses of multiculturalism and secularism. Following Nazarbayev's logic, only multicultural and secular Kazakhstan will be accepted by the international community and only multicultural and secular Kazakhstan can attract foreign investors.

In sum, the secular multiculturalism and internationalism discourses have two functions. First, on the domestic level, they develop as dovetailing parts of the discursive system that protects and legitimizes Nazarbayev's rule in Kazakhstan and, subsequently, his control over national oil resources. Secondly, these discourses are at the core of the self-representation of Kazakhstan on the international level. They are a part of Kazakhstan's international branding. Nazarbayev's discursive construction of Kazakhstan is supposed not only to distinguish it from other petrostates but also to open-up for it as many cooperation opportunities as possible.

One way to think about interconnections between Kazakhstan's state-led secular multiculturalism and pronounced internationalism on one side and its energy politics on the other side is the concept of petro-Islam. Petro-Islam is defined by Syed Manzar Abbas Zaidi (2010, 145) as a specific type of Islam, the first and foremost objective of which is "to protect oil wealth, or, more appropriately, the type of social relations underlying those tribal societies that possess the lion's share of this wealth." Nazih N. Ayubi (1996, 233) notes that in Saudi Arabia and most of the smaller countries of the Persian Gulf "domestically 'petro-Islam' emphasizes an interpretation of religion that is excessively ritualistic in style and conservative in socio-economic content." Consequently, in the case of the Persian Gulf states, a conservative top-down version of Islam served as a legitimacy structure for state control over the oil sector and redistribution of oil revenues. While the readings of Islam by Nazarbayev's regime are the exact opposite, the discursive mechanisms that link oil and religion are the same. As Richard U. Moench (1988, 188) sharply summarizes the essence of petro-Islam as an ideology, it "may be theologically vague, but it is sociologically clear." Indeed, essentializing and mythologizing religion and promoting top-down repressive secularism, Nazarbayev's regime instrumentalizes Islam as a threat to Kazakhstan's oil-driven prosperity. Nazarbayev's regime uses religion policy and multiculturalism as tools in constructing Kazakhstan as a petrostate, and thus its approach to Islam and multiculturalism can be functionally defined as petro-secularism or petro-multiculturalism.

"We" and "they" in Kazakhstan's discursive politics of energy

Nazarbayev repeatedly emphasizes that Russia has never been the Soviet Union itself (2006, 2010a, 2017). Even though Nazarbayev admits that being a part of the Soviet Union, Kazakhstan was constrained by the decision power of the "center," he constructs Kazakhstan as an equal agent of Soviet modernity rather than a powerless colonial subject of Russia (e.g., 2006). In this framework, the "center" is responsible for the fiasco of the Soviet Union and, as the successor of the Soviet Union, Russia represents the failure to provide a viable alternative to the neoliberal development model and the failure to reform the socialist system in the late 1980s. Importantly, such framing of the Soviet past allows Nazarbayev to detach Kazakhstan from the collapse of the hegemonic socialist project. He also does not include Russia in the category of developing countries. Labeling Kazakhstan as a developing country and excluding Russia from this group, Nazarbayev differentiates Kazakhstan's and Russia's experience after the dissolution of the Soviet Union. As a result, the Soviet Union is "we," but Russia is "they."

Nazarbayev (2017, 17) stresses that, unlike many other former member republics of the Soviet Union, Kazakhstan "made the right choice" in the early 1990s and continues to follow "the right path" in the 2010s:

> In just a quarter of a century, a former Soviet republic that in the USSR was unjustly ranked among the laggards turned into a modern country with a national statehood, an effective market economy, a democratic social system, and a high international authority. All this is a complex and dynamic process of modernization of Kazakhstan – breaking the old and obsolete, carrying out bold reforms and innovations, and creating the new and modern.

In this sense, the process of development turns into a competition. Nazarbayev constructs Kazakhstan as an exceptional post-Soviet state, accentuating that in many realms Kazakhstan became "the only" or "the first" post-Soviet state. He contrasts Kazakhstan to other post-Soviet states that, according to him, failed to embrace modernization and globalization. Unlike them, Kazakhstan is open to the world and actively learns from developed countries. The recurring example is the decision to establish NFRK in 2000 that, as stressed in the official energy discourses, was inspired by Norwegian experience (e.g., Nazarbayev 2017, 218).

While official discourses emphasize the advantages of close relations with Russia and other former Soviet states, they construct Kazakhstan as a part of the broader international community rather than the so-called "post-Soviet space" (*постсоветское пространство, postsovetskoye prostranstvo*). Within the international stratification system, Kazakhstan places itself among the developing countries. In this category, however, Kazakhstan is set off against developing countries of Africa and Latin America. Specifically, such petrostates as Nigeria, Venezuela, and Argentina are presented as failures and often serve as examples for what Kazakhstan should never become. In contrast, Singapore, Malaysia, South Korea, and China are commonly pointed out as suitable role models for Kazakhstan (e.g., Nazarbayev 2006, 2017; Suleev 2009). At the same time, Nazarbayev's regime does not present Kazakhstan as an Asian country. Instead, Nazarbayev (2006, 2010a, 2017) introduced and developed his vision of Euarasianism that he has been propagating consistently over the past two decades.

Nazarbayev (2010) locates Kazakhstan both symbolically and geographically "at the heart of Eurasia." In Nazarbayev's conception, being Eurasian means being different from both Asia (East) and Europe (West). Asia is associated with a set of negative stereotypes, including underdevelopment, illiteracy, radicalism, fundamentalism, and violence, whereas Europe designates a modern and superior yet culturally and socially foreign model of development. Besides, the European past represents colonial oppression and imperialism. Following the logic of the East–West dichotomy, being a Eurasian country, Kazakhstan is more civilized and modern than its neighbors in the East but still is not an entirely Western country and thus is entitled to its unique path of development that deviates considerably from the hegemonic neoliberal model.

The logic of Nazarbayev's Eurasianism intersects with Kazakhstan's brand of post-colonialism that distinguishes it from the former Third World. Official post-colonial discourses focus on further delinking Kazakhstan from its Soviet past and strengthening the construction of Kazakhstan as an independent actor of international relations vis-à-vis Russia. Kazakhstan considers itself only semi-colonized and does not identify itself as a victim of imperialism (Beissinger and Young, 2002). Discussing her conversations with Kazakhstani academics in the early 1990s, Bahvna Dave (2007, 2) describes their understanding of colonialism as "quite perfunctory" because they did not disapprove of colonial domination per se but expressed "a feeling of disappointment by the failure of the Soviet state to fully deliver its promised goals." Diana T. Kudaibergenova (2016) accentuates similar trends in Kazakhstan's post-colonial discourse in the 2000s and the

2010s. She points out that Kazakhstan's post-colonial discourse is "as fragile and insecure as the local process of nation-building" (Kudaibergenova 2016, 924). She highlights that her respondents in Kazakhstan were "ambiguous in pointing fingers to the active actors of the past colonization" and avoided "radical anti-colonial and, thus, anti-Russian messages." Colonialism, in general, is associated with humiliation and shame, while a post-colonial status signifies its inferiority. Avoiding associations with this status, dominant discourses separate Kazakhstan from the victims of colonialism, represented by a generalized and homogenized Third World.

In sum, Kazakhstan's "we" still belongs to the Soviet Union, whereas the developing countries are "they." Constructing itself as a part of the former Second World, Kazakhstan also delinks itself from the political legacies of the Third World. Finally, Kazakhstan is presenting itself as a carrier of the unique Eurasian identity. These complex and contradictory identity constructions transform into an even more complex and more contradictory energy identity.

According to the dominant discourses, while Kazakhstan aspires to become "the Kuwait of Central Asia" in the near future, it is not going to be a petrostate forever. Nazarbayev promises that Kazakhstan will have its own distinctive and original path of development and, despite all odds, will not repeat the experience of Nigeria, Norway, Venezuela, Saudi Arabia, and other petrostates that allowed themselves to "drown in petrodollars" (Nazarbayev 2006, 110). In this context, Kazakhstan's construction of Russia as an "other" is particularly revealing.

Some Kazakhstani scholars compare Russia and Kazakhstan as countries that face similar economic challenges related to the dependence on resource rents (e.g., Yelyubayev 2016). Others, on the contrary, avoid such parallels and distinguish Kazakhstan from Russia, using the metaphor of the raw-material appendage to describe Russia's development after the collapse of the Soviet Union (e.g. Bisenbayev 2011). The discursive construction of Russia as a raw-material appendage is particularly interesting. For example, Murat Abdirov of the Gumilyov Eurasian National University (2017, 704–705) argues that in the 2000s Russia "turned into a raw-material appendage of the developed countries, such as Europe, and China" and thus it will eventually lose both "its vast territory and splendid natural resources." Abdirov predicts that by 2030 "not only China but also the international community" will try to gain control over Russia's "immense and unpopulated lands full of natural resources" (706). Particularly, according to him, Russian authorities risk losing Siberia and the Far East: these two regions will turn into "Siberian Africa" where China extracts resources to support its aspirations for global hegemony (622). In the picture so vividly presented by Abdilov, Russia's overreliance on energy resources not only subscribes it to a low status in the international power hierarchy but also jeopardizes its sovereignty and territorial integrity. He warns that, if Kazakhstan follows Russia's steps, it too can "unwittingly become China's resource colony" (754).

In essence, Kazakhstan's dominant energy discourses purposefully and consistently construct other petrostates as "they." Since the 1990s, Kazakhstan has not found a place for itself in the developed First World or the developing Third

World. Staying in between the two worlds as a petrostate, Kazakhstan is exposed to geopolitical threats and risks. Hence, the key goal for Kazakhstan becomes transitioning into the category of a developed country and a gradual abandonment of its dependence on resource incomes.

Kazakhstan's energy paradigm: Nazarbayev's petrostate

The dominant energy discourses identify oil wealth as the foundation of Kazakhstan's independence and prosperity after the collapse of the Soviet Union. At the same time, however, official discourses construct Kazakhstan in the opposition to other petrostates. It is widely recognized in Kazakhstan that the dependence on resource exports constrains Kazakhstan's economic development and inevitably consigns it to a low place in the international hierarchy. At the center of Kazakhstan's energy paradigm is the reading of its oil-driven economic prosperity as a temporary phase in national development. In the discursive framework developed by Nazarbayev's regime, Kazakhstan is a petrostate by destiny but will become a modern innovation-driven economy by choice.

Another important part of Kazakhstan's energy paradigm is the securitization of oil as a globally sought-after commodity. Kazakhstan's official discourses construct its oil wealth as a tasty morsel for the avid great powers. Following this logic, oil becomes a source of various threats to Kazakhstan's independence and sovereignty.

Kazakhstan's discursive politics of oil is intimately connected to the discourses that legitimize and support the Nazarbayev regime, and hence Nazarbayevism plays an instrumental role in Kazakhstan's construction of oil. Nazarbayev is portrayed as the single guarantor of the fair redistribution of oil incomes in the best interests of the Kazakhstani people. Nazarbayev's regime also promises to ensure that Kazakhstan will smoothly transition to the post-oil future. Defining Kazakhstan in relation to oil, Nazarbayev's regime produces and reproduces two broad discursive constructions: internationalism and petro-multiculturalism. Nazarbayev's regime uses religion policy and multiculturalism as tools in constructing Kazakhstan as an exceptional petrostate. According to the official discourses, Kazakhstan's internal unity and openness to Western modernity strengthen its international prestige and, therefore, secure a steady inflow of foreign investment.

In sum, oil is constructed in Kazakhstan as a source of development and a source of multiple vulnerabilities, whereas Nazarbayev's regime represents itself as the only power that can turn oil into a blessing for Kazakhstan. In this sense, Kazakhstan's energy paradigm is subordinated to the discursive politics that sustains and legitimizes Nazarbayev's authoritarian rule.

China–Kazakhstan energy dialogue

China's NOCs in Kazakhstan: The reality vs. perceptions

China's NOCs first purchased equity oil stakes in Kazakhstan in the late 1990s, yet until the mid-2000s China was not a visible actor in the oil sector. In 2005,

China–Kazakhstan energy relations made news when CNPC announced that it had struck an agreement to buy PetroKazakhstan, a Canada-based company, for US$4.2 billion. The news about this deal came three weeks after CNOOC had to drop its bid for Unocal amid opposition from US politicians. Kazakhstani analysts (interview, February 2017, Nur-Sultan) argue that Canadian investors "slammed the door" in the mid-2000s because they did not want "to share" by investing in infrastructure and social projects in Kazakhstan. China's NOCs, on the contrary, took a "more cooperative stance" and thus were warmly welcomed by Nazarbayev's regime. Later the same year, CNOOC signed a memorandum of understanding with KMG to jointly explore the Darkhan field on the shelf of the Caspian Sea that has been estimated to hold about 11 billion barrels of oil.

In February 2006, Kazakhstani media reported that Canada's Nations Energy Company was interested in selling to China's CITIC Group 96.4 percent of shares in KarazhanbasMunai, which held 20-year exploitation rights for the oilfields north of Aktau in Mangystau region.[8] Representatives of Nations Energy Company at first denied that they were negotiating with Chinese investors; however, in November 2006, the company announced that it reached an agreement with CITIC Group to sell its share in KarazhanbasMunai for US$1.91 billion.

After the deal was announced, all key Kazakhstani press agencies, newspapers, and news websites reprinted quotations from the statements made by Valery Kotovich, Victor Egorov, and Alikhan Baimenov, members of the Mazhilis (the lower house of the parliament), who expressed concerns with "Chinese expansion" (e.g., *KazakhstanToday* 2006). Kotovich described the actions of China's NOCs as "persistent and even straightforward." According to him, the acquisition of KarazhanbasMunai would have allowed China to control more than 40 percent of Kazakhstan's oil production. Yegorov and Baimenov warned that China's assertive expansion might threaten the national interests of Kazakhstan. The anxiety voiced by the three Mazhilis members provoked a heated public discussion about the nature and consequences of China's growing presence in Kazakhstan's energy sector. Various commentators shared the belief that Kazakhstan was a "tasty morsel" for energy-hungry China and agreed that Nazarbayev's regime needed to be more cautious in relations with it (e.g., Adilov 2006; Amrekulov 2006; Morzabayeva 2006).

Two years later, Kotovich explained that he "read on the Internet about China's expansion in Kazakhstan" and "became alerted" by this information (Zakon.kz 2008). In retrospect, he calls the public statements that he made in November 2006 "a certain message to the government so that it pondered and developed an approach to minimize threats for the national security." Konstantin Syroezhkin (2010, 287–288) and some other Kazakhstani China experts (interview, February 2017, Almaty), however, speculate that concerns of Kotovich and his colleagues are linked to the interests of unspecified Western and Russian energy companies. Whatever motivated members of the Mazhilis to criticize China's NOCs, their concerns resonated with the public. The government took their "message" and public debates provoked by it seriously. After a review, it approved the deal with the condition that CITIC Group will resell 50 percent of its shares in KarazhanbasMunai to KMG. In October 2007, the parliament approved the amendments to the 1996 Law of Subsoil and Subsoil Use that enabled the government to alter or cancel contracts with foreign companies if their actions pose a threat to the national security by substantial impairment of the economic interests (Law 2-IV, 24 October 2007).

While this legislative change continued the process of institutionalization of resource nationalism initiated after the dispute over Tengiz in 2002,[9] Kazakhstan's authorities presented it as a direct response to the public concerns about China's newest acquisitions. Official discourse emphasized that Kazakhstan needs Chinese money as much as China needs Kazakhstani oil and thus toughening control over the IOCs operating in Kazakhstan would not scare off Chinese investors (Nazarbayev 2006, 2017). Importantly, Nazarbayev's regime was able to discursively reinforce its position as the only guarantor of Kazakhstan's sovereignty over natural resources.

Despite deteriorating phobias and prejudices against China and the Chinese in Kazakhstan, China's NOCs continued their expansion in Kazakhstan's energy sector. During the oil price surge at the end of the 2000s, Nazarbayev's regime welcomed Chinese investment and effectively used Chinese money to renationalize the oil sector. The case in point is the takeover of MangistauMunaiGas by KMG and CNPC in 2009.

Central Asia Petroleum Ltd of Indonesia had controlled MangistauMunaiGas since 1997 and by 2007 its stake in the company had risen to 99 percent. Various sources, however, connect MangistauMunaiGas to a member of Nazarbayev's family, Rakhar Aliyev. While being married to the president's older daughter Dariga Nazarbayeva, Aliyev made a successful career in Kazakhstan's National Security Committee and invested in various assets, including the oil sector (Peyrouse 2012). In 2007, Aliyev fell from grace after he divorced Nazarbayev's daughter. Experts connect the decision of Central Asia Petroleum Ltd to sell its stake in MangistauMunaiGas to Aliyev's downfall (Silk Road Intelligencer 2007; interview, February 2017, Nur-Sultan).

Nazarbayev's regime was determined to regain control over MangistauMunaiGas, but, because of the ongoing economic downfall, KMG did not have enough money to close the deal with Central Asia Petroleum Ltd. In 2009, Nazarbayev visited China and after a meeting with Hu Jintao secured for Kazakhstan a generous US$10 billion loan. While the media often describe the deal as a "loan-for-oil," the two lines of credit extended to Kazakhstan were not backed by a supply contract. China's Export-Import Bank of China (Exim Bank) lent the state-owned Development Bank of Kazakhstan US$5 billion, whereas CNPC extended a US$5 billion loan to its Kazakhstani peer KMG. The two NOCs also signed a separate deal agreeing for joint purchase of the majority stake in MangistauMunaiGas. The MangistauMunaiGas takeover was finalized at the end of 2009 when Central Asia Petroleum Ltd divided its assets between KMG (51 percent) and CNPC (49 percent) for US$2.6 billion, less than the US$3.3 billion originally announced in 2007.

Since 2010, controversial reports that China will soon control most of Kazakhstan's oil sector appear regularly in the national media. As a case in point, in August 2013, the key Kazakhstani news websites reported that "China's share in Kazakhstani oil is greater than that of Kazakhstan itself and greater than that of anyone else in the country," citing an "analyst wishing to remain anonymous" (e.g., TengriNews.kz 2013; Forbes.kz 2013). Even though such information was usually followed by refutations and questions about its credibility, many of Kazakhstan's China experts perpetuate it as a fact, arguing that after the 2009 MangistauMunaiGas takeover China's NOCs control around 40 percent of Kazakhstani oil (e.g., Syroezhkin 2010, 292; Sadovskaya 2015, 22).

On the contrary, China's NOCs did not have assets in Kazakhstan's offshore projects that produce "big oil" for a long time. Only in 2013, CNPC was able to buy a share in the Kashgan oilfield in the Caspian Sea waters.[10] This acquisition cost CNPC US$8 billion: US$5 billion for ConocoPhillips' 8.33 percent share in the North Caspian Operating Company and US$3 billion to finance the second phase of the Kashgan oil project. As in the case of the 2009 MangistauMunaiGas takeover, the two governments were involved in settling the deal. CNPC and the North Caspian Operating Company signed the final agreement after Xi Jinping visited Kazakhstan in September 2013. In Xi's words (2013a), Nazarbayev and he both "hailed and supported" CNPC participating in the Kashagan project.

In parallel with the practice of obtaining equity oil stakes, China was also actively investing in the development of unfractured pipeline in Kazakhstan. The construction of the 2,798-kilometer-long Kazakhstan–China oil pipeline was financed by KMG and CNPC and is operated as a joint venture. The Atasu-Alashankou section of the pipeline (987 kilometers) was completed in just ten months and in July 2006 the pipeline began to pump oil from the fields located near Atasu in northern Kazakhstan to the Dushanzi refinery located in Xinjiang. The current capacity of the pipeline is 14 million tons of crude oil per year, whereas its nominal capacity is 20 million tons (KCP LLP 2018).

The Kazakhstan–China pipeline is not overly significant in addressing China's rapidly growing energy needs (EIA 2017). Likewise, even though the pipeline offers Kazakhstan a direct connection to the rapidly growing Chinese market, the amount of crude oil that comes to China through the pipeline is small in comparison to that shipped to Russia (EIA 2017). However, because it is China's first transnational pipeline and Kazakhstan's first post-Soviet transnational pipeline and, importantly, Kazakhstan's first pipeline that bypasses Russia, many experts consider its construction an important sign of geopolitical changes (e.g. Huo et al. 2013; Yang, C. 2014; Zhao 2014; Yue and Yang 2016). In this framework, the Kazakhstan–China pipeline becomes a symbol of the new era in which Russia's domination in Central Asia is declining, whereas China's influence is rising.

While China's achievements in Kazakhstan are indeed impressive, China's NOCs still do not participate in the development of the Tengiz and Karachaganak fields where around 55 percent of Kazakhstan's oil is produced (see Table 5.1). By investing in smaller projects, China obtained access to a total of around 24 percent of the oil produced in Kazakhstan. However, China's NOCs do not ship their

Table 5.1 Kazakhstan's Largest Oil Producing Companies (With More Than 1,000 Employees, April 2017)

Name of the Company	*Region*	*Ownership*
Ozenmunaygaz	Mangystau Region	KMG (Kazakhstan), 100%
MangistauMunaiGas	Mangystau Region	KMG (Kazakhstan), 51% CNPC (China), 49%
KarazhanbasMunai	Mangystau Region	KMG (Kazakhstan), 50% CNPC (China), 50%
PetroKazakhstan Kumkol Resources	Kyzylorda Region	KMG (Kazakhstan), 33% CNPC (China), 67%
Karachaganak Petroleum Operating B.V. Kazakhstan	West Kazakhstan Region	Royal Dutch Shell (UK, Netherlands), 29.25 % Eni (Italy), 29.25 % Chevron (США), 18 % Lukoil (Russia), 13.5 % KMG (Kazakhstan), 10 %
Nostrum Oil and Gas (former Zhaikmunai)	West Kazakhstan Region	The Netherlands, 100%
Tengizchevroil	Atyrau Region	Chevron (США), 50 % KMG (Kazakhstan), 20 % ExxonMobi (USA), 25 % LukArco (Russia, France), 5 %
North Caspian Operating Company N.V. (NCOC)	Atyrau Region	KMG (Kazakhstan), 16.8% Eni (Italy), 16.8% Total (France), 16.8% ExxonMobil (USA), 16.8% Royal Dutch Shell (UK, Netherlands),16.8% CNPC (China), 8.3% INPEX (Japan) 7.5%
EmbaMunaiGas	Atyrau Region	KMG (Kazakhstan), 100%
CNPC AktobeMunaiGas	Aktobe Region	CNPC (China), 94.5% KMG (Kazakhstan), 5.5%

equity oil back home via the newly built pipeline, as many observers predicted. Between 2005 and 2017, Kazakhstan's oil exports to China have not exceeded 6 percent of its total oil exports (Ministry of National Economy of the RK 2017). According to the customs, Kazakhstan exports its crude oil to 35 countries. The key consumers of Kazakhstan's oil are in the West. The EU members receive more than 75 percent of Kazakhstan's oil, with most of the exports going to Italy (32 percent), Netherlands (15 percent), Switzerland (11 percent), and France (11 percent).

Sinophobia and oil

Sinophobia is becoming an increasingly prominent phenomenon in Central Asia, and China is perceived as yet another great power that threatens the political and economic sovereignty of Central Asian states. While Central Asian states' political leaders all praise China in unison for its reliable and trustworthy partnership, Central Asian societies are divided over China's rise (Peyrouse 2016; Laruelle and Peyrouse 2012). Kazakhstan is not an exception.

Kazakhstani experts see China as a necessary counterweight to both Russia and the US not only for Kazakhstan but for the whole Central Asia (e.g., Basenov and Khafizova 2007; Abdrakhmanov and Kaukenov 2007; Tokayev 2008; Syroezhkin 2010; Bisenbayev 2011). Many of them believe that cultural and educational exchanges between China and Kazakhstan improve the way that young people see Chinese development. For example, the director of the Chinese Studies Center in Almaty Adil Kaukenov (interview, 11 February 2017, Almaty) maintains that university students already see China as an opportunity rather than a threat. Another prominent Kazakhstani China scholar, Ruslan Izimov, argues that in the 2010s China started to invest more in its "soft power" and it had a positive effect on the image of China in Kazakhstan (Omarov 2017). Despite that, the experts agree that Sinophobia is a problem. As Kaukenov (interview, 11 February 2017, Almaty) emphasizes, Sinophobia "comes in waves" and its "outbreaks" parallel with the emergence of social discontent with economic development and the government's decisions. In these cases, China and the Chinese become a scapegoat. In regard to China–Kazakhstan energy relations, the 2010 and 2011 labor protests in the oil-rich Mangistau region provide a vivid example that even gossip can trigger Sinophobic sentiments.

In 2010, in the city of Zhanaozen 6,000 employees of OzenMunaiGas, owned by KMG, went on strike to demand unpaid danger money, higher wages, and better working conditions. After two weeks of negotiations, the oil workers ended the strike as the company agreed to satisfy almost all their demands. In May 2011, a similar labor conflict between the management and employees of KarazhanbasMunai led to a mass strike. Activists called for a general strike across the Mangistau region and soon protests broke out in Kuryk and Aktau (Salmon 2011). The three companies involved in the disputes with oil workers – KarazhanbasMunai, Ersai Caspian Contractor, and OzenMunaiGas – refused to negotiate with independent labor unions and eventually dismissed the employees who actively participated in the strikes. Local authorities took the side of oil companies in the conflict, which only aggravated the tension, turning the labor dispute into a grand battle between the workforce on one side and the oil companies and authorities on the other. The movement also acquired a political dimension, when many strikers in Zhanaozen collectively resigned from Kazakhstan's ruling political party Nur Otan.

On 16 December 2011, the day when Kazakhstan celebrated its 20 years of independence, oil workers laid off by OzenMunaiGas disrupted festivities in Zhanaozen. Protests of oil workers quickly transformed into mass riots. Rioters burned down several administrative buildings, including the mayor's office and the offices of OzenMunaiGaz, as well as private houses of the company's top-managers. Police responded by shooting at the rioters, killing 14 and injuring over 90 of them (General Prosecutor's Office of RK 2012; see also Salmon 2012).

The day following the clash between police and protestors, Nazarbayev delivered a speech at a meeting of the Security Council, identifying the events as "criminal actions of a group of individuals" that "resulted in mass disorders" (Akorda 2011). He emphasized that "labor disputes of oil-workers should not be associated with the deeds of hooligans who wanted to use the situation for their criminal intentions" and ambiguously warned the "masterminds" of the riots that the authorities would soon identify them. While official discourses attributed the violence to the actions of unspecified evil Others, blogosphere, social media, and opposition news websites produced information and opinions critical of Nazarbayev's regime, creating several contradictory versions of the events in Zhanaozen. Along with Islamic fundamentalists, the Oralmans,[11] the West, and the Russians, commentators also blamed Chinese NOCs for the oil workers' strikes and riots.

Chinese investors only participated in the negotiations with oil workers of KarazhanbasMunai in Aktau, whereas OzenMunaiGas is wholly owned by KMG and Ersai Caspian Contractor is a Kazakhstani–Italian venture. Nevertheless, some commentators speculated that it was the unfair labor policies and practices introduced by China's NOCs that contributed to social discontent and pushed Kazakhstani oil workers to go on strike (e.g., Kurmanov 2011; Rumer 2011; Torguzbayev 2013). Even the sources that did not focus on the role of Chinese investors in the conflict emphasized that it was a Chinese manager who filed a suit on behalf of KarazhanbasMunai against the lawyer of the striking oil workers Natalia Sokolova[12] (e.g., Torguzbayev 2011).

The oil workers strikes and the Zhanaozen tragedy undermined Nazarbayev's long-standing efforts to present Kazakhstan as a democratic and politically stable state, damaging its international image. On the level of domestic discursive politics, these events caused a "discursive dislocation" (Torfing 1999, 301) because official constructions that portray Nazarbayev's regime as a source of economic prosperity and security were not able to domesticate and explain the events in Zhanaozen (for a detailed analysis see Lewis 2016). In this sense, it is quite indicative that not only Nazarbayev's regime but also its critics attributed the escalation of the conflict to the actions of ambiguous evil Others. The discursive politics around the oil workers' strikes and the Zhanaozen tragedy also reveals how easily Kazakhstani latent Sinophobia turns China into one of the Others.

China's Kazakhstan policy in the mid-2000s and China's construction of Kazakhstan

In an attempt to build a foundation for mutual discovery and create new socio-economic and political links, since the mid-1990s China has promoted itself in Central Asia under the brand of the Shanghai Cooperation Organization (SCO). According to China's officials, an essential and novel attribute of the SCO is the "Shanghai spirit" (上海精神, *Shanghai jingshen*), a set of shared values, such as peace, cooperation, openness, and striving toward harmony (e.g., Yang, J. 2008; Xi 2013b). China also emphasizes its status as the SCO founder, as well as its major inspirer and ideologist, and offers Central Asia a partnership based on foreign policy pluralism, cosmopolitism, mutual benefits, common developmental goals, and equality. Energy resources are listed as one of many possible areas for "pragmatic cooperation," along with sociocultural exchanges and a joint struggle against the "three evils forces" (三股势力, *sangu shili*) that are drug-trafficking, transnational crimes, and cybercrimes (Xi 2014, 2015). In sum, China promotes itself as a senior, yet still an equal partner, in Central Asia and stresses that it will offer "no strings attached" relations.

In the mid-2000s, China's representatives framed China's bilateral relationship with Kazakhstan and the four other Central Asian states as a logical extension of multilateral dialogue with the SCO.[13] However, despite the lofty rhetoric and China's repeated attempts to improve the SCO's competency, the organization failed to become an effective platform for multilateral cooperation and is often accused of "talking too much and doing too little" (e.g. Lukin 2007; Germanovich 2008; Kaukenov 2013). In other words, the SCO became a gateway for China to Central Asia but was largely ineffective in institutionalizing political and economic ties between China and the Central Asian states. Importantly, China approached Central Asia as a single country.

For example, China's representatives often highlight that "Central Asia is rich with hydrocarbon resources," whereas only Kazakhstan and Turkmenistan could be considered oil- and gas-rich.[14] A similar trend is evident in the academic literature on China's relations with Central Asian states, where all five states are portrayed as having identical populations, cultures, development potential, challenges, and sociopolitical systems (e.g. Wei and Liu 2006; Wang 2008; Yue and Yang 2016). Some Chinese scholars end up with a discussion of "China's oil cooperation with Central Asia" that is "mainly concentrated in Kazakhstan" (Yang, C. 2014, 89). Kazakhstan becomes "the treasure-house of Central Asia" (Huo et al. 2013, 15), and, as a result, it is presented not as an independent and sovereign entity but as a part of the region. In this framework, Kazakhstan's energy cooperation with China has become a part of China's relations with Central Asia.

China–Kazakhstan energy relations and China's new diplomacy

In the mid-2010s, Xi Jinping designated Central Asia as China's "inland gateway" to Europe and the Middle East in the framework of the Belt and Road Initiative (BRI). The concept of the Silk Road Economic Belt was first officially announced in September 2013, at Nazarbayev University, during Xi Jinping's official state visit to Kazakhstan (Xi 2013a). The fact that this initiative was first officially presented in Kazakhstan underlines Central Asia's significant symbolic status for the development of BRI. It also signals that China offers Kazakhstan one of the central roles in building the new Silk Road, responding to Nazarbayev's ambitions for regional leadership.

Introducing the Silk Road Economic Belt, Xi Jinping (2013a) remarks that he "could almost hear the camel bells echoing in the mountains and see the wisp of smoke rising from the desert" and that these images "have brought [him] closer" to Central Asia. Eventually, camels became one of the major symbols of the Belt and Road project. Camels traversing the desert in caravans regularly appear not only on official websites and newspaper articles but also in the speeches of China's officials. For example, Li Zhaoxing (2015) argued that camels "have epitomized the trade and cultural exchanges across the Eurasia continent and beyond into the vast oceans." China's officials also frequently refer to the legacy of Zhang Qian, a Chinese explorer of the Han Dynasty who is credited with "discovering" Central Asia (e.g., Xi 2013a, 2016a, 2017a, 2017b). Mythologizing and romanticizing the history of the ancient Silk Road (Sidaway and Woon 2017), China's official discourses link BRI to the past that Central Asia shares with China. In doing so, they present BRI not as a novelty but as an opportunity to revitalize the historical economic, social, and cultural networks that connected China and Central Asia for centuries. Under this framework, the Chinese and Central Asian "community of destiny" (命运共同体, *mingyun gongtongti*) becomes timeless and timely, while the narrative of the mutually beneficial relationship between China and its immediate neighbors moves to the center of discursive politics of BRI.

Defining Central Asia in the context of BRI, China's representatives often use such words as "bridge," "crossroad," "corridor," "hub," and "strategic location." Under the brand of the "belt," China offers Kazakhstan and other Central Asian states an "all-of-the-above" cooperation strategy. As a *People's Daily* editorial summarizes it, the Silk Road Economic Belt is a strategy that will improve qualitatively the development of China's relationship with Central Asian states: "By strengthening policy communication, road connectivity, trade links, currency circulation, and connections among their peoples, the countries involved can tighten their economic links, deepen cooperation among them, and expand the space for development" (Zhong Sheng, 2014). Importantly, China promises to respect Central Asian states' political independence and, specifically, to preserve the status quo vis-à-vis Russia:

> China is committed to the path of peaceful development and the independent foreign policy of peace. We respect the development paths and domestic and foreign policies chosen independently by the people of every country. We will in no circumstances interfere in the internal affairs of Central Asian countries. We do not seek to dominate regional affairs or establish any sphere of influence. We stand ready to enhance communication and coordination with Russia and all Central Asian countries to strive to build a region of harmony.
>
> (Xi 2013a; see also Xi 2016b, 2017a, 2017b)

In this discursive framework, all five Central Asian states have a space for their discursive models of cooperation with China and can frame their participation in BRI as stemming from their independent choice. Importantly, Central Asian states are not forced to respond to China's initiative as an integrated unit but can join it as autonomous entities. In this sense, under the brand of BRI, China consolidates the existing bilateral ties rather than build a new multilateral network in Central Asia.

Nazarbayev's ambitions for Kazakhstan not only to be Central Asia's regional leader but also to play a greater role in international politics shape his regime's responses to BRI. First and foremost, Nazarbayev seeks to use China's interest in Central Asia to his sovereign advantage, kick-starting the development of non-resource sectors and reinforcing his political control at home and in the region. At the end of 2014, Nazarbayev's government announced a new development program called Bright Path (*Нұрлы жол, Nurly Zhol*). This program is designed as an anti-crisis plan and an extension of Kazakhstan-2050, the long-term development strategy presented in 2012 (Akorda 2015). However, it is best described as a smaller customized version of Russia's "linking up" proposal (Kuteleva and Vasiliev 2020).

At the end of 2015, China's Silk Road Economic Belt and Kazakhstan's Bright Path were merged by the leaders of the two states. The joint plan focuses on three priorities: transportation infrastructure, trade, and manufacturing industries. This strategic and highly ideologically charged merger allows Nazarbayev to position Kazakhstan as an actor with independent decision-making power in the framework of BRI. Simultaneously, the merger supports the official Chinese discourses that present BRI as a collaborative effort and a basis for win-win cooperation, reinforcing the idea that BRI is not China's "solo" enterprise but a "chorus of nations." As a case in point, the official glossary of China.org (2017) defines Kazakhstan's Bright Path program and BRI as "complementary and mutually reinforcing" projects. In this framework, Kazakhstan is a willful international agent rather than a loyal powerless subject of China's new geopolitical ambitions.

On the discursive level, security and energy cooperation ceases to be the key priorities in China–Kazakhstan relations, giving way to the "multi-vector cooperation" that includes five areas: (1) strengthening policy communication and coordination, (2) development of transport infrastructure, (3) creation of new trade routes and improvement of the business environment, (4) enhancement of currency circulation and creation of new financial networks, (5) and the "people-to-people bond [*sic*]" that will ensure the public support for BRI (State Council of the PRC 2015). Consequently, in the discursive framework of BRI energy relations between China and Kazakhstan are fading into the background. This new logic of cooperation corresponds well with the discursive politics of Nazarbayev's regime that tends to obscure the role of energy resources in Kazakhstan's development and foreign affairs. On the other hand, it helps China to repair its image in Kazakhstan.

In addition to rebranding relations with Kazakhstan along the lines of BRI, China's representatives started to openly address the issue of Sinophobia in Kazakhstan, rebutting the popular myths about China's expansion and resource grabbing. Zhou Li (2012), China's ambassador to Kazakhstan (2010–2013), for example, complained about the lack of confidence in China's peaceful rise around the world:

> The US worries that China can claim world leadership. India and the countries of South-East Asia are afraid that China will use its growing military power to resolve territorial disputes. Tokyo is concerned about the threat to its security and the reduction of its influence in the region in connection to the rise of Beijing. In Russia, some Central Asian countries, and even in faraway Africa one can hear about the "threat of Chinese migration" or "China's resource grabbing."

According to Zhou, those fears are groundless. He claimed that China does not pose a threat to Kazakhstan and the rest of Central Asia because "China is not the Soviet Union" and China's rise is not going to unleash a new Cold War. He also highlights that China needs Kazakhstan's "understanding and support" as a fellow developing country. His successor Le Yucheng (2013a) used the idiom "a close near neighbor is better than a far-off relative" (远亲不如近邻, *yuanqin bu ru jinlin*) to describe China–Kazakhstan relations, implying that both countries are equally attracted to each other and thus need to "invest in the mutual trust." Elsewhere (2013b), Le argues that the China Dream is compatible with Kazakhstan's development aspirations and hence China's ongoing transformation into a "powerful and prosperous state" brings Kazakhstan (as well as all other countries in the world) only benefits (see also Le 2013c).

China's reaction to Kazakhstani discourses that portray it as a threat gradually became more forceful. In August 2013, China's response to Sinophobia in Kazakhstan hit the headlines of the major national newspapers, when Zhang Hanhui, at that time the director-general of the MFA's Department of European and Central Asian Affairs,[15] abruptly criticized pronouncedly anti-Chinese remarks by Murat Auezov, the first ambassador of Kazakhstan to China (1992–1995) and renowned Kazakhstani sinologist (Burdin 2013). In an interview with a popular Kazakhstani weekly newspaper, Auezov argued that "today China needs Kazakhstani oil and gas," whereas in the nearest future China will occupy its territory to "solve its problem of overpopulation" (Batsiyev and Omelchenko 2013). Auezov also told the journalists that he repeatedly raised the issue of China's expansion and possible aggression with Kazakhstan's leadership but never received a proper response. Zhang replied to the retired diplomat, accusing him of spreading "false information" about China and calling him a "lunatic"[16] (Burdin 2013). Zhang blamed the Kazakhstani media for not covering the "American threat," even though "NATO gained a foothold on the territory of Kazakhstan" and conducted military exercises near the Chinese border. He also boldly pointed out that the Kazakhstanis are more interested in China than the Chinese are interested in Kazakhstan:

> Some [Kazakhstani] media report that a million illegal Chinese immigrants freely live in Kazakhstan. Others claim that there are special settlements – three million people – in Xinjiang on the border with Kazakhstan that could be turned into an army in a wink and occupy Kazakhstan in three days. Can you imagine this! But the Kazakhstani people believe that China can attack

> them. However, I am telling you that [in 2012] only 180 thousand Chinese citizens visited Kazakhstan. This is the exact statistics. In contrast, half a million Kazakhstanis went to China, and this number is growing. So, who will occupy who?
>
> (Burdin 2013)

Zhang's appointment as China's ambassador to Kazakhstan in 2014 indicates that the MFA approved his tough stance on China's critiques. Zhang's unambiguously assertive and straightforward response to Auezov and other opponents of Kazakhstan rapprochement with China highlights the new trend in China's Kazakhstan policy and, more broadly, a turn toward harder-edged "Wolf Warrior" diplomacy (Gill 2020). Framing China–Kazakhstan relations as mutually beneficial and synergetic, China's representatives present Sinophobia as a common problem. Accordingly, Kazakhstan should be interested in a decrease of Sinophobia no less than China because Kazakhstan needs China. Consequently, China wants to be recognized and respected as a valued partner not only by Kazakhstan's authorities but also by Kazakhstan's society. At the same time, China recognizes its image of a "resource grabber" in Kazakhstan as a problem and seeks to reframe China–Kazakhstan relations, creating a new discursive construction within which its interest in Kazakhstani oil and other resources is less obvious.

Energy cooperation between Xi Jinping's China and the post-Nazarbayev Kazakhstan

In the mid-2000s and the 2010s, with the strong financial and political backing of the state, China's NOCs were able to make good deals with Kazakhstan's KMG. Even though China's NOCs were able to invest only in "leftover" assets, by 2017 they gained control over a total of around 24 percent of the oil produced in Kazakhstan. Their investments brought the financial resources much-needed by Nazarbayev's regime in the wake of the global financial crisis but did not transform Kazakhstan into China's "resource colony" as many Kazakhstani observers feared. Despite the increase in equity production volume and the rapid development of the pipeline infrastructure, China's NOCs do not send substantial amounts of Kazakhstan's oil back home, and hence the dynamics of regional energy supply patterns did not change. In this sense, China's NOCs build an "overseas Daqing" in Kazakhstan rather than solve China's "Malacca dilemma."

At the same time, even though energy relations between China and Kazakhstan have so far been mutually beneficial and corresponded to the interests of both states, China's expansion in Kazakhstan's oil sector promotes a Sinophobic backlash and increasing neo-colonial concerns in Kazakhstani society. Kazakhstan's energy paradigm securitizes oil as a globally sought-after commodity, and, as a result, China's interest in Kazakhstani oil is constructed as a potential threat to Kazakhstan's independence and sovereignty.

The securitization of oil is a result of Kazakhstan's energy paradigm being subordinated to the discourses that legitimize and support Nazarbayev's regime. Kazakhstani public, critiques of Nazarbayev's regime, and local experts see China's growing presence in Kazakhstan's oil sector as a sign of the weakness of the state and its inability to protect Kazakhstan's national interests. In this sense, Sinophobia becomes a byproduct of oil securitization, and hence it not only creates risks for China's NOCs but also poses a legitimacy challenge for Nazarbayev's regime. To resolve this paradox, Nazarbayev's regime is trying to reposition Kazakhstan as an actor with independent decision-making power vis-à-vis China and reframe China–Kazakhstan relations in accord with the broader construction of Kazakhstan's development, according to which the country is moving away from its dependence on resource incomes.

The turbulences in Sino-Russian relations, as well as the growing animosity between China and the US, will in meaningful ways shape Kazakhstan's future and add extra pressure on the political regime. China's representatives consistently frame China–Kazakhstan energy relations as an example of win-win cooperation. In the mid-2010s, the "Shanghai spirit" gave way to the new narrative that fits China's relations with Kazakhstan into the framework of BRI, within which China still positions itself as a peer of Kazakhstan. The frame of shared regional history is bridged with the frame of market rationalism through the emphasis on China's reputation as a reliable partner that has been built over decades of cooperation. At the same time, in the 2010s, China became sensitive to the allegations of neocolonialism and started to employ assertive public diplomacy tactics to respond to those who doubt the win–win nature of China–Kazakhstan relations. China's representatives aggressively denied that China might use the investment of NOCs in Kazakhstan as geopolitical leverage and rejected the allegations of neocolonialism. The new president of Kazakhstan, Kassym-Jomart Tokayev, inherited profoundly complex challenges. As China is becoming increasingly more assertive in its international dealings and communication, Tokayev will have to balance the demands of Kazakhstan's resource-cursed development and attempts to preserve the status quo vis-à-vis China's rise.

Notes

1 West Turkestan, also known as Russian Turkestan, is a region colonized by the Russian Empire. It comprised the vast territory to the south of the Kazakh Steppe. In the Soviet era, the region was known as Middle Asia (*Средняя Азия, Srednyaya Aziya*) and was divided between Kazakhstan in the north, Uzbekistan across the center, Kyrgyzstan in the east, Tajikistan in the southeast and Turkmenistan in the southwest.

2 Russian and Kazakh languages distinguish "Kazakh as nationality/ethnicity" from "Kazakh as citizenship/territorial affiliation." The term "Kazakh" (*казах, kazakh*) is only used for the nationality and for ethnicity. "Kazakhstani" (*казахстанец, kazakhstanets*) is designated for the state and territorial belonging and thus includes many other ethnicities and nationalities (e.g., Russian Kazakhstani, Uzbek Kazakhstani, Korean

Kazakhstani). The later term – Kazakhstani – was introduced in the early 1990s after the collapse of the Soviet Union.

3 I retrieved 68 academic works published in Russian between 2006 and 2016 from the social science databases of the National Academic Library of the Republic of Kazakhstan (Nur-Sultan) on 12 February 2017. The search was based on the keywords: "нефть" (oil), "ресурсы" (resources), "развитие" (development), and "Казахстан" (Kazakhstan). The results included academic articles published in the national peer-reviewed journals (43), graduate dissertations (17), and monographs (8). In 52 out of 68 works, the authors quoted Nazarbayev as an authority on diverse topics (e.g., economic development, foreign policy, energy security, environmental policies, to name just few), with 19 works using his quotes as epigraphs.

4 The idea of energy and environmental crises is further developed in *Global Energy and Ecological Strategy of Sustainable Development in the 21st Century* (2011). According to the library abstract, this book summarizes Nazarbayev's "theoretical and methodological research on the problems of building a global energy security and environmentally sustainable development of the world and the Eurasian Economic Community." The book is also described as Nazarbayev's "message" to the developing world and its publication was timed with the 2012 United Nations Conference on Sustainable Development.

5 Nazarbayev used here the expression "*проесть деньги*" (*proyest' den'gi*), which literally means "eat the money."

6 Upon the collapse of the Soviet Union in 1991, Tselinograd (also known as Aqmola) was a remote industrial town in the middle of the Kazakh steppe. In the early years of independence, Nazarbayev decided to transform this small town into the capital of his newly sovereign state, giving it a new name, Astana (means "capital" in Kazakh). The capital was formally moved to Astana in 1997. Back in 2006, the authorities moved the Capital City Day from 10 June to 6 July, which coincides with Nazarbayev's birthday. The official explanation claims that the new date references the 6 July 1994, and commemorates the decision of the Kazakhstan Supreme Council to designate the city as the new capital. In 2019, the parliament renamed the capital Nur-Sultan in honor of Nazarbayev.

7 The most recent example includes girls being banned from school wearing head scarfs. On 1 September 2018, in the village of Firdaus in Turkestan province 32 teenage girl attempted to enter the school building but were stopped by the administration. In the public statement, the Minister of Education and Science Yerlan Sagadiyev promised to make sure that "no pupil in a head scarf will enter the school building" (Zakon.kz, 2008). Another official emphasized that because "the President [Nazarbayev] says that we are civilized secular state, we must raise [the children] as secular people" (Informburo.kz, 2018).

8 Renamed as CITIC Canada Petroleum Limited in 2007.

9 A dispute arose in November 2002 when the Western companies that controlled Tengizchevroil sought to finance a US$3.5 billion expansion of the Tengiz oilfield using oil revenues. Kazakhstan's government protested, as the plan would erode its tax receipts. In 2004, the amendments to the 1996 Law on Subsoil and Subsoil Use granted the government to claim priority purchase rights in all energy projects (Law 2-III, 1 Dec. 2004). In 2005, the goverment toughened its contract terms (Law 79-III, 14 October 2005).

10 Kashagan is the largest super giant oilfield discovered in the past three decades. Even though Kashagan has suffered from eight-year delays and cost increase since 2005, many experts still consider it an oil market game-changer in the making. The Kashagan oil project is operated by North Caspian Operating Company owned by Eni, KazMunayGas, Royal Dutch Shell, Total, ExxonMobil, CNPC and INPEX. Production started in September 2013, some eight years after the original schedule, but was halted

in just a few weeks because of gas leaks in its pipelines. Production was restarted in October 2016 and the field reached actual production levels of over 200.000 barrels per day by mid-2017.

11 Oralmans are Kazakh repatriates. Most of them immigrated to Kazakhstan from Uzbekistan, Turkmenistan, Mongolia, and China.

12 Natalia Sokolova acted as the official representative of the independent trade union of oil workers of KarazhanbasMunai in the conflict. In August 2011, the court found Sokolova guilty of violating two articles of the Criminal Code of Kazakhstan, by inciting social, national, tribal, and racial irreligious enmity (Article 164) and violating the regulations of organizing and holding meetings, rallies, pickets, marches and demonstrations (article 334). The labor lawyer was sentenced to six years of imprisonment. In March 2012, Sokolova pleaded guilty on all charges and her penalty was reduced to three years of probation.

13 Kazakhstan, Kyrgyzstan, Tajikistan, and Uzbekistan are members of the SCO, with Turkmenistan attending most of the summit meetings in a status of a special guest.

14 Uzbekistan is often described as resource rich; however, it does not belong on the same plane as Turkmenistan with gas and Kazakhstan with oil. Uzbekistan's oil production has seen steady decline over the past decade. The situation with natural gas is slightly better. In 2015, Uzbekistan was the third largest natural gas producer in Eurasia, following Russia and Turkmenistan. However, existing gas fields are depleting faster than new discoveries are coming online, spurring the need for further investment and modernization of the gas sector. Kyrgyzstan and Tajikistan do not have substantial deposits of oil and gas. Both countries have potential for hydroelectricity and wind energy production but fail to make the most of their endowments, using only about 5 percent of the available reserves.

15 In 2014, Zhang Hanhui became the new China's ambassador to Kazakhstan. In 2018, Zhang left Kazakhstan to become the assistant foreign minister.

16 Zhang Hanhui is a fluent Russian speaker, and the interview was conducted in Russia without a translator. Criticizing Auezov, Zhang used a colloquial Russian expression "fall from the Moon" (*как с луны свалился, kak s luny svalilsya*). This expression is quite strong and implies that Auezov's comments are inappropriate and reveal his ignorance about the subject.

References

Abdirov, M. Z. (2017). *Otkrytiye drugoy Ameriki, Kitaya, Rossii i Kazakhstana: Nauchno-populyarnoye issledovaniye blagonamerennogo avtora* [The discovery of another America, China, Russia and Kazakhstan: a popular science study by a well-meaning author]. Astana: Qazaq universiteti.

Abdrakhmanov, A., and Kaukenov, A. (2007). Otnosheniya Kitaya i stran Tsentral'noy Azii glazami kazakhstanskikh ekspertov [Relations between China and Central Asian countries through the eyes of Kazakhstani experts]. *Kazakhstan v global'nykh protsessakh*, 3, 119.

Adilov, M. (2006). V politike ne byvayet druzey i vragov, a yest' tol'ko interesy [There is no friends in politics but only interests]. *Respublika-Delovoye obozreniye*, 3 Nov. Retrieved from https://centrasia.org/newsA.php?st=1162804740. [Accessed 1 June 2018].

Akorda (2011). Segodnya v Akorde pod predsedatel'stvom Glavy gosudarstva Nursultana Nazarbayeva sostoyalos' soveshchaniye s rukovodstvom Administratsii Prezidenta, Pravitel'stva, partii "Nur Otan" [A meeting with the leadership of the presidential administration, the government, and the Nur Otan Party was held today in Akorda, chaired by the Head of State Nursultan Nazarbayev]. 26 December. Retrieved from http://www.akorda.kz/ru/special/events/segodnya-v-akorde-pod-predsedatelstvom-glavy-gosudarstva-nursultana-nazarbaeva-sostoyalos-soveshchanie-s-rukovodstvom-administracii-preziden. [Accessed 1 March 2018].

Akorda (2015). Gosudarstvennaya programma infrastrukturnogo razvitiya «Nұrly zhol» na 2015 – 2019 gody [The state program of infrastructural development "Nurly Jol" for 2015 – 2019]. 6 Apr. Retrieved from: http://www.akorda.kz/ru/official_documents/strategies_and_programs. [Accessed 26 July 2018].

Alff, H. (2015). Profiteers or moral entrepreneurs? Bazaars, traders and development discourses in Almaty, Kazakhstan. *International Development Planning Review*, 37(3), 249–267.

Amrekulov, N. (2006). Damoklov mech kitayskogo drakona [Damocles Sword of the Chinese Dragon]. *Svoboda Slova*, 8 February.

Anacker, S. (2004). Geographies of power in Nazarbayev's Astana. *Eurasian Geography and Economics*, 45(7), 515–533.

Ayubi, N. N. (1996). *Over-stating the Arab state: politics and society in the Middle East.* New York: IB Tauris.

Azam, M., and Ahmed, A. M. (2015). Role of human capital and foreign direct investment in promoting economic growth: evidence from commonwealth of independent states. *International Journal of Social Economics*, 42(2), 98–111.

Azattyq (2012). Kitay postroit v Kyrgyzstane neftepererabatyvayushchiy zavod [China will build an oil refinery in Kyrgyzstan]. *Radio Azattyk Kyrgyzstan*, 6 June. [online] Retrieved from https://rus.azattyk.org/a/24605180.html. [Accessed 26 July 2018].

Basen, J., and Khafizova, K. (2007). Kazakhstan i Kitay v XXI veke: strategiya sosedstva/ ZH. Basen// Ekonomicheskiye strategii Tsentral'naya Aziya [Kazakhstan and China in the 21st century: neighborhood strategy]. *Ekonomicheskiye strategii Tsentral'naya Aziya*, 1(2), 15–17. Retreived from http://www.inesnet.ru/article/ kazaxstan-i-kitaj-v-xxi-veke-strategiya-sosedstva/. [12 June 2018].

Batsiyev, D., and Omelchenko, A. (2013). Murat Auezov: Kitaytsy v Kazakhstane prisutstvuyut v gorazdo bol'shey stepeni, chem ob etom govoritsya [Murat Auezov: the Chinese in Kazakhstan are present to a much greater extent than is stated]. *Megapolis .kz*, 7 Aug. Retreived from http://shymkent.kz/print.php?id=40293. [Accessed 11 June 2018].

Beissinger, M., and Young, M. C. (2002). *Beyond state crisis? Post-colonial Africa and post-soviet Eurasia in comparative perspective*. Washington, DC: Woodrow Wilson Center Press.

Bisenbayev, A. K. (2011). *Ne vmeste: Rossiya i strany Tsentral'noy Azii* [*Not together: Russia and the countries of Central Asia*]. St. Petersburg: Izdatel'skiy dom Piter.

Burdin, V. (2013). "Auezov svalilsya s luny." Interv'yu s Chzhanom Khan'khueyem ["Auezov fell from the moon" interview with Zhang Hanhui]. *Vremya*, 23 Aug. Retreived from http://www.time.kz/articles/zloba/2013/08/28/auezov-svalilsja-s-luni. [Accessed 27 July 2018].

Cherdayev, R. (2012). *Neft' Kazakhstana. Vekovaya Istoriya* [Oil of Kazakhstan. The century old history]. Astana: Aldongar.

China.org. (2017). Kazakhstan: "Bright Road" initiative. *China.org.cn.* 20 Apr. Retrieved from http://www.china.org.cn/english/china_key_words/2017-04/20/content_40657154.htm. [Accessed 26 July 2018].

Dave, B. (2007). *Kazakhstan: ethnicity, language and power*. New York: Routledge.

EIA, Energy Information Administration (2017). Kazakhstan. Retrieved from https://www.eia.gov/beta/international/ analysis.php?iso=KAZ. [Accessed 27 June 2016].

Eurasian Development Bank (2017) *EAEU and Eurasia: monitoring and analysis of direct investments*. [PDF file] Retreived from https://eabr.org/upload/iblock/3f8/EDB-Centre_2017_Report-47_FDI-Eurasia_ENG_1.pdf. [Accessed 17 March 2018].

Forbes.kz (2013). Dolya kitayskikh kompaniy v kazakhstanskoy neftyanoy otrasli v 2013 godu prevysit 40%, soobshchil istochnik v neftegazovoy otrasli [The share of Chinese companies in the Kazakh oil industry in 2013 will exceed 40%, a source in the oil and gas industry said]. 8 January. Retrieved from https://forbes.kz/process/ economy/kazahstanskuyu_neft_budet_kontrolirovat_kitay. [Accessed 11 May 2018].

Franke, A., Gawrich, A., and Alakbarov, G. (2009). Kazakhstan and Azerbaijan as post-Soviet rentier states: resource incomes and autocracy as a double "curse" in post-Soviet regimes. *Europe-Asia Studies*, 61(1), 109–140.

General Prosecutor's Office of RK (2012). *Zayavleniye General'nogo Prokurora Respubliki Kazakhstan po sobytiyam, imevshim mesto v g. Zhanaozen 16.12.2011 goda* [Statement by the General Prosecutor of the Republic of Kazakhstan on the events that took place in Zhanaozen on 16 December 2011]. 25 January. Retrieved from http://prokuror.gov.kz/rus/novosti/press-releasy/zayavlenie-generalnogo-prokurora-respubliki-kazahstan-po-sobytiyam-imevshim. [Accessed 1 March 2018].

Germanovich, G. (2008). The Shanghai cooperation organization: a threat to American interests in Central Asia? *China & Eurasia Forum Quarterly*, 6(1), 19–38.

Gill, B. (2020). China's global influence: post-COVID prospects for soft power. *The Washington Quarterly*, 43(2), 97–115.

Huo, M., Yang, R., and Xu, H. (2013). Zhong-Ha nengyuan hezuo huli shuangying zhanlue lun xi [An analysis of China-Kazakhstan energy cooperation and mutual benefit win-win strategy]. *Handan zhiye jishu xueyuan xuebeo*, 26(3), 15–18.

Isaacs, R. (2010). "Papa"–Nursultan Nazarbayev and the discourse of charismatic leadership and nation-building in post-Soviet Kazakhstan. *Studies in Ethnicity and Nationalism*, 10(3), 435–452.

Jessa, P. (2006). Aq Jol soul healers: religious pluralism and a contemporary muslim movement in Kazakhstan. *Central Asian Survey*, 25(3), 359–371.

Kalyuzhnova, Y., and Patterson, K. (2016). Kazakhstan: long-term economic growth and the role of the oil sector. *Comparative Economic Studies*, 58(1), 93–118.

Karyenov, R. S. (2014). Toplivno-energeticheskiy kompleks kak vazhnyy komponent ekonomiki Respubliki Kazakhstan [Fuel and energy complex as an important component of the economy of the Republic of Kazakhstan]. *Problemy Prava i Ekonomiki*, 4, 19–30.

Kaukenov, A. (2013). Vnutrenniye protivorechiya Shankhayskoy organizatsii sotrudnichestva [Internal contradictions of the Shanghai Cooperation Organization]. *Tsentral'naya Aziya i Kavkaz*, 16(2), 73–89.

KazakhstanToday (2006). Deputaty parlamenta vyrazili ozabochennost' uvelicheniyem doli inostrannogo uchastiya v neftegazovom sektore Kazakhstana [MPs expressed concern over the increase in the share of foreign participation in the oil and gas sector of Kazakhstan]. 1 November. Retrieved from http://www.kt.kz/rus/economy/deputati_parlamenta_virazili_ozabochennostj_uvelicheniem_doli_inostrannogo_uchastija_v_neftegazovom_sektore_kazahstana_1153402827.html [Accessed 12 August 2018].

KCP LLP, Kazakhstan-China Pipeline LLP (2018). About the company. Retrieved from http://www.kcp.kz/company/about. [Accessed 26 July 2018].

Khalid, A. (2014). *Islam after communism: religion and politics in Central Asia*. Berkley and Los Angeles, CA: University of California Press.

Koch, N. (2010). The monumental and the miniature: imagining "Modernity" in Astana. *Social & Cultural Geography*, 11(8), 769–787.

Koch, N. (2013). Kazakhstan's changing geopolitics: the resource economy and popular attitudes about China's growing regional influence. *Eurasian Geography and Economics*, 54(1), 110–133.

Kudaibergenova, D. T. (2015). The ideology of development and legitimation: beyond "Kazakhstan 2030." *Central Asian Survey*, 34(4), 440–455.

Kudaibergenova, D. T. (2016). The use and abuse of postcolonial discourses in post-independent Kazakhstan. *Europe-Asia Studies*, 68(5), 917–935.

Kurmanov, A. (2011). Zhanaozen – proobraz budushchikh sobytiy v Rossii [Zhanaozen: a prototype of future events in Russia]. *Vzglyad-Info*. 21 Dec. Retrieved from http://www.vzsar.ru/special/2011/12/21/aynur_kurmanov__zhanaozen__-__proobraz_buduschih_sobytiy_v_rossii.html. [Accessed 4 March 2018].

Kuteleva, A., and Vasiliev, D. (2020). China's belt and road initiative in Russian media: politics of narratives, images, and metaphors. *Eurasian Geography and Economics*, 1–25.

Laruelle, M. (2014). The three discursive paradigms of state identity in Kazakhstan. In M. Omelicheva (Eds.), *Nationalism and identity construction in Central Asia: dimensions, dynamics, and directions* (pp. 1–20). Lexington: Lexington Book.

Laruelle, M., and Peyrouse, S. (2010). *L'Asie Centrale à l'aune de la mondialisation: une approche géoéconomique*. Paris: Armand Colin.

Laruelle, M., and Peyrouse, S. (2012). *The Chinese question in Central Asia: domestic order, social change, and the Chinese factor*. New York: Columbia University Press.

Le, Y. (2013a). Iskrennost' otnosheniy: blizhayshiy sosed luchshe dal'nego rodstvennika [Sincerity of relationship: the nearest neighbor is better than a distant relative]. *Embassy of the PRC in the RK*. 2 Dec. Retrieved from http://kz.china-embassy.org/rus/sgxx/sgdt/t1104694.htm. [Accessed 15 Aug. 2018].

Le, Y. (2013b). Interv'yu gazete Novoye Pokoleniye [Interview to the Novoye Pokoleniye newspaper]. *Embassy of the PRC in the RK*. 1 November. Retrieved http://kz.china-embassy.org/rus/sgxx/sgdt/t1095107.htm. [Accessed 15 August 2018].

Le, Y. (2013c). Iskrennost' otnosheniy: Blizhayshiy sosed luchshe dal'nego rodstvennika [Sincerity of relationship: the nearest neighbor is better than a distant relative]. *Embassy of the PRC in the RK*. 2 Dec. Retrieved from http://kz.china-embassy.org/rus/sgxx/sgdt/t1104694.htm. [Accessed 15 Aug. 2018].

Lewis, D. (2016). Blogging Zhanaozen: hegemonic discourse and authoritarian resilience in Kazakhstan. *Central Asian Survey*, 35(3), 421–438.

Li, Z. X. (2015). Building the maritime silk road of the 21st century with open mind and bold courage. *China.org.cn*. 9 Feb. Retrieved from http://www.china.org.cn/world/2015-02/09/content_34774918.htm. [Accessed 26 July 2018].

Loring, B. (2014). "Colonizers with Party Cards": soviet internal colonialism in Central Asia, 1917–39. *Kritika: Explorations in Russian and Eurasian History*, 15(1), 77–102.

Lukin, A. V. (2007). Shankhayskaya organizatsiya sotrudnichestva: chto dal'she? [Shanghai cooperation organization: what is next?]. *Rossiya v Global'noy Politike*, 5(3), 78–93. Retrieved from https://www.globalaffairs.ru/number/n_8818. [Accessed 2 April 2018].

Ministry of National Economy of the RK (2017). Committee on statistics. Retrieved from http://stat.gov.kz. [Accessed 11 May 2018].

Moench, R. U. (1988). Oil, ideology and state autonomy in Egypt. *Arab Studies Quarterly*, 10(2), 176–192.

Morzabayeva, Zh. (2006). Kazakhstanu grozit "kitaizatsiya"? 40% kazakhstanskoy nefti kontroliruyut kitaytsy [Is Kazakhstan threatened with "Chinazation"? 40% of Kazakh oil is controlled by the Chinese]. *Respublika-Delovoye Obozreniye*. 3 November. Retrieved from https://centrasia.org/newsA.php?st=1162796820. [Accessed 11 May].

Nazarbayev, N. (2005). Kazakhstan na puti uskorennoy ekonomicheskoy, sotsial'noy i politicheskoy modernizatsii. Poslaniye narodu Kazakhstana. Fevral' 2005 [Kazakhstan on the way of accelerated economic, social and political modernization. Address to the people of Kazakhstan. Feb. 2005]. Retrieved from http://www.akorda.kz/ru/addresses/addresses_of_president/poslanie-prezidenta-respubliki-kazahstan-na-nazarbaeva-narodu-kazahstana-fevral-2005-g. [Accessed 4 Apr. 2018].

Nazarbayev, N. (2006). *Kazakhstanskiy put'* [Kazakhstan's path]. Astana: Zhibek zholy.

Nazarbayev, N. (2009). Pyatyy put' [The firth way]. *Izvestiya*, 22 Sept. Retrieved from http://personal.akorda.kz/ru/category/stati/pyatyi-put.

Nazarbayev, N. (2010a). *V serdtse Yevrazii* [At the heart of Eurasia]. Almaty: Zhibek zholy.

Nazarbayev, N. (2010b). *Strategiya radikal'nogo obnovleniya global'nogo soobshchestva i partnerstvo tsivilizatsiy* [Radical renewal of global society and partnership of civilizations]. Astana: Zhibek zholy.

Nazarbayev, N. (2010c). Novoye desyatiletiye – Novyy ekonomicheskiy pod"yem – Novyye vozmozhnosti Kazakhstana. Poslaniye narodu Kazakhstana. Yanvar' 2010. [New decade – new economic growth –new opportunities of Kazakhstan. Strategy "Kazakhstan-2050." Address to the people of Kazakhstan. Jan. 2010]. Retrieved http://www.akorda.kz/ru/addresses/addresses_of_president/poslanie-prezidenta-respubliki-kazakhstan-n-a-nazarbaeva-narodu-kazakhstana-29-yanvarya-2010-goda_1340624693. [Accessed 4 Apr. 2018].

Nazarbayev, N. (2011a). Interv'yu informatsionnym agentstvam RIA Novosti i Interfaks [Interview to RIA Novosti and interfax news agencies]. 19 November. Retrieved from http://www.akorda.kz/ru/speeches/external_political_affairs/ext_interviews/intervyu-prezidenta-kazahstana-nanazarbaeva-informacionnym-agentstvam-ria-novosti-i-interfaks. [Accessed 27 March 2018].

Nazarbayev, N. (2011b). Postroim budushcheye vmeste! Poslaniye narodu Kazakhstana. Yanvar' 2010. [Let's build the future together! Address to the people of Kazakhstan. Jan. 2011]. Retrieved from http://www.akorda.kz/ru/addresses/addresses_of_ president/poslanie-prezidenta-respubliki-kazakhstan-n-a-nazarbaeva-narodu-kazakhstana-28-01-2011-g_1340624589-. [Accessed 4 Apr. 2018].

Nazarbayev, N. (2012). Strategiya "Kazakhstan-2050." Poslaniye narodu Kazakhstana. Dekabr' 2012 [Strategy "Kazakhstan-2050." Address to the people of Kazakhstan. Dec. 2012]. Retrieved from http://www.akorda.kz/ru/events/astana_kazakhstan/participation_ in_events/poslanie-prezidenta-respubliki-kazahstan-lidera-nacii-nursultana-nazarbaeva-narodu-kazahstana-strategiya-kazahstan-2050-novyi-politicheskii-. [Accessed 4 Apr. 2018].

Nazarbayev, N. (2013). Protsvetaniye, bezopasnost' i uluchsheniye blagosostoyaniya vsekh Kazakhstantsev. [Prosperity, security, and welfare of all Kazakhs. The President's message to the people of Kazakhstan]. *Official Site of the President of the Republic of Kazakhstan*. Retrieved from http://www.akorda.kz/ru/page/kazakhstan-2030_1336650228.

Nazarbayev, N. (2017). *Era Nezavisimosti* [The era of independence]. Astana: QAZaqparat.

Nurmaganbyetov, K. R. (2011). Osnovnyye napravleniya provedeniya forsirovannoy industrial'no-innovatsionnoy politiki v Kazakhstane [The main directions of the forced industrial innovation policy in Kazakhstan]. *Organizator proizvodstva*, 48(1), 1–5.

Omarov, A. (2017). Ruslan IZIMOV: Dlya nas rost voyennoy moshchi Kitaya ne neset pryamykh ugroz [Ruslan Izimov: for us, the growth of China's military power does not bear direct threats]. *Karavan*. 4 Apr. Retrieved from https://www.caravan.kz/gazeta/ruslan-izimov-dlya-nas-rost-voennojj-moshhi-kitaya-ne-neset-pryamykh-ugroz-392991/ [Accessed 7 May 2018].

Omelicheva, M. Y. (2013). Central Asian conceptions of "democracy": ideological resistance to international democratization, 81-104. In Vanderhill, R. and Aleprete, M. (eds) *The international dimensions of authoritarian persistence in the former Soviet Union*. Lanham: Lexington Books.

Omelicheva, M. Y. (2015). *Democracy in Central Asia: competing perspectives and alternative strategies*. Lexington: University Press of Kentucky.

Omelicheva, M. Y. (2016). Authoritarian legitimation: assessing discourses of legitimacy in Kazakhstan and Uzbekistan. *Central Asian Survey*, 35(4), 481–500.

Ondash, A. O. (2012). Kontseptsiya "Proklyatiya prirodnykh resursov" i perspektivy ekonomicheskogo razvitiya Respubliki Kazakhstan [The concept of "natural resource curse" and the prospects for the economic development of the Republic of Kazakhstan]. *Mezhdunarodnyy zhurnal eksperimental'nogo obrazovaniya*, 12(1), 58–62.

Ondash, A. O. (2013). Aktual'nyye problemy diversifikatsii natsional'noy ekonomiki i kontseptsiya resursnogo proklyatiya (na materialakh Respubliki Kazakhstan) [Challenges of diversification of the national economy and the concept of resource curse (on the materials of the Republic of Kazakhstan)]. *Aktual'ni problemy ekonomiky*, 7, 405–411.

Ostrowski, W. (2009). The legacy of the "coloured revolutions": the case of Kazakhstan. *Journal of Communist Studies and Transition Politics*, 25(2–3), 347–368.

Ostrowski, W. (2010). *Politics and oil in Kazakhstan*. London: Routledge.

Ostrowski, W. (2011). *Rentierism, dependency and sovereignty in Central Asia*. Edinburgh: Edinburgh University Press.

Peyrouse, S. (2012). The Kazakh neopatrimonial regime: balancing uncertainties among the "family," oligarchs and technocrats. *Demokratizatsiya*, 20(4), 345.

Peyrouse, S. (2016). Discussing China: Sinophilia and Sinophobia in Central Asia. *Journal of Eurasian Studies*, 7(1), 14–23.

Ross, M. (2001). Does oil hinder democracy? *World Politics*, 53(3), 325–361.

Ross, M. (2012). *The oil curse: how petroleum wealth shapes the development of nations*. Princeton, NJ: Princeton University Press.

Rumer, B. (2011). Kazakhstan s kitayskoy spetsifikoy? [Kazakhstan with Chinese characteristics?]. *Exclusive*. 7 November. Retrieved from http://www.exclusive.kz/votum_separatum/boris-rumer/7134/. [Accessed 4 March 2018].

Sadovskaya, Y. (2015). The mythology of Chinese migration in Kazakhstan. *Central Asia Caucasus Analyst*, Retrieved from http://www.cacianalyst.org/publications/field-reports/item/13112-the-mythology-of-chinese-migration-in-kazakhstan.html. [Accessed 10 March 2021].

Salmon, P. (2011). Repression intensifies against Kazakh oil workers' uprising. *Debatte: Journal of Contemporary Central and Eastern Europe*, 19(1–2), 507–510.

Salmon, P. (2012). Police massacre has opened a dark chapter for Kazakh workers' movement. *Debatte: Journal of Contemporary Central and Eastern Europe*, 20(1), 73–77.

Schatz, E. (2005). Reconceptualizing clans: kinship networks and statehood in Kazakhstan. *Nationalities Papers*, 33(2), 231–254.

Schatz, E. (2010). Reconceptualizing clans: kinship networks and statehood in Kazakhstan. *Nationalities Papers*, 33(2), 321–254.

Sidaway, J. D., and Woon, C. Y. (2017). Chinese narratives on "One Belt, One Road" in geopolitical and imperial contexts. *The Professional Geographer*, 69(4), 591–603.

State Council of the PRC (2015). *Vision and actions on jointly building silk road economic belt and 21st century maritime silk road.* 28 March. Retrieved from http://en.ndrc.gov.cn/newsrelease/201503/t20150330_669367.html. [Accessed 4 August. 2018].

Suleev, D. (2009). Lider natsii – eto real'nost, interview s Darkhanom Kaletayevim [Leader of the nation: it is reality, an interview with Darkhan Kaletayev], *Izvestia,* 25 September.

Sullivan, C. J. (2017). State-building in the steppe: challenges to Kazakhstan's modernizing aspirations. *Strategic Analysis*, 41(3), 273–284.

Syroezhkin, K. (2010). *Kazakhstan – Kitay: ot prigranichnoy torgovli k strategicheskomu partnerstvu. V formate strategicheskogo partnerstva* [Kazakhstan–China: from cross-border trade to strategic partnership. In the framework of a strategic partnership]. Almaty: Kazakhstan Institute of Strategic Studies.

Temirkhanov, M. (2014a). Za chto Kazakhstan poluchil resursnoye proklyatiye [How did Kazakhstan receive a resource curse]. *Forbes.kz*. 28 August. Retrieved from https://forbes.kz/process/economy/za_chto_kazahstan_poluchil_resursnoe_proklyatie/. [Accessed 16 May 2018].

Temirkhanov, M. (2014b). Kazakhstan idet po grablyam neftyanykh arabskikh stran [Kazakhstan repeats mistakes of oil Arab countries]. 20 January. Retrieved from https://forbes.kz/process/economy/kazahstan_idet_po_grablyam_neftyanyih_ arabskih_stran/. [Accessed 16 May 2018].

Temirkhanov, M. (2015). Kak Kazakhstanu izbavit'sya ot resursnogo proklyatiya [How can Kazakhstan get rid of the resource curse]. *Forbes.kz.* 29 August. Retrieved from https://forbes.kz/process/expertise/kak_kazahstanu_izbavitsya_ot_resursnogo_proklyatiya/. [Accessed 16 May 2018].

TengriNews.kz (2013). Dolya kitayskikh kompaniy v neftyanoy otrasli Kazakhstana v 2013 godu prevysit 40 protsentov [The share of Chinese companies in the oil industry of Kazakhstan in 2013 will exceed 40 percent]. 1 January. Retrieved from https://tengrinews.kz/money/dolya-kitayskih-kompaniy-neftyanoy-otrasli-kazahstana-2013-226309/. [Accessed 17 July 2018].

Tokayev, K-J. (2008). *Svet i Ten': Ocherki kazakhstanskogo politika* [Light and shadow. Essays on Kazakhstani politics]. Almaty: Vostok-Zapad.

Torfing, J. (1999). *New theories of discourse: Laclau, Mouffe and Žižek.* Oxford: Blackwell Publishers.

Torguzbayev, K. (2011). Volny zabastovki v kompanii «Karazhanbasmunay» doshli do Almaty [Waves of the strike at Karazhanbasmunai reached Almaty]. *Azattyq*. 30 May. Retrieved from https://rus.azattyq.org/a/karazhanbas_oil_workers_strike_/ 24209265.html. [Accessed 17 March 2018].

Torguzbayev, K. (2013). Zakash Kamalidenov: "V otlichiye ot Zhanaozena v dekabre 86-go my ne pozvolili strelyat'" [Zakash Kamalidenov: unlike the 1986 Zhanaozen we were not allowed to shoot]. *Azattyq*. 26 January. Retrieved from https://rus.azattyq.org/a/zhakash_kamalidenov_zhanaozen_iojzen_/24462775.html. [Accessed 17 March 2018].

Wang, X. (2008). Zhong Ya shiyou hezuo yu Zhongguo nengyuan anquan zhanlue [Central Asia petroleum cooperation and China's energy security strategy]. *Guoji jingji hezuo,* 6, 41–46.

Wei, L., and Liu, Q. (2006). Zhong Ya diqu de nengyuan zhengduo yu Zhongguo nengyuan anquan [Energy competition in Central Asia and China's energy security]. *Shijie jingji yu zhengzhi luntan*, 6, 73–78.

World Bank (2018). *Kazakhstan. Overview*. Retrieved from https://www.worldbank.org/en/country/kazakhstan/overview. [Accessed 10 March 2017].

Xi, J. (2013a). Promote friendship between our people and work together to build a bright future. Speech at Nazarbayev university. *Ministry of Foreign Affairs of the PRC*. 7 September. Retrieved from http://www.fmprc.gov.cn/mfa_eng/wjdt_665385/zyjh_665391/t1078088.shtml. [Accessed 26 July 2018].

Xi, J. (2013b). Hongyang "Shanghai jingshen" cujin gongtong fazhan – zai Shanghai Hezuo Zuzhi chengyuan guo yuanshou lishi hui di 13 ci huiyi shang de jianghua, Bishenkake [Promote the "Shanghai Spirit" and promote common development. Speech at the 13th meeting of the Heads of State Council of the Shanghai cooperation organization, Bishkek]. *Renmin Ribao*. 13 September. Retrieved from http://cpc.people.com.cn/xuexi/n/2015/0721/c397563-27338283.html.

Xi, J. (2014). Ning xin ju li jingcheng xiezuo tuidong Shanghai Hezuo Zuzhi zai Shang xin taijie [Concentrate on cooperation, promote the Shanghai cooperation organization to a new level]. *Renmin Ribao*. 13 September. Retrieved from http://cpc.people.com.cn/n/2014/0913/c87228-25653522.html. [Accessed 11 October 2017].

Xi, J. (2015). Towards a community of common destiny and a new future for Asia. Speech at the 2015 Boao forum for Asia. *Xinhua*. 28 March. Retrieved from http://www.xinhuanet.com/english/2015-03/29/c_134106145.htm. [Accessed 26 July 2018].

Xi, J. (2016a). Goujian chuangxin, huoli, liandong, baorong de shijie jingji – Xi Jinping zhuxi guanyu 20 guo jituan lingdao ren Hangzhou fenghui de zhongyao lunshu [Building an innovative, vigorous, linked and inclusive world economy. Speech at the summit of the G20 leaders in Hangzhou]. *Renmin Ribao*. 17 August. Retrieved from http://cpc.people.com.cn/n1/2016/0817/c64094-28641538.html. [Accessed 2 November 2017].

Xi, J. (2016b). Puxie Zhong-Wu youhao xin hua zhang [Writing the new chapter in Sino-Uzbekistan friendship]. *Renmin Ribao*. 22 June. Retrieved from http://cpc.people.com.cn/n1/2016/0622/c64094-28467564.html. [Accessed 11 August 2018].

Xi, J. (2017a). Work together to build the silk road economic belt and the 21st century maritime silk road. *The Opening Ceremony of the Belt and Road Forum for International Cooperation*. 14 May.

Xi, J. (2017b). May China-Kazakhstan relationship fly high toward our shared aspirations. Signed article in the Kazakh newspaper Aikyn Gazeti. 8 June.

Yang, C. (2014). Zhongguo he Eluosi zai Zhong Ya de nengyuan guanxi ji qianjing zhanwang [Energy relations and prospects of China and Russia in Central Asia]. *Xinjiang shehui kexue*, 3, 87–92.

Yang, J. (2008). "Shanghai jingshen" de yongheng meili – jinian Shanghai hezuo zuzhi chengli 7 zhounian [The eternal charm of "Shanghai Spirit." commemorating the 7th anniversary of the establishment of Shanghai cooperation organization]. *Renmin Ribao*. 16 June. Retrieved from http://world.people.com.cn/GB/1030/7383613.html [Accessed 12 September 2017].

Yelyubayev, Z. H. S. (2016). Voprosy obespecheniya natsional'noy bezopasnosti v sfere nedropol'zovaniya v Respublike Kazakhstan [Issues of ensuring national security in the area of subsurfaction in the Republic of Kazakhstan]. *Russian Juridical Journal Rossijskij Juridiceskij Zurnal*, 108(3), 77–83.

Yemelianova, G. M. (2014). Islam, national identity and politics in contemporary Kazakhstan. *Asian Ethnicity*, 15(3), 286–301.

Yue, L., and Yang, F. (2016). "Sichou zhi lu jingji dai" Zhongguo yu Zhong Ya wu guo nengyuan hezuo de jingyan jiejian ji lujing tanxi – jiyu diyuan jingji shijiao [Experience and development of "Silk Road Economic Belt" energy cooperation between China and five Central Asian countries. Based on geo-economic perspectives]. *Renwen zazhi*, 9, 23–32.

Zaidi, S. M. A. (2010). Tribalism, Islamism, leadership and the Assabiyyas. *Journal for the Study of Religions and Ideologies*, 9(25), 133–154.

Zakon.kz (2008). Valeriy Kotovich: "V poiskakh zolotoy serediny" [Searching for a golden mean]. 26 February. Retrieved from: https://www.zakon.kz/105470-valerijj-kotovich-v-poiskakh-zolotojj.html. [Accessed 12 August 2018].

Zhao, W. (2014). E – Mei – Zhong Ya zhengce dui Zhongguo nengyuan anquan de yingxiang [The impact of Russia-US-Central Asia policy on China's energy security]. *Xiboliya yanjiu*, 6, 48–51.

Zhong, Sheng (2014). Fuxing si lupu xin pian [Writing a new chapter on the silk road]. *People's Daily*. June 28. Retrieved from: http://opinion.people.com.cn/ n/2014/0628/c1003-25211591.html. [Accessed 26 July 2018].

Zhou, L. (2012). Kitay ne mozhet razvivat'sya v otryve ot vsego mira, takzhe i mirovoye razvitiye neotdelimo ot Kitaya [China cannot develop in isolation from the whole world and also the world development is inseparable from China]. *Embassy of the PRC in the RK*. 9 July. Retrieved from http://kz.china-embassy.org/rus/sgxx/sgdt/t967240.htm. [Accessed 18 May 2018].

6 Conclusions

Examining oil as a discourse

This book explores the nexus between politics and sociocultural contexts in international energy politics by drawing on the development of bilateral energy relations between China and two oil-rich countries – Kazakhstan and Russia. Its goal is to challenge conventional assumptions about energy politics and, particularly, China's global quest for oil by demonstrating how oil becomes an idea and how this idea is mobilized in the realm of international relations. Firstly, I sought to offer a nuanced, dynamic, and diverse picture of international energy politics and China's participation in it. Secondly, I wanted to show that mainstream IR theories are too limited in their analytical scope and thus not able to explain the complex nature of energy relations.

Energy (in)securities and discursive politics of oil

This book offers a valuable theoretical and methodological addition to the study of energy politics in the realm of IR. I show that China's energy relations with Russia and Kazakhstan are simultaneously enabled and constrained by the discursive politics of energy. I am also able to demonstrate that a critical constructivist approach to the examination of China's energy politics provides an original contribution to the understanding of the development of China's energy relations with major oil exporters.

My analysis reveals that the commonly used concept of energy security lacks explanatory power. Instead, the notions of security and insecurity in energy politics are contextual. Focusing on the social logic of energy relations, I move beyond the concept of energy security and the dichotomy of conflict and cooperation reproduced through the dialogue between realist and liberal IR approaches. My analysis focuses on discourses and their constitutive role in the development of relations between states. I develop a constructivist conceptual framework and adopt the poststructuralist discourse analysis methodology inspired by Lene Hansen's work. Discourse analysis is preoccupied with what people know about diverse material and social realities and how they articulate this knowledge because its aim is to uncover how these realities are constructed, negotiated, and interpreted through the processes of social interaction. A structured, systematic, and focused intertextual discourse analysis of a heterogeneous collection of texts allows me to show how the material realities of energy acquire their meanings in the process of narrative-making and discursive symbolization. Social context, intersubjective meanings, and identities acquire characteristics of explanatory variables. The concept of the energy paradigm links national discursive politics of energy to the practice of international relations and hence becomes a constructivist roadmap to relations between exporters and importers.

While constructivist and poststructuralist analysis of energy politics tends to focus on policy discourse, this book goes much further. It brings textual documents and diverse cultural artifacts (e.g., works of fiction, popular song lyrics, paintings, photographs, films, museum exhibits, and architecture) to map and elucidate societal discourses of energy. My research is multilingual, with textual documents in Chinese and Russian being the major sources of data. I take language seriously and explore its power to construct social reality. Moreover, I show that diverse competing discourses about extraction, production, and consumption of energy and redistribution of energy revenues emerge and disseminate themselves through different forms of visual art, popular entertainment, architecture and city planning, museums, cultural spaces, and other sociocultural structures and practices. This allows me not only to advance the nuanced understanding of energy policy-making and diplomacy but also to unravel critical discourses about economic, environmental, social, and political impacts associated with the expansion of the energy industry and the increase of energy exports that define a broader understanding of energy in our societies.

China's quest for oil

At the core of China's energy paradigm is the notion of development. The availability of energy resources, and specifically fossil fuels, is instrumentalized as a prerequisite for development. Importantly, China's energy paradigm defines energy development as a right of every nation. Hence, the global distribution of energy resources is neither a purely economic issue nor a security issue but first and foremost a matter of international politics. China's official energy discourses emphasize the fundamental and persistent inequality of the current world order and, using it as a starting point, call for reducing the gap between the Global North and the Global South.

Accordingly, the focus of China's concept of energy security is development, and thus its definition corresponds with the concept of development that in the mid-2000s was encapsulated in the aspiration for "harmonious society/world" and "China's peaceful rise." Following the new development strategy, China's energy paradigm broadened, and now the concept of energy security includes sustainable and environmentally conscious development. In addition to it, the concept of energy security began to internationalize, and, as a result, the energy deficit became more politicized. The de-securitization of energy deficit presupposes that the distribution of energy resources should be regulated by binding international rules and regulations. It also implies that international energy relations can and should be a positive-sum game.

On the domestic level, however, China's official discourses associate the deficit of energy with the reliability of oil supply, and thus oil is still a securitized object. As was the case 60 years ago, China treats the deficit of oil as an existential threat to its national development and a source of dangerous security vulnerabilities. Therefore, China's oil strategy on the domestic level is defined as the quest for a new Daqing.

In sum, China's energy paradigm is bifurcated: while on the global/ international level the energy deficit is now politicized, on the domestic/national level it remains largely securitized. China actively promotes a cooperative mode of energy development on the international level and does not call for urgent and exceptional measures to deal with the energy deficit, yet, when it comes to oil, China still does not rush to trade its self-reliance for interdependency.

Throughout the 2000s and 2010s, "win-win" is the most frequently repeated epithet for "cooperation" in China's energy discourse. China frames its relations with Russia and Kazakhstan as mutually beneficial and based on common developmental goals. The balance of interdependence in the relations between China and these oil-rich countries is assumed to be created and sustained by market incentives that transcend political and ideological differences. Building relations with Russia and Kazakhstan, China aspires to become a strategic business partner and trusted friend for them. The two cases demonstrate that China is determined to desecuritize energy and separate its cooperation with oil-rich countries from geopolitics.

At the same time, China is becoming more assertive and sensitive to the allegations of neocolonialism as well as to the doubts about its peaceful intentions. When Xi Jinping became the general secretary of the Chinese Communist Party in 2012, he announced that China is dreaming about the "great rejuvenation of the Chinese nation." By the middle of the 21st century, Xi asserts, China will become "a global leader in terms of comprehensive national power and international influence." Xi offers China as a model for other developing nations, demonstrating extreme confidence in China's achievements during the past two decades and in the superiority of China's development, compared to both the Global North and the Global South. This growing confidence transfers into China's energy policymaking on the international level. Under Xi's leadership, we see China seeking not only to build an "overseas Daqing" but also striving to be recognized as a new trendsetter and a global player of consequence in international energy politics.

The analysis of China's bilateral energy relations with Russia and Kazakhstan also reveals a lot about the ways discursive politics of energy influences foreign policy and international strategies of petrostates. Russia is a former empire recovering after a collapse and seeking revenge. Kazakhstan, on the contrary, is a young post-colonial state. While its geopolitical position in the international system is uncertain, Kazakhstan can be safely identified as a part of the Global South. As much as these two states seem to be different from each other, they are significant net oil exporters and share the identity of an oil-rich country. As the analysis of their discursive politics of energy demonstrates, they both instrumentalize oil as a source of liveliness, national development, sovereignty, independence, and power. At the same time, notwithstanding their obsession with oil, they do not consider themselves petrostates. Both Russia and Kazakhstan securitize the energy sector, and their energy diplomacy is heavily affected by the dominant dichotomies of "we" and "they."

China is "they" for Russia and Kazakhstan. Both countries see China as striving to control their energy sector and, subsequently, as a threat to their sovereignty in the realm of international energy politics, which is key to their sense of identity. As a result, Russia and Kazakhstan do not consider China as a priority partner. Overall, Russia's and Kazakhstan's energy cooperation with China simultaneously exposes contradictions within their energy paradigms and acts as a conduit through which perceptions of China as a threat find a stronger voice.

In sum, my study shows that the external energy strategies of China and its oil-rich counterparts are crucially dependent on their discursive politics of energy. Hence, building collaborative and constructive energy relations with China, its partners in Russia, Kazakhstan, and elsewhere must consider not only material realities of China's energy industry (e.g., the amount of energy resources available in China, its mining, refining, and storage capacity, and the existing and planned transportation routes) and institutional settings of China's energy policy (e.g., China's legal frameworks and the structure of China's energy government) but also multiple symbolic meanings that energy resources acquire in China. Likewise, my best advice to China's representatives is to be conscious about the way China is perceived in other states and take the world of words and ideas as seriously as the world of pumpjacks, pipelines, tankers, price charts, and long supply chains.

Limitations and directions for future research

Four directions for future research are most apparent. Firstly, my study concerns itself with the underexamined topic of oil, and thus it only superficially covered discourses related to decarbonization and energy transition. A study of discursive politics of energy with a focus on renewable resources (e.g., biomass, hydropower, geothermal, wind, and solar) would offer important and valuable insights into the current state of international energy politics and likely would also allow us a glimpse into its future. Moreover, the analytical scope of my study is defined by its emphasis on the state. Accordingly, the next logical step is to have a closer look at the energy discourses produced by various actors within the state (from NOCs to the CEOs of private refineries) and diverse transnational actors.

Secondly, while China's energy relations with Russia and Kazakhstan are a fertile source for the analysis of China's discursive politics of energy, these cases allow covering only one side of it. An examination of the recent examples of China's engagement with international institutions on energy-related issues, therefore, would help to show how China's energy discourses evolve to represent the latest shifts in China's foreign policy strategy (e.g., China's foreign policy-making on climate change) and power realignments in the international energy politics in general (e.g., the US withdrawal from the Paris Agreement and Xi Jinping's determination to "strive for achievement" in international affairs).

The third direction involves a study of the complex issues related to political legitimacy and national branding. My analysis of Russia's energy politics reveals the discursive constructions that are essential to the way Putin's regime has been actively positioning Russia as an antagonist to the West on both domestic and international levels. The case of Kazakhstan demonstrates that Kazakhstan's energy paradigm is subordinated to the discursive politics that sustains and legitimizes Nazarbayev's authoritarian rule. In this sense, a critical examination of the evolution, transformation, and limits of Russia's and Kazakhstan's official discursive politics of energy would be fruitful for a more nuanced understanding of domestic practices and strategies of nation branding adopted by the ruling regimes. Importantly, the conflict between different discursive representations of oil exposes fractures in Putin's and Nazarbayev's ideologies, pointing out to new possibilities for the emergence of strong counter-hegemonic discourses that will challenge the legitimacy of their regimes.

Finally, as a constructivist and somewhat critical student of international relations, I was struck by the fact that the discursive politics of energy reinscribes the wide varieties of masculinist hierarchies. In China, the official discussion of energy poverty and the quest for energy efficiency never considers gendered energy usage. In Russia, the aggressive expressions of the energy superpower discourse in Russia's diplomacy are linked to Putin's masculinity cult. Doing fieldwork in Kazakhstan, I witnessed many examples of structural and institutionalized gender discrimination that left me wondering whether the disempowerment of Kazakhstani women is connected to or affected by the dominance of the energy sector in Kazakhstan's economy. Lastly, in all the three countries that I studied, women's experiences were absent in the dominant narratives of the oil industry development. On illustrations to newspaper articles about oil, at oil museums, and in the documentaries about oil, I saw men digging, drilling, and squeezing out oil, as well as men smiling and shaking hands over the signed international contracts. I can hardly find a dozen texts in my dataset that are produced by women. In other words, it seems that the world of oil belongs to men. While I am not sure how exactly we should study the women–oil nexus in the realm of international energy relations, I am confident that this nexus deserves more attention from scholars in the fields of politics, international relations, and political economy.

This research project was challenging and extremely rewarding. The experience and new knowledge that I gained affected my view of the aims and methods of the discipline of political science. As a way of concluding, I want to summarize the major lessons that I have learned as a political scientist throughout this research project. First, diversity is beautiful and exciting. The diversity of ideas about energy inspired me to pursue this study, and further this diversity became an essential source of creativity and established an exigency for critical thinking. We should celebrate differences rather than try to neutralize them. In a world suffering from multiple social breakdowns and divided by political polarity, an appreciation for diversity will challenge us to search for new paths toward compromise and cooperation. Second, traveling across different languages, cultures, and countries, I encountered a great variety of politics, practices, types, and modes of knowledge production. I believe that by creating, reproducing, preserving, sharing, and celebrating knowledge we can embrace diversity and help other people to do so as well. This is the only way how we can learn and teach others to accept and respect political and sociocultural norms distinct from our own. Finally, we indeed live in the "world of our making," and, to a large extent, we talk this world into being. We must acknowledge that our language is political and recognize its power to shape our lives and the lives of others. I hope my work will inspire both scholars and practitioners to take the constitutive power of language seriously and reflect on how the language they choose to use influences the way they study and practice politics.

Index

Taylor & Francis Group
an informa business

Taylor & Francis eBooks

www.taylorfrancis.com

A single destination for eBooks from Taylor & Francis with increased functionality and an improved user experience to meet the needs of our customers.

90,000+ eBooks of award-winning academic content in Humanities, Social Science, Science, Technology, Engineering, and Medical written by a global network of editors and authors.

TAYLOR & FRANCIS EBOOKS OFFERS:

- A streamlined experience for our library customers
- A single point of discovery for all of our eBook content
- Improved search and discovery of content at both book and chapter level

REQUEST A FREE TRIAL

support@taylorfrancis.com

Routledge
Taylor & Francis Group

CRC Press
Taylor & Francis Group

For Product Safety Concerns and Information please contact our EU
representative GPSR@taylorandfrancis.com
Taylor & Francis Verlag GmbH, Kaufingerstraße 24, 80331 München, Germany

www.ingramcontent.com/pod-product-compliance
Ingram Content Group UK Ltd.
Pitfield, Milton Keynes, MK11 3LW, UK
UKHW020001200926
475702UK00015B/2418

* 9 7 8 0 3 6 7 6 5 1 4 6 6 *